For many years Engineers in the Royal Navy were called Plumbers. Over the years, as types of engineer proliferated, the mechanical or marine engineers acquired the sobriquet of Clankies, to distinguish them from the weapons engineers, referred to as Greenies, reflecting the coloured cloth that they wore between their gold lace, denoting rank, from 1947 to 1956.

ADMIRAL CLANKY ENTERTAINS

An Alternative Naval Memoir

PATRICK MIDDLETON

Matador
5 Weir Road
Kibworth Beauchamp
Leicester LE8 0LQ, UK
Tel: (+44) 116 279 2299
Fax: (+44) 116 279 2277
Email: books@troubador.co.uk
Web: www.troubador.co.uk/matador

ISBN 978 1848763 852

British Library Cataloguing in Publication Data.
A catalogue record for this book is available from the British Library.

Typeset in 12pt Perpetua by Troubador Publishing Ltd, Leicester, UK

Matador is an imprint of Troubador Publishing Ltd

Printed in Great Britain by the MPG Books Group, Bodmin and King's Lynn

Dedicated to Janey, my love.

Preface

It is not uncommon for former military people to lay down their muskets and reach for their pens, and I suppose that in this respect I am no exception. But perhaps unlike those of so many of my peers and predecessors, this is no tale of derring-do and high adventure, nor is it a fearless exposé of What's Wrong With Today's Armed Forces, though that book needs to be written and rewritten on a frequent and regular basis.

But if war is too serious a business to be left to the politicians, then peace is too comical a business to be left to the entirely serious commentators, still with an axe or two to grind. My time in the RN has been filled with humour and incident, of a lower case nature, but none the worse for that. So I am at variance with my erstwhile colleagues in avoiding the great policy issues and the sweep of events in this memoir, which reports some of the lesser quiddities and oddments that occurred in the margins of my own personal history.

A good friend once said to me "I've never really thought of you as a NO", and that is an observation that I took as a complement at the time, without really considering what it might mean. Being a touch out of the ordinary in a conformist service is a dangerous flirtation, which can pay off or can end in tears. Certainly, many of my earlier, more individualistic friends found that the straitjacket of conformity was a little too uncomfortable for extended wear and left the RN early on. In my own case I never really found the pressure to conform to be intolerable. It seemed to me that service life gave you a frame of reference which defined the edges of what was acceptable whilst leaving plenty of room inside to be your own person. An early demonstration of an independent turn of mind was all that was necessary to set you free, albeit watched with a mixture of envy and schadenfreude by your mates.

As time went by, and I clawed my way slowly up the ladder of seniority and promotion, the frame pressed ever less upon me in a personal sense, but the rigours of working in a public service with, each year, a little less to spend on a slightly smaller operation, became increasingly wearisome. To spend the major part of your working life constantly revising downwards may be good for the soul, but it is not a recipe for novelty, expansion and fun, and the laughs grew noticeably fewer as the years passed. For much of my service career, I had been protected from these necessary economies by the nuclear submarine programme, which may turn out to have been one of the last genuinely expansionist revolutions that the Royal Navy will have experienced. For me, it set a standard of high endeavour, innovation and job satisfaction which was never subsequently matched. Such is life, but it meant that when the time finally came to hang up my uniform, I had few regrets, but a quiver full of warm and happy memories.

So much has changed that already the Navy that I have described in this book is history. But if it serves as a footnote to the social history of the time, whilst at the same time giving the reader the odd smile, I shall be content.

I have included a fair amount of unexplained technical jargon in this account, because it enlivens and may even inform. Readers would be wise to go with the flow, without straining to understand every obscurity!

Some of my erstwhile colleagues I have probably treated with rather less than the respect that they deserved, all of course in the cause of trying to tell an entertaining story. To them I apologise, not least because they constituted collectively a fine Band of Brothers (Nelson's phrase), but also because in one's mellowed-out later years one wishes good to all mankind and lays the acerbities of youth to rest. Still and all, I can't abide blandness, so their involuntary sacrifice has been in the just cause of piquancy.

I am indebted to all those I mention and to many more that I don't, and above all to my wife, to whom I dedicate this slender piece with all my love. Enough! Let's get started.

CHAPTER 1

The Primordial Soup

It is not given to many people to remember their own conception, and I would not claim to be one of them. But perhaps I have a better feel than some for the ambience surrounding that auspicious event, since I returned to the land of my birth – and conception – as a young Naval Officer many years later. That land was Malta, where my father John was serving as the Engineer Officer of a destroyer – HMS Ilex. He and my mother Tessa had spent much of their married life up to that point in Malta. Earlier on, he had been the Engineer Officer of HM Submarine Oxley which, following the pattern of the times, spent her days in local running, surfaced and dived, around Malta, and came back home usually in the evenings and certainly at weekends. Tessa used to go down to the boat on Saturday mornings to sit in the tiny wardroom, deal with and type the week's correspondence, and drink horses' necks with the other officers.

Malta was heavily Italianised before the war, but its essential character has survived the many external influences upon it. It was and remains an island of light, most of the buildings constructed of wonderfully honey-coloured limestone, and round every corner a brilliant, twinkling arm of the sea, impossibly blue. The language, a mish-mash of many nationalities, even more cryptic in written form than when spoken, was fortunately often supplemented by rather fractured English.

Three iconic forms of transport flourished then. Dghaisas constituted the maritime element, and were at their most numerous in the stunningly picturesque Grand Harbour. Somewhat akin to the gondola, with high stem and stern posts, and brightly painted in primary colours, their boatmen stood up, facing forward, and pushed on two oars mounted in rowlocks in the usual way. They were plentiful, cheap, and were a fine colourful sight, particularly when sporting awnings or canopies in summer.

The dghaisa's land-borne equivalent was the gharry, a tall two wheeled carriage drawn by a single - often rather spavined - horse urged on by its driver. The poor horses slipped and slithered on some of the steeper hills around Valletta, particularly the notorious Crucifix Hill, which led down to the principal landing place, the very splendid Customs House Steps. The other way down was via the Barracca lift, which clawed its way up to the gardens at the top, with many an alarming creak, groan and faltering progress.

Finally there was the substantial population of buses, which combed the island from one end to the other. A crucifix swung prominently above the windscreen, and was much prayed to, not least by the drivers as the coach shuddered on the edge of disaster.

The extensive waterfront around Valletta was dominated by Royal Naval craft and activities. Grand Harbour itself, the home of the big ships — battleships, carriers, and cruisers - led into the dockyard, with its deep water berths at Parlatorio and several large graving docks. Senglea Point led round past the senior dockyard officers' houses to an area known as the Barbary Coast, full of bars and generally preferred by senior ratings. Youngsters on the other hand made for the Gut, running through the centre of Valletta. Not a place of beauty or of style, as basic and slightly sad as they come, but a necessary rite of passage and the scene of some formidable inter-ship wars over the years. Looking down serenely over all, Bighi, the great RN hospital, matched across the harbour at the time by its civilian equivalent King George V Hospital for Seamen at Floriana, where I was born on 15th March 1938. The KG V is no more.

To the north and east of Valletta lies the inlet of Tax Biex where the Submarine depot ship and its chicks used to be moored. The littoral led onto Manoel Island, the Fleet Recreation Centre, and base for the Fleet Repair Ship. Then, away to the north was

Sliema Creek, in which the destroyers, glamour boys of the piece, used to moor in pairs between two buoys. It was a narrow and serpentine bit of water, and the ships used to bustle up stern-first, so that they were ready to go on the next occasion. Not the easiest of manoeuvres, and there were some spectacular near-misses, as well as a few collisions.

Sliema was a favoured residential area, with a vibrant waterfront, stylish bars and cafes, and easy access to the Tigne Club, a swimming club on a rocky promontory where young officers and a multitude of girls met, paraded and fell in love — sometimes. When the sun set, the gilded and sometimes rather pink young moved onto to the City Gem, a fashionable Sliema bar.

Long before the days of serious tourism the island's population was swelled each summer by the arrival of what was known as the Fishing Fleet. This was a sizeable cohort of middle class girls, often accompanied by their dear mothers, who spent the summer in Malta to find a husband. Somewhat artificial and unpleasant as this manifestation was, it was generally recommended to young officers that engagement to a member of the Fishing Fleet was infinitely preferable to a liaison with a Maltese girl; oh yes, they were frequently cultured, beautiful and fun, but, the wisdom went, they all came with a great deal of baggage, to whit numerous relatives, all with an eye on little Johnny's (non-existent) estate and (minimal) prospects!

All in all the Navy's presence and influence in this small island was enormous. The Mediterranean Fleet was second only to the Home Fleet in size and firepower and the Commander-in-Chief was one of the most senior Admirals serving. Ashore he lived in considerable splendour, second only to the Governor, who was often a previous Commander-in-Chief himself! Between the wars the CinC had, quite apart from his Royal Marine Band, a large orchestra, made up of Maltese civilians who were seldom out of their dinner jackets. In 1920 a Treasury audit had recommended that this orchestra constituted an unreasonable expense, and should be disbanded. The CinC of the day achieved a softening of this position; the Treasury eventually agreed that the members of the orchestra could continue to serve until they retired at the appropriate age. Thereafter, whenever a member was due to retire, a successor was secretly appointed, on the understanding that he took the name of his predecessor. When war broke out in 1939 there had been no reduction in the number of players in the orchestra.

If life was agreeable for the CinC and it emphatically was, it was pretty good for the lesser mortals in the Fleet. Warm seas, sunshine, fascinating places to visit and very few wars — it is what sailors join for, even if the down side was a fanatical insistence on spit and polish and long hours spent cleaning, painting and polishing every aspect of uniform and ship.

Ashore there were complementary benefits. There was an intense - if one-dimensional - social scene, well lubricated by the execrable local beer — Cisk. There was some similarly dodgy local wine — Marsovin — which many held was only made drinkable by the addition, 50-50, of Plymouth Gin. There was a great amiability about the Maltese, who recognised clearly the important place the Navy occupied in the Maltese economy. There was English food — of sorts! And there was every form of sport: great swimming and water-skiing, good sailing, walking, climbing plus all the usual ball games; and then there was horse racing at the Marsa. The trotting races, with high-stepping horses pulling skeletal rigs at great speed, were a popular spectacle, but not as popular as the dreaded Naval Officers' race, an event of low comedy at each meeting. My dad, no horseman, unwisely entered on one occasion, urged on his recalcitrant mount with his heels; the nag promptly stopped, turned round and bit him on the foot. Cue loud applause from the stands.

La vie en rose perhaps, but scarcely for me. Dad was appointed to Ramillies, a clapped out First World War battleship (once he could walk again!). So, when I was three months old, I set off for home in a steamer with Mum and Sister Broom. Brush, as she was known in the family, appeared and disappeared over the years as I and my sister were born. I can't remember much about her apart from a very bristly chin — Brush was entirely appropriate.

Mum must have enjoyed the trip. With me safe in the arms of Brush she could indulge her social proclivities to the full. She had been born in Rangoon, Burma, but her father Walter Hitchings soon vamoosed to pursue a new life (and the bottle) in Canada, never to be seen again, though during the war gift parcels would

4

occasionally appear. I seem to remember that spam, peanut butter and, of course, maple syrup were principal constituents. Only child Tessa and deserted mother Margaret formed the inevitable team, scratching a living where they could, and always mutually supportive.

Somehow they struggled for Mum to go to Berkhamsted School, and subsequently to university in Madrid, where she developed a fierce and life-long affection for Spain, for Spaniards (male variety) and for the bull-fighting world. Her language skills got her a job in London at Glaxo's (South American desk). This eclectic upbringing had produced a most attractive young woman with a warm and easy manner and an intense interest in people and in their opinions (not always the same thing!).

Back in England we settled in the Plymouth area, though I have no real recollection of this period of my life. Dad was certainly not much in evidence. The rusty Ramillies was in the Indian Ocean, and on the outbreak of war was instructed to locate and destroy the new German pocket-battleship the Deutschland. The Captain, a notorious firebrand, and the Gunnery Officer were the only two out of the ship's company of 1100 who had any confidence in winning such an engagement. The other 1098 fervently prayed that the Deutschland would *not* be found. Their prayers were answered.

Down below, Dad struggled with old fashioned design, overlaid with a patina of neglect. As the Senior Engineer he was responsible for the operation and maintenance of all the machinery, plus the structure and watertight integrity of the rest of the 30,000 ton leviathan, *and* of course for the huge team of artificers and stokers embarked. True there was a Commander (E), his boss, but his only perceived function was to act as an apologist to the Captain for the manifold shortcomings of his department. Meanwhile, Dad's twin ogres were the Main Condensers, and many auxiliary heat-exchangers, all sea water cooled and therefore potent sources of salt contamination of the Boilers. There were 18 of these brutes, all highly prone to tube failure and every form of steam and water leakage, not to mention brickwork failures within the furnaces (which were quite spectacular in themselves; it was not uncommon to hear a sustained rumble and, on peering into the furnace, observe the best part of a three bedroomed house in bricks collapsed on the furnace floor;

time to move swiftly on). Dad told me that, on one occasion, when preparing to go to sea, his Night Order Book read: "at 2200, flash up all 18 boilers, and when ready connect the best 15". Poor Dad, it was a Sisyphean task on which he always blamed his subsequent ill-health, but it got him promoted to Commander (at the time the youngest engineer officer to be so rewarded). Now he could become an apologist – except that he never would.

Meanwhile Mum and I enjoyed Devon. There's a photo of us both sauntering jauntily along the front at Torquay, she in a saucy hat and highish heels, me in a smart woollen coat which I somehow think of as blue. And some more grey images of our house at Yelverton, on the edge of Dartmoor.

You never know if your first memory *is* your first memory or if you have succumbed to being repeatedly told that it *is* your first memory. Mine, I do believe, concerned a visit to Paignton Zoo. Half way round, I desperately needed a pee. "Go behind those bushes," said Mum "no-one'll see you there".

I scuttled into a rhododendron grove, away from prying eyes. Hauling up the leg of my shorts (not for years was I able to work out the complexities of flies and underpants) and letting fly with my tiny member, I was horrified to see, right in front of me, a peacock with tail fully deployed, a thousand eyes on my little stream.

When the Commander returned, complete with shiny oak leaves on the peak of his cap, hence known as a brass hat, he was appointed as Chief Engineer of HMS Hornet, the Coastal Forces base at Gosport, across the harbour from Portsmouth. This was a brilliant job for a newly promoted commander. Now well into the war, Motor Torpedo Boats were streaming off the slips at an amazing rate, and were immediately flung into the Battle of the Narrow Seas, as Peter Scott's magisterial book on the campaign was called. The majority of people involved in this rather alternative navy – dubbed the Costly Farces by some of the disdainful regulars – were Hostilities Only or RNVR, and were as eclectic a bunch as you could find. They virtually invented a new form of warfare, harrying the enemy up and down the Channel and beyond with great flair, a lightly worn professionalism and immense bravery. There were many losses.

Before the war broke out the few precursor vessels of the MTBs were powered by Isotta-Franchini engines, and when these were subsequently withheld by the Italians, United States Packards became the universal prime-mover. Dad's team were mostly drawn from garages up and down the country and were excellent motor mechanics, though persistently forgot which hand to salute with – possibly on purpose.

We moved to Hampshire, and first alighted in a farm bungalow called Sunny Corner, on the coast road from Titchfield. Now a smart commuter enclave in the Solent linear city, Titchfield was at the time a simple rural community. I remember walking in with Mum the mile or so to buy food and to get our wet accumulators for the wireless charged at the cycle shop. Titchfield was also the destination for my first break-out, when I retraced our steps alone, and later, in the panic, was discovered deep in conversation with my friend the butcher.

Sunny Corner would have been better called Smelly Corner for it was cheek by jowl with the farm. I made friends with Rosemary Harris, the farmer's daughter, who allowed me to play on the tractor and contrived, rather ingeniously, to bite me right between the shoulder-blades. Dad spent hours sticking diagonal crosses of brown paper on every window – the Government's jejune prescription for minimising blast damage. Strangely he retained an affection for this repulsive material, and ever after our house was full of broken bits and pieces held together by brown sticky paper. I took particular exception to the taste.

But apart from the smell and the flies, there was another reason to move on from Sunny Corner – it was about to become too small. Though I did not know it at the time, Mum was pregnant. Whilst the bungalow could have accommodated the extra baby, it certainly couldn't contain, or receive the approval of, Brush, who had already been alerted.

We moved a mile further down the road, to a handsome Edwardian house overlooking the Meon estuary and the Solent. It was called, appropriately enough, Meon Marsh, and a walk through the Scots pines in the garden took you straight into the marsh itself. The house was well equipped with verandas and dormers and, most excitingly, gas central heating. Like Sunny Corner it had no electricity so our that our now extensive stock of Aladdin lamps, with their tall glass chimneys and beautiful gossamer mantles, came with us together with boxes of candles and torches.

We drove down the road in the Morris 8. Half way a platoon of the Home Guard was drawn up in the road, opposite the Anti Aircraft gun emplacement. There wasn't room for us to pass, but the Sergeant said "drive over the men's boots, sir, they won't mind". And so we did, and so they didn't. Amazing. When we arrived at Meon Marsh Dad disappeared inside the shed at the side of the house, rattling his matches, to flash up the boiler. At the time he had a bushy black beard (Irish origins) with eye-brows to match. As we dragged our cases from the car there was a loud explosion from the shed, and Dad came running out, his beard now ginger and eye-brows non-existent. If all else fails, consult the handbook.

I loved Meon Marsh. The owners, called Hughes, had left a large collection of butterflies, beautifully mounted and displayed in multi-drawer mahogany cabinets – very classy! I was allowed to look at them, 'very carefully'. My room overlooked the garden, where Mum had started her first (of many) love/hate relationship with a flock of hens, a necessary wartime adjunct. From my window I saw a lustrous red fox making off with a chicken, but was so frozen with excitement that I couldn't raise the alarm.

When the gales blew, we could watch Dad driving to work along the coast road. The trusty Morris was covered with spray as he went. It was along that same road that I first travelled to school, at Miss Croad's in Hillhead. A somewhat down-market woman, Mrs Downes, had come to do for us, and I sat on the flat, pressed steel carrier of her bike, holding on tight to her waist, whilst she warned me to keep my feet out of the spokes.

It was a time of seeing more of Dad for the first time, and we often went out on the Marsh, where he rather ineffectually waved a shot-gun at the snipe. He impressed on me how hard they were to shoot; true, he never got one. On one such trip I lost a welly in a particularly gooey bit of marsh, and stood on one leg wobbling and crying for help. It seemed a long time coming. Another time, surely in contravention of some regulation, Dad brought his service revolver home and we shot at tin cans on the beach. I had to use both forefingers to pull the trigger.

We could see the low profile of the Isle of Wight clearly across the grey waters of the Solent, and on more than one occasion I was got up late at night, it seemed, to watch the bombing raids on Cowes, and the anti-aircraft tracer and searchlights crisscrossing the sky. It was a wonderful spectacle, but I never felt threatened or alarmed. It was too distant, and I was too innocent.

There was always a lot of naval activity in the Solent, though we left before the big build-up to D-Day. Dad's MTBs were often tearing up and down, and the first components of Mulberry were being slowly gathered together; we saw them being towed westwards to Pegwell Bay in ones and twos from the dockyard, great concrete slabs without - to us - any obvious use.

In due course my sister was born, at Meon Marsh, with the local quack and, of course, Brush in attendance. No dramas that I can recall. She was a dark baby, with a sharp face and a triangular head of black hair sticking straight upwards, very much Dad's Irish colouring. I took more after Mum, with blonde hair and a round, grinning face. Still the same today, without the hair! Rather charmingly, the little lass was named Meonetta, a made-up name to reflect her birth-place. It was, I suppose, unfashionable to have an Italian sounding name at that time, but in any case she soon became Netta to the family, and, from university onwards, all her friends called her Min. Neither diminutive quite lives up to the original.

We all had three Christian names in the family. Dad was John Henry Dudley. The Dudley came from Irish connections, but he never liked it, and used to sign himself 'JH Middleton'. Many years later I met one of his watchkeepers from Ramillies. He told me that Dad had been referred to there as 'Deadly Muddleton' — possibly a simple transliteration, or perhaps redolent of some perceived shortcoming. Senior Engineers were seldom popular. Anyway, it could hardly have helped his regard for his name. Mum was Norna Mary Tessimond. I'm not sure how much she liked the Norna, though she liked Norma, which she was frequently miscalled, considerably less. She was certainly attracted to the mythology, possibly Norse, which links the name with the swan. She was very thrilled, in her elder years, to discover a North Sea Supply vessel called the Norna, and she exchanged long letters with the Steward on board. His picture was on the sideboard at home. Dad normally called her Tessa, again a diminutive without the beguilement of the full name. I (and Netta) were cursed by not having our used name at the front. I was John Patrick Windsor, and she was Mary Meonetta Tessimond. On many occasions I found it really tiresome not to be called by my first name, and even as I write I have to masquerade as John at my doctor's surgery, because the NHS cannot fathom the complexity of calling you by your second name.

Life at that age was pretty simple – home, school, walks on the beach. But once a week I went to dancing lessons in a room above Woolworths in Fareham, where I became adept at the polka, a life skill I have regrettably lost since. We used to venture out in the Morris to see Dad's mother, a rather formidable old lady who lived nearby. The trip itself was exciting, in darkness, our way inadequately lit by headlights masked by triangular tin shields: the lights, not great to start with, shed their feeble glimmer about three feet in front of the car. Similarly equipped motorists groped their way past us in the opposite direction. I suppose it may have confused the Nazis overhead.

My father's father had died when he was in his early teens in Dublin. His mama, another of those indomitable Victorian dames, had brought him, her only son, to England, where they settled in Devon, and he went to Kingsbridge Grammar School, a well-placed and recognised stepping stone to the Navy. Mum was extremely wary of her.

HMS Hornet, although entirely accommodated in wooden huts, was good for a children's party, having liberal supplies of bunting, sticky cakes and sailors who enjoyed being silly – show me one who doesn't. Mum and I were at one of these happy occasions and settled down to watch a Mickey Mouse film – a real treat. An extremely drunk sailor sat down next to Mum and in a moment was fast asleep, head on what was left of her lap – Netta was not far off. She endured this throughout the film show, as she didn't have the heart to disturb him. Heroes come in all shapes and sizes!

Soon after Netta's birth we were on the move again, this time to Bath. Dad had a job in the Engineer-in-Chief's Department, with the rather grand title of Inspector of Machinery (Diesel Engines). He did well to get it, for the naval element of the Department at that time was almost exclusively the Daggers, engineer officers who had completed further academic studies after qualifying – often thought to be 'clever but useless'. Their dominant grip on the upper reaches of the branch was slowly loosening, in favour of less clever but arguably more useful officers. Dad was in the latter camp.

The very small cadre of naval engineering HQ had been based in London at the beginning of the war. A civil servant was sent out to find somewhere for them to go. His wanderings took him to Bath, comfortably remote from the sea, where a number of large hotels were available for requisition, and a couple of hutted sites, built almost overnight as emergency hospitals for Dunkirk, stood empty.

It's lucky for the civil servant that he arrived in daylight. Just outside Bath station is a bridge over the river Avon, with flat parapets at platform height. At night, in the pitchy black, trains frequently stopped on the bridge before entering the station. Several promising careers were terminated by those who disembarked prematurely, and plunged forty feet down to their death. The arrangement is the same to this day, though there is more light, and the trains have fewer doors.

A bit of money must have come from somewhere, for our house in Bath was bought, not rented, and was a fine Edwardian dwelling in Bath stone, 92 Newbridge Hill, near the Royal United Hospital on the western extremity of the city. Further along the road was a secluded estate, said to be the hideout of Haile Selassie, of whom there were various sightings reported, not all of them convincing. No. 92 rejoiced in the name of Revelstoke, possibly after the eponymous Lord R who was something of an adventurer in 18th century Italy. It had a large garden, greenhouse, garage and cellars. Mum's mum Margaret moved in with us, and there was enough room for her to have her own sitting room. Resourceful woman that she was, she promptly joined the Bath Bridge Club, which continued its busy programme throughout the war, even when the next door building was bombed. Granny proceeded to bring home £20 every week thereafter. She was a canny player.

Dad's office was the other side of town, in the requisitioned Spa Hotel. It was a lot better than most of the Admiralty office space, and he enjoyed views over the city from his window. I only remember the grotto in the grounds which featured in the inevitable children's parties. Another requisitioned hotel was the Grand, an undistinguished building with an incomparable position, overlooking Pulteney Bridge and the Avon weir, with the Parade Gardens and the Recreation Ground (home of Bath rugby) also in sight. Undistinguished it may have been, but it did have a marvellous wooden staircase, so exceptional that it was listed, although the building wasn't. At some stage during the war a near-miss went off, and the precious staircase sighed and moved a bit. Men from the Ministry of Public Buildings and Works (MPBW) rapidly arrived and erected a web of scaffolding to support the staircase. Forty years later the scaffolding was still there, and had, it was supposed, in its turn been listed too.

The cadres of civil servants who worked in these various buildings rapidly developed a culture and conditions of service of their own. Thirty years later when I was, in my turn, a shiny young Commander working at Foxhill – one of the Dunkirk hospital sites – I noticed that a sizeable proportion of the more elderly draughtsmen were leaving the site half an hour before packing up time.

"What are they doing?" I asked Len Coath, my wonderfully indulgent Senior Draughtsman.

"They're off home", he replied "They're Spa Hotellers".

"And?" I said.

"And they leave half an hour early, to avoid the traffic".

"What traffic?"

"The traffic in North Road."

"But we're nowhere near North Road."

"No, but the Spa Hotel was."

"And when did they leave the Spa Hotel?"

"Twenty seven years ago."

"I see."

Life in suburban Bath was interesting after the wilds of Meon Marsh. Newbridge Hill abounded in elderly ladies who seemed to enjoy a small blonde boy causing a public danger by dominating the pavements on his Fairy cycle. There were occasional jaunts to the city, where, despite the war, Jolly's tearooms still produced some exceptional chocolaty treats. There were also a number of toyshops which, just now and then, might have Dinky toys in stock, rationed to one on each visit. ("There's a war on, you know"). In Kingsmead Square there were itinerant displays of militaria, and I remember sticking postage stamps (2 ½ d.) on 1000 lb bombs. Or perhaps bigger still. They seemed enormous to me. Above the Square was the Theatre Royal, where I went to see my first play ever, "Where the Rainbow Ends". It was half panto, half pageant, full of St George, dragons, explosions, smoke, music and pretty young women, sometimes dressed as men. Pure magic!

I was going to another little school along by the hospital. Shrouded in clouds of amnesia, apart from three startlingly good-looking little classmates, Rosemary Burgess and the Exton girls – Denise, willowy and dark, and Carol, short with blonde curls. I also made a new friend, John Cole, who lived round the corner in Penn Lea Road. There was an air of frothy affluence about the Coles. I often went out with John and his parents in their huge car, and our excursion usually ended, after a big lunch, in some railway siding where his dad disappeared into some hut or other, to re-emerge wreathed in smiles and cigar smoke. It all seemed good to me, but my own parents were critical of what they thought of as a spiv in the black market – they were probably right.

Dad had acquired a BSA 250 motor bike and it was a special treat to have a ride on the back. One warm summer's day we took a picnic to Stonehenge, about an hour's run. When we arrived we rode over the rough grass and leant the bike against one of the great stones. There were no Soviet-style guards, no plastic grass, no depressing visitors' centre smelling of urine – just us and our picnic under the stones. Dad's picnics were always the same, a hardboiled egg and bread and butter, with a bottle of stout for him. He never ventured forth without a folded wad of loo paper in his top pocket 'in case we're taken short'.

On other summer days we used to go and row on the Avon. I was taught by my godfather Frank Windsor, a Cambridge blue in his time, who, after a lifetime in the Indian Army as a doctor, had retired to Emmanuel College. He was a good-looking, amiable man, and he had a very smart cream, open Lanchester, complete with red leather upholstery. Dad was unimpressed – or envious! I quickly got the knack of rowing the rather nice skiffs let out from a boat-house on the river, and felt important at the oars whilst Mum, Granny and Netta giggled on the cushions in the stern, and steered using twin ropes attached to the rudder head. A pause half way, this time for one of Mum's picnics – Madeira cake.

Amongst all this picnicking the war rumbled on, not making a great impression on my small introverted life. There was a fair amount of aircraft activity, as Bristol was a major strategic target for the Luftwaffe. For a short period Bath too was included in the Baedeker raids. The city featured an exceptional number of iron railings, and these were remorselessly harvested by the authorities for recycling. Sadly very few were ever replaced, as they added a look of elegance to otherwise quite ordinary streets.

As the war stuttered towards its conclusion, and the first bananas were spotted with incredulity in the greengrocers, it was time for Dad to go to sea again, this time to the cruiser Diadem. This should have been a pleasant appointment, but he developed a gastric ulcer which went wrong, and had to be hastily landed in Copenhagen days after it had been liberated. Here he was accommodated in a military hospital, where he promptly contracted pneumonia. Fortunately a 19 year old Danish nurse, Isse Bronnée, had taken a shine to him and announced with Danish candour "if you stay here you will die." Isse used her friends and family influence to get Dad moved to a civilian hospital. Placed on the danger list, he nevertheless managed to get a wavering message home "come quickly, and bring cycle inner tubes".

At home Mum and I scoured the cycle shops of Bath, and when she had a bagful she set off to Black Bushe aerodrome to become the first 'ordinary civilian' to fly into Copenhagen. Here she found Dad slowly recovering, and was greeted by his new Danish friends, who fell upon the consignment of rubber goods with ecstasy. Dad made a long convalescence, minus half a lung and some of his stomach, and was eventually repatriated to Barrow Gurney Hospital near Bristol, to complete the process. Isse became a lifelong family friend, and I met her and her family when I went to Denmark as a Midshipman.

In 1946 I went off to St Christopher's Preparatory School, oddly enough almost next door to the aforementioned Spa Hotel in North Road. I hated boarding for the first couple of terms, feeling violently homesick, wetting the bed, which of course made things worse, and generally getting in a state. Eventually all that wore off, but I still find it strange that I was made to be a boarder just the other side of town. The zeitgeist I suppose.

Schools were struggling in 1946 with so many potential teachers still being tied up with the Armed Forces. St Christopher's was run and owned by a patrician classicist, Ted Pryor, with flowing grey locks and a vein throbbing in his temple; and by his rather less patrician wife Mavis, a large untidy woman with, we fondly thought, a taste for gin. She did however play the piano, an essential requirement. The baby classes, through which I transited, were taught by Miss Florence (a plump, amiable woman) and later by Mrs Boardman, sterner stuff! Miss Moore, the maths teacher, was small, dark and a very good, unemotional teacher. But for me there was one outstanding teacher, Squadron Leader Kefford, who taught English and Geography. He had spent much of the war in Ceylon and had a delightful, low key, Celanese wife. He taught as to the manner born, but his real forte was to talk about nature; he was entirely captivating, drawing on his own youth for many of his stories and observations. He and his wife took me to my first ever concert, where we heard the L'Arlesienne Suite by Bizet. For many years I loved this piece – but seem to have gone off it now!

There were about 100 boys, mostly accommodated in the school buildings, though the senior boys had a boarding house a few hundred yards along the road. We wore bright red blazers, ties and caps, and grey otherwise. We used to proceed into Bath in crocodiles for the functions that I can recall, church at the Abbey, swimming and gym at Captain Olsen's basement in Pulteney Street. Otherwise we didn't leave the school very often, except for away matches. Not being much of a sportsman, I seldom went.

This was no loss, as the school had large grounds with plenty to do. Above the lower playing field was a long bank, out of which a 'Burma Road' had been carved. We each had our own section – allocation process forgotten – which we kept in good condition by carving and smoothing the earth, and where our treasured Dinky toys toiled to and fro.

Perhaps following Mum's example, I became involved in the Hen Party, a bunch of boys responsible under the groundsman for feeding and mucking out the flock of hens which provided our eggs, otherwise still rationed. We had a large hand-cart which, when loaded with chicken-shit, could be raced down the hill to the compost heap, a terrific helter-skelter.

There was a row of poplars which were alive with poplar hawk moths, and in the autumn we each had one these large, mournful caterpillars, slowly turning from green to purple in a jam-jar, and munching a few leaves before spinning their chrysalises. I can't remember them hatching out the next spring, but I suppose that they must have.

Perhaps the best bit of the grounds was several hundred acres of downs at the back of the school land, which ran up to Sham Castle, a one-dimensional Victorian structure designed to add drama to the sky-line. Here we could run free, building lairs, damming streams and getting filthy. I had been admitted to the Mounties, the top secret society – some secret! Everyone knew about it! – and we remained supreme whilst I was there.

We were looked after quite well, I suppose, though the food was dreadful. For most of our married lives Janey has been re-introducing me to dishes which I swore I'd never touch again. We seemed to spend a lot of time in the kitchens either working the antediluvian spud-basher or washing up. Mavis and the Matrons used to issue us with the dreaded malt every morning, queuing up for a spoonful of Vimaltol or Radio Malt, according to taste. What's to taste, both were pretty vile?

We were allowed home every third Sunday, taking with us friends whose parents were far away. On one occasion I took a rather smooth boy with me, who obviously came from a moneyed background. Dad, of whom the best that could be said was that he was a niche gardener, had persuaded a nectarine to flourish in the greenhouse, despite its lack of glass. Flourish is perhaps a relative term, for it eventually produced just one highly prized fruit, whose progress was minutely chronicled. I shall never forget the look on Dad's face when my chum, who had been prowling round the garden, sauntered in and said cheerfully "that nectarine was delicious!"

Parents were not greatly in evidence at St Christopher's, though they turned up for the usual sports days and other festive occasions. A friend of mine, Mickey Rouse, had a most glamorous mum who the boys all adored. She was married to a successful bookie, and thus had no shortage of nylons and other sought after bits of clothing which made her look even more exquisite. Thus, doubly hated by all other mums, poor creature.

After his long convalescence, Dad started a new job — at the Admiralty Engineering Laboratory in West Drayton. This consisted of a fine old house surrounded by a slew of sheds, warehouses, lean-tos and temporary buildings scattered throughout the grounds in flagrant disregard of any planning constraints that might have been applicable. "The Lab" as it was known, carried out a wide variety of fairly obscure experiments. It struggled for years with components for the Admiralty Standard Range of light diesel engines, but these, eventually fitted in O & P class submarines and in numerous frigates and destroyers, never really met the criteria of low maintenance and high reliability effortlessly delivered by commercial designs — a theme I might return to!

Years later I visited the Lab and was shown the arrangements for testing the high voltage equipment (33 kV) being intended for the Carrier Replacement programme of the 1960s. These big carriers, being designed to replace Eagle and Ark Royal, were eventually cancelled, not least, it was said, because the Royal Air Force contrived to "move" Australia, to prove that all areas of the Indian Ocean could be covered by shore-based (RAF) aircraft. It sounds ridiculous enough to be true. The Lab had eight submarine batteries — acres of 2.1V cells in harness in a shed the size of — oh yes — a football pitch. This was described as the largest electrical storage facility in Europe, comprising I suppose about 60,000 ampere-hours. I was shown the results of the experiment in which they had applied the collective voltage across a piece of armoured ring-main cable and then fired a six inch nail through it. I saw a hole surrounded by the spelter of vaporised cable, which whilst impressive was hardly surprising. That perhaps was the Lab for you!

Dad by this time had acquired a pre-war London Talbot, a sturdy open car with a tatty hood and terrible yellow talc side screens, much patched with surgical tape. It did have a very smart tonneau cover, a town and country horn (soft and loud respectively), a handle under the dash to cut out the silencer, and a fly-off hand brake lever to the right of the driver. For Mum's hair, a disaster; for Dad's and my street-cred — cool.

Whist he was weekly commuting to West Drayton, Mum took in a lodger, namely Dad's old friend Geoff Cowland. Short, round, balding always with a twinkle and a cigarette, he was a delightful man, well contrasted with Isobel, his Scottish, dry, sandy wife who was 'something at the BBC'. Mum was thought of by the ladies of Newbridge Hill as 'the woman with two husbands', which tickled her immensely.

As is the way, I was finding St Christopher's increasingly enjoyable, and all trace of homesickness had now disappeared. So I was not downhearted when Dad was invalided out of the Navy and found a job with ICI in Cheshire. The family moved to Haslington, a village near Crewe, and for my last three years at St Christopher's I used to get the Pines Express down from Crewe to Bristol Temple Meads, then a local train across to Bath. These trips were of course preceded by the ritual of PLA — Personal Luggage in Advance. My trunk was picked up from home by railway transport — a three wheeler Scammell towing a trailer. At the start of term a huge consignment of trunks was delivered to the school playground, to be fallen upon by the odd-job man, the Matron, and eventually the boys themselves.

The house in Cheshire was in the village of Haslington, two miles from Crewe, and slap in the middle of the Cheshire plain. Haslington was a work-a-day dormitory for Crewe, largely built of brick in Victorian times. It was by the standards of modern villages well appointed. Church, chapel, garage, forge, pub and half a dozen little shops — oh, and the Hall of the local branch of the Ancient Order of Foresters — a perpetual puzzle to me. Our new abode, Harmel House, had been built in the 30s and was a large pebble-dashed house with an acre of grounds, including an orchard, bumpy tennis court and an area of swampy ground, known romantically, if not strictly accurately, as the Ha-ha. It had a small pond alive with crested newts where I spent a lot of time. There was a 'little sitting room' for granny, and a permanently leaky 'sun-lounge' with a flat roof on which Dad spent many hours and much money dressing the leaking seams with a variety of black tarry liquids. A hopeless cause. We only found out where the house got its strange name from when we got a Christmas card from the previous owners, a pair of music teachers. It wished us "a *har*monious Christmas and a *mel*odious New Year".

After the heady social scene in Bath, Haslington was a bit of a backwater. The forge, run by young Mr Brereton (old Mr Brereton, the former blacksmith, now confined himself to running the ironmonger's attached to the forge), was always a good place to hang out, and was probably where I first met the Watts family.

A war widow with two young daughters they lived in some style in the Hall, a beautiful black and white house near the village. I spent quite a lot of time up there, jumping their ponies bareback over one foot high jumps and enjoying my friendship with Sizza, the younger daughter — née Victoria. Joan Woodcock used to squeeze through the orchard fence from the council estate beyond, and was my theatrical partner in the shows that we put on. Netta, five years younger, always had a somewhat menial role!

Relations with the village boys were not quite so cordial. They were intent on fighting me, an option I declined until school friends came to stay, when we would go out looking for trouble, and a bloody good time was had by all.

That part of Cheshire was not the smart bit, and Mum and Dad's social life was as circumscribed as mine, with a few locals and a smattering of work colleagues. There was rather a dearth of reasonable restaurants in the area, and surprisingly the Dining Room on Crewe station was one of the best. I remember clambering off the train at 6 pm to see the local gentry descending on the Dining Room on Platform 3 in evening dress, clearly intent on a wild and gastronomic evening. O tempores!

In my final year at St Christopher's, Ted Pryor, Headmaster, decided, largely for his own amusement I suspect, that my chum O'Connor and I should form a set of two to study Greek. We didn't get very far as it was conducted in odd half-hours when there was nothing else on, but it enabled me to recite $\lambda\upsilon\omega$, $\lambda\upsilon\epsilon\iota\sigma$, $\lambda\upsilon\epsilon\iota$ with reasonable competence, and to decode the Greek alphabet. This modest accomplishment turned out handy when, later on, I was studying nuclear physics, and the equations were of such hideous complexity that every Greek letter was brigaded, and one needed to know one's ϕs from one's ψs, and ζs from ξs.

Dad announced out of the blue one day that he thought that I'd go on to Cheltenham. I later discovered that this apparently arbitrary decision was based on Cheltenham's proximity to Prescott (some ten miles to the north), where the Bugatti Owners' Club ran a hill climb for all manner of hairy motors. Dad had always greatly admired Bugattis (who had not, at that time?) but of course never aspired to one; ownership was not a condition of membership, oddly. Actually he did surprise us all by buying a very quick Connaught sports car, with leather bonnet straps, individual windscreens (like half glasses) and an exhaust note to waken the dead. Cool, as my granddaughters would say, or what?

We did go on a reconnoitre and meet the Headmaster, an utterly charming man called Elliott-Smith who had previously run the British School in Egypt – I bet that *that* was fun. Needless to say, by the time I got to Cheltenham Elliott-Smith had been replaced by the considerably less charming Reverend Pentreath, a beaky academic who soon made his mark by drastically reducing sport in favour of extra lessons. Even the boys noticed – and disapproved.

It was decided (as was so often the case, I seemed to be unaccountably missing from the decision making process) that I should sit the Scholarship exam, and duly arrived at the College one Monday morning, for four days of written papers, culminating in an interview. I noticed that I had been 'put down for' Greek, and quickly decided that to sit that would be an alpha-class mistake. When the time came for the exam I strolled down town and was delighted to find a cinema screening Monsieur Verdoux, starring Charlie Chaplin. When, at the interview, they enquired of my failure to attend the Greek exam, I told them, which resulted in a thoughtful silence. I was eventually awarded a small Exhibition, more for initiative than for academic excellence, I imagine.

Leaving St Christopher's was no great sadness, for all of us in the top year were on our way, and five years there had been enough. I said goodbye to many good friends, including Richard Penfold, my blood brother. I hardly saw any of them ever again, with the exception of two. David Smeeton, whose father had been lost with the Royal Navy during the war, became a journalist in Devon when I was there later on, and we met each others' new wives in a boozy reunion. Michael Rowse, son of the bookmaker and the glamorous mum, appeared in Wiltshire running a pub in the 80s, and, after the shock of mutual recognition he rushed up stairs and returned with a school photo, with us all in our little grey suits and shorts. I felt vaguely uneasy, as if he had admitted keeping a dossier on me!

The step change from St Christopher's to Cheltenham College where I went in September 1951 was one of scale. St Christopher's had one hundred boys; Cheltenham College had six boarding houses of a hundred each, plus a day boys' house of sixty. There was also a junior school in close consort. The College was sometimes called, with heavy irony, the Gentlemen's College, to distinguish us from the Ladies' College, with whom we had absolutely nothing to do – officially. Huge opportunities were pushed away in those chauvinist days; it now seems extraordinary and unforgivable.

The college had been well endowed by its Victorian founders. It had a magnificent chapel whose highlight was a mighty organ. A story much relished by the boys was that if the deepest note was played at full power the entire building would collapse; sadly none of the organists were up to giving it a go. The chapel's architectural pigeon pair was the dining hall, presided over by Miss Penman, who continued the tradition of revolting food that I had become acclimatised to at St Christopher's. If we went off for a day at the weekend we could ask for a picnic lunch, whose principal component was a Penman Special, a large dry bun filled with 'elephant's tool'. All our meals were taken here, for there was no catering in the houses. But of course that was where our tuck-boxes were, well stocked by doting mothers. To this day the smell of boot polish reminds me of eating toast in the boot room, accompanied by drinking sweetened condensed milk through a small hole in the top of the tin. It seemed like heaven then.

Many of the other college buildings were in tune with the Victorian gothic of the chapel, and included a cloister, a good theatre and library and, of course, a multitude of classrooms. The sports field, still good enough to stage county cricket matches, was ringed on three side by college buildings, including the hideous striped brick gym, and the apologetic little tuck-shop alongside it.

Some years later I went to see the film "If", a delightful fantasy by Lindsay Anderson. Unknown to me the film was shot at Cheltenham, a shock to see my familiar environment on display.

The boarding houses had been acquired, built or modified later and were all a bit different, though they shared the essential features. A large sweatroom for the younger boys, a senior sweatroom for the fifth form and a long row of 'shacks' — studies for the sixth form boys. Dormitories, bathrooms and staff accommodation and, outside, a large tarmac playground. In my house, Cheltondale, the playground was overlooked by the geriatric wing of a hospital, and we used to spend much time, particularly around November the fifth, in trying to fire rockets through the open windows. In due course, no doubt exasperated by this behaviour, the superior purchasing power of the NHS allowed them to buy Cheltondale and then demolish it. I'm sure that Cheltondale was replicated elsewhere, perhaps with some more tempting targets.

Cheltenham College had been identified as the alternate seat of government during the war, and it was planned that the college should collocate with Shrewsbury. Nothing came of it, except the establishment of GCHQ near the town. The boarding houses were scheduled to become MPs' offices, and in Cheltondale the shacks had been wired, for but not with telephones, so that they could all talk to each other. We spent many happy hours trying to do the same by clipping various bits and pieces onto the wires they had left behind, but the technology of the time was not on our side, and we soon discovered that our preferred suppliers – Government Surplus – only dealt in equipment that was surplus to any conceivable requirement.

The social life of the boarding house was a defining feature, and we combined only in our scorn of the day-bugs who were denied it. Our housemaster was Dr Johnston, or HJ, and I can still manage a passable stab at his signature, useful for all sorts of slightly dodgy activities. He was a small, precise man with huge glasses and a habit of clicking his teeth. His wife was even smaller, and was assisted by Matron, an almost identical woman; these two midgets presided over the cleanliness and laundry of the house, and occasionally took a half-hearted crack at our moral cleanliness, without noticeable effect. There was also an assistant housemaster, Mugs Miller, a second row forward in his day, since passed, whose single but substantial claim to fame was that he had reduced a colleague's priceless viola d'amore to matchwood by inadvertently sitting on it at a concert in the town.

In the house we did prep – three hours a night, loosely supervised by a sixth former, spent many hours in the playground, prepared weird meals in the boot room, and played and listened to music. My love of jazz started there with an excellent pianist – George Purves – and a record of Humphrey Lyttelton playing 'The Onions'. We polished, inefficiently, our "Corps" uniform, and paraded on Wednesdays, in the playground before marching up to Coll for the larger parade. We kept our prized bikes there, and these formed a major part of the weekend, with expeditions all over Gloucestershire. In the summer the twelve mile ride to Tewkesbury, where the college rowing took place on the Severn, was a favourite outing.

We made forays into the town, ostensibly to buy toiletries and the like, using HJ's chit, or to have a haircut at Cav House, the upmarket store, much approved of by mums and disparaged by dads. In fact we more often were after cigarettes, at a penny apiece at the corner shop, or VP Ruby Wine, the gut-rot sold only at chemists; well, it certainly had no wine content. What a way to start a drinking career!

Friendships waxed and waned, often with an exciting hint of sexuality. We were, I suppose, the classic testosterone time-bombs, all ticking away like mad. Beautiful little boys were called 'bijoux', and were discussed endlessly. The fagging system, in its dying gasp, was intertwined with sexual ambition, and those of us who were definitely not bijoux tended to get off more lightly.

During my time there I did have one girl friend at the Ladies' College, who I had met on a sailing holiday. There was a loophole in their Colditz-like security, and we were able to see quite a lot of each other, but only in the many churches in the town during services, sitting at the back and holding hands. Comparative religion it wasn't. Mum and Dad used to come down occasionally, and I remember rather severe meals at their hotel, Sunday chapel (no holding hands), and, if Dad had his way, a day out at the Prescott hill-climb.

Despite all these diversions there was a bit of academic work going on, though at this remove it made little lasting impression. Six or seven years after the war the teaching staff were still split between the old and the young, with nothing much in the middle. I do remember Pot Mosley, an immensely fat man who tried to teach us Latin, but he is remembered more for his belly than for his teaching. Good teaching in English and Maths, Science scrappy, History and Geography minimal, and the Arts almost non-existent. Par for the course perhaps at that time. Anyway it seemed to be good enough.

At fifteen, without very much ado, I took the Dartmouth exam, and in due course heard that I had passed, and was called forward for interview. It would have been pleasant to have stayed for another two years as a sixth former enjoying the modest privileges of seniority, but I felt that I was already inexorably trundling along the rails of a career, and finally left Cheltenham College with scarcely a backward glance. It was time to move on.

CHAPTER 2

The Cradle of Neptune?

Mum took me to London for the Dartmouth interview, and a pretty sorry figure I cut too. It was a miserable cold day in January 1954, and, in addition to a statutory winter cold of seemingly Niagara proportions, I had a large boil on my lip, winking and glistening like a Bessemer converter. Nor did the agony end there. Dad, who had generally taken little interest in the prospect of my interview, had decreed at the last moment that the one necessity for me to impress the Board was that my socks should not wrinkle. Accordingly, I was wearing a pair of his sock suspenders, a form of apparel that I hadn't hitherto encountered, and which seemed bound to cut off all circulation below the knee. So, snuffling and throbbing above, and numb and elasticated below, I felt gloomily that this was unlikely to be one of my better performances.

I also had my Guilty Secret. The previous year, when reading, en famille, the apparently endless list of interesting medical conditions that would debar entry to the Naval College, we had come across the item - Hammer Toes. It so happened that I had one of these, lying innocently alongside its other less distinguished fellows. It had never caused me any trouble, but it was resolved that it would have to go. So I went to see Mr Mitford, a private consulting surgeon in Newcastle-under-Lyme who, no doubt rubbing his meticulously manicured hands at the prospect of a bit of serious money for old rope, agreed to carry out a minute operation to straighten the offending toe. We were, collectively, less clear about whether a toe that had formerly been hammer but was now straight but unbending would pass the stringent requirements of the Royal Navy, and Mr Mitford, he of the silk and tasselled tie, was of the view that "they" would probably never notice, but to be on the safe side he would make the incision, which must have been all of half an inch long, in a curve, and I was to say, but only of course if asked, that I had cut my toe on a piece of glass on the beach. I approached the Medical convinced that my toe would be a major item of forensic study, and that the relentless questioning of hawk-eyed doctors would blow my cover story apart.

If only I had known. Naval Medical Officers have never enjoyed much of a reputation for perspicacity or indeed for sobriety, and things were worse then. It is likely that the examining Doctor, apart from being somewhat perplexed by the blue hue of my lower legs caused by the sock-suspenders, would have been pleased to be able to distinguish an individual toe let alone observe some trivial micro-surgery. My secret has been safe to this day, and Mr Mitford's artwork has never really had the audience it deserved.

The Medical itself was held in the forbidding atmosphere of Queen Anne's Mansions, long since pulled down, only to be replaced by the present Home Office, a dubious genuflection in the direction of progress. I can't remember much about the examination itself, which seemed pretty cursory apart from the optical section, which made heavy weather indeed of the requirements for colour perception. Eyes filled with drops which did nothing for visual acuity, we peered at tiny lights in red, green and white in a simulation of a ship's lights at sea, whilst the lights got steadily smaller and fainter the while. In many years at sea subsequently I never saw anything so difficult to resolve, and indeed if lights were ever that distant it was comfortably assumed that they were too far away to worry about (whatever their colour).

Finally, after we had trailed round the building for some hours, coughing and bending, breathing deeply and repeating "ninety-nine", denying that we had ever suffered from dengue fever, chilblains or syphilis, we were brought together for the "intelligence tests". It was strenuously denied that the results of these would have any bearing on The Interview, but nevertheless they must be completed so that the Psychologist on the interviewing panel could consult them "if he wished", a signal for much rolling of eyes and shared dark glances amongst the Candidates, as we had learnt that we were called. So we fought our way through the usual collection of gallimaufry, spotting the odd man out, decoding primitive ciphers, matching obscure shapes with others which were inverted, flipped over or reversed, and completing a number of increasingly unlikely catch-phrases or sentences. It was with considerable relief that we were bundled, still weeping gently from the eye-drops, into taxis bound for Paddington - and the West.

Once installed on the train, in groups of three or four scattered throughout the third-class compartments, we began to explore our individual relationships, pleased to be people again after a long day acting as ambulatory medical specimens. We were after all herded together in the same boat, united by our common desire to join the Navy, and more immediately by our common fear of the unknown. We pooled all manner of unlikely stories garnered from our various schools. We were under continuous surveillance whilst on the train; the ticket collector was a Navy spy, checking for signs of weakness or decadence; members of the interview board were travelling on the train disguised as old ladies; our purchases from the buffet would be reported to the board and evaluated for evidence of un-officer-like tastes. Having frightened ourselves pleasantly, we decided that it was all a load of nonsense, and passed round a packet of ten Rhodian No 3s, one of the thinnest and foulest cigarettes known to man, though pride of place in that department must go to a Central American product called a Mexicana, which had to be held horizontally to prevent the contents, unconvincingly masquerading as tobacco, from falling out.

The long train journey thus passed pleasantly. The candidates had been batched up alphabetically, so I found myself in the company of fellow sporters of the middle letters - Innes, Melhuish, Midgely, Milne Home, Neville-Rolfe and Pitt amongst others. These early contacts were to survive into Dartmouth where we felt bound together by the ordeal we had shared.

We disembarked eventually at Kingswear, the railhead on the eastern side of the River Dart, and sampled the brief ferry ride across the river to Dartmouth Station. As we gazed up at the huge bulk of the College, brilliantly illuminated in its commanding position above the town, and reflected in the black waters of the Dart, we felt that we were already part of the maritime tradition, and swayed nautically, we hoped, at the guardrails. These tenuous links with Nelson et al were rapidly swept away by being bundled unceremoniously into a bus by a disgruntled Chief Petty Officer and driven up the hill to the College where we were immediately treated to that most traditional of Naval snacks - a cup of Kye and a Ships' Biscuit.

Kye is an early precursor of cocoa, but there the similarity ends. Provided in the form of large powdery blocks of bitter chocolate of an unrivalled hardness and an unusually high melting point, this staple diet of the watchkeeper at sea is prepared by some minion such as the Midshipman of the Watch attacking the giant slab with as big and sharp a knife as he can find and hacking it into submission. By the time it is ready to be dissolved in boiling water, he is exhausted - and covered in chocolate. When consumed, best at night when its dun colour and mottled appearance caused by the floating blobs of cocoa-fat cannot be seen, it is without sweetness, and gritty from some thankfully undisclosed impurity. It is faintly addictive, and has the unique property of being one of the few substances known to man that can reduce ships' biscuits to an edible state.

The ships' biscuit itself has a long history, and is perhaps most famous as a domicile for weevils, which were classically dislodged by rapping the biscuit sharply on the table. An assembly of cognoscenti issued with this fare made a noise like a Mah Jonghh party as they indulged in formation de-weevilling. Having purified the biscuits, it was necessary to render them edible, for they were so solid and hard that no teeth could crack them unaided, hence the juxtaposition of Kye.

Having enjoyed this heady foretaste of things to come, and made our first acquaintance with the doughty Miss Bulla, famed and feared Catering Manager to the College, we were led off for a fitful night of anticipating the morrow. Weary as we were, we knew that the Selection Process had not yet started. . . .

The Board, which consisted of an Admiral, two Captains, a Headmaster brought in from a public or grammar school and a Psychologist, had two separate interrogation chambers: they had a suite of offices, interview rooms and the like high on the hill above the College, and they had The Gymnasium. This last was a windowless building half way down a long run of steep stairs into the woods known as Britannia Steps. Later I was to find that these same steps down which we strode with such innocent insouciance were a principal punishment ground for erring Cadets, and many was the unhappy hour I spent bunny-hopping up them, usually with a rifle sagging above my head.

The Gym, sour with the smell of fear and sweat, was sparsely kitted out with a few ropes dangling overhead, some oil drums, and a variety of baulks of timber. However the most salient feature was not these modest artefacts, but two parallel chalk lines drawn perhaps fifteen feet apart on the floor. These delineated the Bottomless Chasm. The Interview Board were ranged, clipboards in hand, around the walls, and a couple of naval Physical Training Instructors, immaculate in white singlets, blue trousers and pristine gym-shoes, stood ready for any eventuality. Into this alarming space we were herded, as into a corrida. I feel sure that, like the poor bulls, we were breathing heavily and rolling our eyes until the whites showed.

It was explained to us that we would be set a variety of tasks, most of which were almost identical, involving moving equipment and/or people from one side to the other of the Bottomless Chasm without "falling in" (heavy humour, provoking smirks from the Board, sycophantic simpers from us). It was of course axiomatic that none of the planks was long enough to span the divide, none of the oil drums was light enough, none of the ropes were thick enough etc., etc. A leader would be selected for each task, and points would (doubtless) be awarded for the soundness of the plan, for the excellence of the leader, and for the individual performance of each candidate.

It seemed a not unreasonable approach at the time. It was of course consonant with the Navy's continuing preoccupation with what is called Action-Based Leadership, which is effectively the abseil made flesh. A curious choice, you might very well think, for a service where so much time at sea is the antithesis of action.

The nature of the test naturally favoured those who had done it before, were good at forcing through a plausible plan, and were reasonably athletic. This was not my strong suit. I had never taken to the gym, despite the blandishments of Captain Olsen of Bath, and had given up vaulting after a couple of noisy collisions with the box-horse. Later on at Dartmouth nemesis caught up with me, and I was classified as a 'backward vaulter', therefore requiring extra practice. I was rather proud of this accolade, though it sounded less impressive than my chum, who was a 'backward rope-climber'. I think that some schools prepared their boys for this ordeal, but Cheltenham, now in the grasp of the Reverend Pentreath, was certainly not one of them.

We eventually trailed back up to the college, and into the interviews proper, gloomily aware that our cards had already been marked with a poor performance in the gym and probably in the psychological tests. The spies on the train had also reported by now, we imagined. The interviews were predictable – one-to-one sessions with each Board member followed by exposure to the whole lot. The members played their parts perfectly:

Admiral: gruff, benign, unfocussed.

> "Were any of your people in the Services?"
> (Nine years after the war, what do you think?)

Captain (X): fierce, probing; in naval terms: anchor–faced.

> "What makes *you* think that you'll make a good naval officer?"

Captain (E): pleasant, encouraging, bland.

> "What famous engineers can you name?"
> (Answer: not many, then or now")

The Captain (E) had a contraption on his desk which he asked some candidates to dismantle and then put together again. He did not ask me, which was a pity, as I would have been good at it, after years of Meccano. I had the No 6 set, bright red and green, augmented by many older parts resulting from a vigorous swapping regime at St Christopher's. The older parts were generally pre-war, and were maroon, dark blue and gold. It all lived jumbled up in a large box at home. (Mum used to say that the sound of me rootling through the Meccano box was instantly and intensely evocative.)

Headmaster: determinedly academic.

"What texts did you study for your Latin O level?"
(Answer: Hillard & Blotting's Latin Primer, at the last moment.)

Psychologist: slightly mad.

"What does the pattern on the curtains make you think of?"
(Answer: curtains.)

My sessions seemed to go quite well, with the exception of the Board interview. We had been asked to write an essay about The Sea, and the Headmaster seemed to be convinced that I had plagiarised it. "Where did you get it from?" he kept asking, as I patiently insisted that it was all my own work, as it was. All the Board members started writing, probably not their own essays on The Sea.

In the margins of the interviews, the man from Gieves was hovering, taking our measurements. "Sir," he said, ingratiating even at that early stage, "if you are lucky enough to pass we shall have to make your uniforms very quickly." We really could not comprehend all that, and submitted, cowlike, to his practised hands running the tape up the inside leg. They did that on and off throughout my service life — you'd think that that was one dimension that would not change. Gieves was always pricey: I bought a splendid greatcoat from Ikey Goode of Portsmouth. The story was that, prudent Jewish tailor that he was, every evening during the war he would load his entire stock from his shop into a removal van which he then drove into the South Downs and spent the night. I like to think of him fast asleep on a pile of his own greatcoats, surrounded by quizzical sheep. As an impecunious Lieutenant Commander in Chatham I commissioned a new uniform from Burtons, the original fifty shilling tailor, though those days had long passed. I think that I paid thirty pounds. When the spotty youth had finished his measurements he turned to me with a ghastly smile (the best he could manage, poor chap) and said "Now, Sir, the sleeves; would you prefer the stripes or the buttons?"

At last the interviews were over and we returned to our schools, uncertain whether we would ever see each other again. I went home to report on events, celebrate my sixteenth birthday and take my motor bike road test – freedom at last? I had recently acquired a 49cc BSA Bantam, a cocky little number in pale green, with an absolute top speed of 49mph. The test took place in Sandbach, a small market town a few miles from home. I rode there through light rain; slightly worrying, as my brief practice sessions had so far always been in the dry. At the Test Centre I met the Examiner, a lugubrious man in a beige mackintosh and a pork-pie hat. He explained to me that I was to ride round a route through the town, and that he would observe me from the pavement, and might (portentously) signal to me. I duly set off on my series of laps, indicating left and right, looking over my shoulder, and changing up and down at every opportunity. I spotted the Examiner on each lap, as he lurked in the doorways of Woolworths and the Co-op. Suddenly he stepped out with a hand imperiously upraised. It was the Emergency Stop. My practice sessions had not extended to the use of the front brake. I stamped on the rear brake. The Bantam pirouetted in the wet, and I and the bike ended up at his feet. Impassively the Examiner looked down at me, wrote out a yellow failure slip, and let it flutter down onto my chest. Neither of us spoke a word – it would have been de trop.

However, when I got home somewhat crestfallen and nursing a grazed knee, there was a letter waiting for me from Gieves. Wrapped in fulsome congratulations, this told me that I had passed into Dartmouth, and that they looked forward to being of further service. A rather drier communication arrived from the Admiralty the next day, bearing the same message.

Britannia Royal Naval College, built high on the hill above Dartmouth in the early 1900s when the two officers' training hulks Britannia and Hindustan were finally condemned, had seen many varieties of entry in its fifty years of existence. Perhaps the most abiding one had been the 13-year-old entry, drawing directly on the tradition of midshipmen first going to sea when they were about twelve. For this entry Dartmouth was very much a nautical public school, educating the boys until they were 18 and could join up with those who only joined at that age, the so-called Special Entry. A few years before I arrived, the Admiralty (in its customary wisdom) succumbed to the public view that sending boys to Dartmouth at 13 was akin to sending them up chimneys. The obvious thing to do would have been to change to one entry at 18, but inevitably there was a compromise, and the 13 entry became the 16 entry. Like most compromises it satisfied no one, and almost as soon as we arrived there we were being told that our entry was a failure, though I doubt if this was ever borne out statistically.

After the traumas of the interview, it transpired that 44 of us had passed, and we were allocated to the four 'houses' in the College: Blake, Grenville, Exmouth and St Vincent. The old school-based nomenclature held on for a few more years. The civilian teaching staff were 'masters', the Headmaster had not yet become the Director of Studies, and we went to 'lessons', not study periods. House Officers took the place of housemasters, and anything remotely nautical was invariably in the hands of an officer. Collectively the staff were referred to as the Officers and Masters (O & M).

The primary building of the college was a handsome confection in Portland stone and mellow brick. Three storeys high, abundantly windowed (or should I say fenestrated?) the building extended for over a quarter of a mile in length, starting at the right hand end with the Captain's House and the Chapel, leading to two houses, separated by the Main Entrance, and ending on the left with the Cadets' Dining Hall and the Wardroom (for the O&M). It is possible that the building was so long so that it could accommodate the somewhat unwieldy (if admirable) slogan carved along the front elevation:

"It is upon the navy under the good Providence of God that the safety, honour and welfare of this realm do chiefly depend".

A quotation from the Articles of War preamble, attributed to Charles II.

In front of the building was the Parade Ground, scene of many experiences, not all pleasant; the wide encircling ramps swept up to the Main Entrance, and were very suitable for all forms of ceremonial. Closest to the town was the mast, where colours were paraded every morning and evening, and challenging flag-hoists to test the Cadets appeared every so often. Within the building, on the centreline behind the main entrance, stood the Quarterdeck, a galleried hall with an immaculately polished wood block floor. Here indoor parades were held, most notably Evening Quarters, each day before we all doubled off for our supper.

The space behind the splendid frontispiece was largely taken up with classrooms, rising eventually to a much newer brick building in which the other two houses were situated. The planners should have been shot, for there could have been no possible case for crown exemption. Behind this monstrosity a cluster of much less conspicuous buildings nestled, constructed as the need arose. Amongst these were the swimming pool and the gymnasium.

The gym, apart from its customary and (as far as I was concerned) unwelcome usage had another infinitely more glamorous function. It was the scene of the ceremony of Official Cuts, one of the most anachronistic of many anachronistic practices at Dartmouth, being a lineal and close descendant of sailors being lashed at a grating. OCs were awarded for the more heinous of domestic offences, outside the Cadet Captains' powers of sentencing, which were considerable. Cuts, non-official, were the currency of punishment, awarded in threes and administered by a Cadet Captain in the bathrooms after evening rounds; pyjama bottoms remained up, and padding was not allowed. We habitual miscreants infinitely preferred cuts to their alternative – the Slack Party. This was a complicated routine of parading in a variety of different clothing at every spare moment of our crowded day. The Catch 22 was that the Slack Party was so demanding that we could never get it right; penalty – another Slack Party. Kafkaesque. The only escape from this Hindu wheel was that all outstanding punishments were cancelled at the end of each term.

No Cadet ever saw the OC ceremony unless he was the subject of it. Bent over a vaulting horse in his PT kit, he would receive three to six strokes on the bottom administered by the Chief Physical Training Instructor, seldom a shrinking violet. What was extraordinary was the Ruritanian collection of dignitaries in attendance to observe. The Captain, Commander, House Officer and possibly a Cadet Captain represented the judiciary; the Principal Medical Officer and Chaplain were there as consultants of the last resort; and the Royal Marines Officer was the Chief PTI's boss. There may have been more – we only heard from the victims. After each blow, the Chief PTI would report to the Captain, "One official cut administered, permission to proceed?"

The smallest inclination of the Captain's head gave the affirmative.

These occasional recipients of OCs (one or two a term) were feted and lauded by their peers. We listened, breathless, to the recital of the rubric. We inspected with clinical interest the cuts themselves, the height and colour of the welts, and their positioning and spacing. We had to agree that the CPTI was generally more proficient than most of the Cadet Captains. One in particular, Benjy Bathurst, later my close colleague when he was Commander-in-Chief, was especially inept, and his enthusiastic blows could fall anywhere from neck to ankle. Much respected were two squash players, Sharpe and Gambier, who could lay on telling shots within half an inch of each of other. Richard Sharpe, an ascetic, was later known as the Navy's Jesuit and, not surprisingly, ended up editing Jane's Fighting Ships, and writing their annual, excoriating editorials.

Did we mind? Not a bit. As I've mentioned, cuts were over quickly, and the pain did not last. Did we feel abused or diminished? No, we regarded cuts as rites of passage and badges to be worn without embarrassment. Did it brutalise us? On the contrary I would class our cohort as having ended up as liberal and caring souls. Has it a place today? I think society has moved too far, not necessarily for the better, and corporal punishment, whatever its merits, must be consigned to history. A pity.

Arrival at Dartmouth was a major culture shock for us. At fifteen or sixteen we had probably made the lower sixth at our schools and were used to being reasonably well treated. When we hit Dartmouth, not only were we the newest, most junior Cadets but we had unwittingly assumed some of the roles of the thirteen year olds who we had supplanted. We were on the bones of our arses, and it hurt. A majority of us had come from public boarding schools so at least we were used to being away from home. But we all had to do what we could to alleviate the oppressive regime.

Many of us drew much succour from new friendships, as I did myself. My particular buddy in Blake house was Mike Tuohy, a scrawny lad (weren't we all?) with a mischievous Irish sense of humour. We shared a certain difficulty with authority; a liking for - and some competence at - English; marked incompetence at most ball games; and a generally anarchic attitude. We particularly enjoyed night exploits, in which we crept out of bed late at night and slipped down to the town, either to have a drink – if the pubs were still open – or simply to wander through the darkened streets, luxuriating in being 'out'. The pensioner Chief Petty Officers (Chiefs), who provided much of the College infrastructure, used to wear naval caps with a plain brass foul anchor at the front. Mike and I managed to acquire a couple of these, and wore them on our own caps together with our naval raincoats for our nocturnal forays. We were convinced that we could easily pass for these weathered old seafarers, probably at least three times our age. The secret path down to the town led across a field, often grazed by cattle. It was easy, in the pitch dark, to trip over a sleeping cow, with much subsequent commotion, and a return to College well covered in cowshit was not uncommon.

We managed to be appointed as curators of the SRE – the sound reproduction equipment which piped radio programmes to all parts of the College. This gave us a key to a small, lockable room which housed the equipment. Late at night we could sneak in there, have a cigarette and thrill to the new music beginning to come out of the States. The film of 'The Twist' came to Dartmouth whilst we were there, and we duly danced in the aisles of the local fleapit. Radio Luxembourg seemed decadent and exotic – just what we were after.

We soon found ourselves in a slightly arty pseudo-intellectual clique across the College, involving some Am-Dram and writing for the College magazine, and interminable conversations in the canteen over the nature of life etc. If there was a touch of Oscar Wilde in our mannerisms (well short of green carnations) it certainly did not extend to our sexuality. We were all resolutely hetero (Dartmouth could not have contemplated any alternative) and desperate for female company. Occasional dances at the College were arranged and large numbers of rather hearty girls were bussed in from Stover School, but there was no opportunity to establish any relationship. I exchanged letters with a girl I'd met on a sailing holiday at Burnham-on-Crouch. She was Judy Innes, whose sister Jocasta became an interior decoration guru, and she had beautiful handwriting, but the lack of opportunity for human contact soon terminated the affair.

I was not completely without sporting ability. I was good at sailing, and even better at the minority sport of .22 shooting. Sailing stood head to head with cricket and rugby as a principal College sport, but many potential sailors were permanently turned off by their baptism, which consisted of being put in the bows of a Montagu 27ft whaler, shouted at repeatedly to "dip the lug", and drenched with seawater until, tired, wet and confused, they were seasick. Cricket and cucumber sandwiches seemed a much better bet. As I had sailed before I bypassed the 'dip the lug' bit and got straight into dinghies, the dreadful RNSA 14' — all moused hooks and hairy sheets — the delightful Dart One Designs, little scows perfect for one, and the Fireflies, top of the heap but fiercely held onto by the top sailing heavies. I was occasionally allowed to crew.

One of the aforementioned heavies was a chap called Peter Court-Hampton, so obsessed by sailing that he used to tack down the wide corridors of the College, uttering little cries of "lee-oh" and "water". I last saw him many years later when he was Harbourmaster at Newton Ferrers; he seemed to have given up tacking.

The river was not merely a place for recreation, but also for important elements of our naval training. These consisted of formal instruction for all in service boat handling, pulling and sailing for largely historical reasons, and power boat handling because this was the portal to the greatly admired skill of Ship Handling.

The Montagu whaler was a wretched beast. At 27ft., and so narrow gutted that its five oars were deployed three and two starboard and port, it was an unwieldy boat for pulling, though this was its function in almost every ship of the fleet, the seaboat to effect transfers, and retrieve flotsam and people from the water. Rigged as a yawl, with its mizzen mast mounted through a ring in the rudder, none of the sails were of a size or cut to provide much in the way of propulsion. It was later replaced by a contrivance called the three-in-one whaler, a reference to an engine which had been mounted in a similar hull form, though of carvel not clinker construction. Early unreliability of this engine meant that the boat was often referred to as the 'one-in-three'.

The cutter on the other hand was a completely different kettle of fish, though withdrawn from active service. It was 32ft. long, and broad enough to accommodate twelve oarsmen seated two by two. (Possibly this explains the traditional expression for an outsize Cornish pasty, or tiddy oggie, as a 'twelve-oared job'). Simply sloop rigged, though still with the disappointing dipping lug, these heavy boats could really crack on with a force six abaft the beam. A popular race (well, with me) was the 'Crash Cutter Race', when the cutters were alternately pulled, then sailed. At the end of each sailing leg, the mast was dropped with a mighty crash onto the iron horse built into the transom – most satisfying if you didn't get hit.

Power boats, seen by some of the executive cadets as their natural inheritance, had their distinctive features too. At the bottom of the heap was the humble motor cutter, a single screw boat powered by a little Dorman engine, which produced clouds of black smoke on starting, and a distinctive donk-donk thereafter. A bowman stood with his upper half sticking out of the forward canopy, flourishing a boathook. Under the main canopy crouched a cadet carrying out the duties of stoker. That is to say, his simple tasks were to open or close the throttle, and throw the gearlever into ahead or astern. Though the coxswain of this little vessel stood only three feet from the stoker, and within easy earshot, protocol insisted that engine orders were to be passed by whistle – one blast for slow, two for fast, and three for astern. But there was also the requirement for the coxswain to communicate with the bowman, which he did by shouting at him, although he was a lot further away than the stoker. The first, principal and abiding shout was "Fenders!" – an important part of naval mystique. Fenders were only to be out just before, during or immediately after being alongside something. Any boat seen pootling along in clear water with fenders out would attract furious shouting of "Fenderrrs!" from the jetty. If the coxswain had his whistle in his mouth at the time, chaos could ensue.

Coming alongside was perhaps the most demanding of all power boat manoeuvres, and the most practised. To save the boats and the jetty from excessive wear and tear most of the practices were carried out on the Beagle Barge. This was an immensely solid open barge occasionally used to transport the College pack of beagles upriver to some inland meet. It stayed out in all weathers, uncovered, and was a favourite perch for cormorants and seagulls. It was only cleaned out immediately before and after a beagle transit, and was thus usually rank with guano. It swung round a single buoy, lying by wind and tide. The phrase, "Stand by to come alongside the Beagle Barge, starboard side to" will still cause the hairs on the back of his neck to rise on every officer who passed through Dartmouth at that time.

It takes a certain finesse. A gentle curve of approach at a reasonable speed (no creeping), followed by a quick burst of astern power should bring the boat directly alongside the Beagle Barge, with the slightest creak of the fenders as they touch the barge. The bowman should be holding on with his boathook, the coxswain should have secured his stern rope, and the imaginary VIP should be able to step simply from one to the other.

There can be snags. Wind and tide may be vigorous and variable. The Beagle Barge can swing on its mooring and change the angle of approach. The stoker may be slow on his response to the whistle. The bowman may miss with his boathook. When the engine goes astern to take the way off it kicks the stern to starboard or port depending on the propeller's direction of rotation. This can help tuck the stern in for an approach on the "right" side, but requires an approach with a vigorous swing on the "wrong" side. All the parameters need to be in accord for a successful manoeuvre. Imperfections result in:

* An impressive crash, which can throw the crew off their feet,

* The boat ending up at right angles to the barge, held on by the bowman. He will shortly be forced to let go, and will probably drop the boathook. (Boathooks usually float vertically, their metal hook downwards. The foot or so clear of the water has been mistaken for a submarine periscope in open anchorages; another story.)

* The boat will end up parallel with but six feet away from the barge. The only answer is to "go round again", another evocative cry.

The next boat in the pecking order was a curious aberration – the Kitchen Rudder Cutter. Dr Kitchen's concept was simple: the engine and propeller ran at a constant speed in one direction. The water flow round the propeller could be diverted anywhere from right astern to right ahead by two curved buckets. The idea was brilliant and I have seen it used with great success in a larger vessel, steered by a wheel, with the handwheel operating the KR gear nearby. In the Dartmouth cutters the handwheel was under the tiller, and it was absolutely necessary to face aft to operate it – always at the time of maximum danger. Cue: another almighty crash, and "round again".

The absolute peaches of the Dartmouth flotilla were the Picquet Boats. Elegant in black and white, capacious and quick, they were driven by two smooth Gardiner engines, quite without vice. Bridge controls, so no whistles. Once we had our PB tickets we could take them up to Dittisham or Totnes, or out and around the coast. Greatly loved, and for good reason.

The grand prix member of the stable was a single FMB – fast motor boat. Low, flat and fast, driven by two screaming Perkins, it was like most grand prix steeds, exciting but unreliable. It was supplanted in the fleet by the Fairey Huntress, which wasn't much better.

There was one final element in the maritime inventory and that was the Offshore Yachts. These consisted of five 50 square metre "windfall" yachts, which had been captured from the Germans at the end of the war as reparations. They had been built for and used by the Luftwaffe for recreation in the Baltic, probably mostly day sailing. They were good looking, fast, very wet and primitive (no engines, or loos). When I say very wet, this refers partly to their design – the Baltic is pretty smooth compared to the Channel – and partly to the fact that everything leaked, and plastic had not really become available. As seawater seeped, squirted and dripped inboard there was an overwhelming smell of mildew and, even on fine days, everything down below was damp to the touch. The few bits of electrics never had a chance!

Despite all this, and because we didn't quite realise that there was an alternative world out there, we had a great time in the yachts. We used to race round a triangular course outside the harbour mouth, and at weekends thrash over to the Channel Isles, retrieve some duty-free, and return home. The lack of an engine made these expeditions somewhat uncertain. I remember drifting for three days in mid-channel with no hint of a zephyr. Although the tides run quite hard there are no currents; every twelve and a half hours you are back in the same place. Before we got back to Dartmouth we'd run out of everything including water, except for red wine and cornflakes – hardly a winning combination.

Each house sailed its own yacht; Blake's was Martlet. We were accompanied on our cross-channel jaunts by various staff officers, including John Robertson, an immensely tall Lt Cdr (L), and Lt Cdr Brett-Knowles, an even taller bearded Instructor Officer or 'Schoolie' with a taste for the outward bound life. One of the things that I remember all too clearly (though I wish that I didn't) is BK, his immensely long and hairy legs naked from waist to ankle, leaning against the boom in an al fresco alternative to the communal bucket below. Too many arctic expeditions I fancy.

During my time at Dartmouth, three of us, Roddy Innes, Mick Milne Home and I, entered the Public Schools and Universities Dragon Championship on the Gareloch. Every Dragon on the Clyde was made available, and we drew for boats each day. Each precious yacht had a brave owner's rep crouching below, on hand to avert disaster if it threatened. What a job! We did well, and were lucky to win the championship, thanks to Roddy's excellent helmsmanship. After a week of non-stop sailing by day and non-stop socialising at night we were happy but exhausted. We all ended up as submariners so got to know the waters of the Gareloch all too well.

The River Dart was really the College's jewel, its Unique Selling Point. Wooded to the waterline with garlic-smelling forests, it drained much of Dartmoor, passing through lively Totnes and picturesque Dittisham (locally pronounced Ditsam); it skirted Agatha Christie's house, high on the hill, before debouching between the twin towns of Kingswear and Dartmouth. As the river, flowing more slowly now, reached the sea it passed the much painted Dartmouth Castle. The College's flotilla of small craft was an excellent mix, well secured in neat lines of moorings, and all serviced by a devoted team of naval pensioners at Sandquay. Here too were the workshops where we learnt some rudimentary engineering. One of our group tasks was to take apart and reassemble small diesel engines. Although they had been worked on so many times that the nuts and bolts had almost lost their hexagons, each time we ended up with a handful of bits that had somehow been missed out on reassembly. Behind the workshops were windowless classrooms where we named the parts of the Admiralty Three Drum Boiler and its arterial partner the Closed Feed System.

Should the structural repairs to the College boats, usually necessitated by an attack of beaglebargeitis, be beyond Sandquay's capability a small civilian ship-yard, Philips, lay across the water, reached by a floating bridge or chain-ferry. The Floating Bridge Inn, on the Dartmouth side, was the closest pub to the College and was immensely, and deservedly, popular. It was there that we heard, with bated breath, a staff officer lieutenant incautiously boasting of his adventures with a Commander's wife. He left the College abruptly the following week. I also overheard two pretty 'yachtie' girls in oilskin jackets recounting that they had spent all afternoon 'making baggy-wrinkle'. Ingénue that I was, I thought that this was some delicious sexual activity, until I learnt that, more prosaically, it was simply a form of anti-chafe for a yacht's rigging.

But it was not all watery fun. Back up the hill we had a bit of work to do, and this was conducted by the Chiefs, the Officers and the Masters.

The Chiefs were the best, since their subjects were artisanal rather than intellectual. Chief Gunnery Instructor 'Dodger' Long, our parade training instructor, was their doyen, mainly because gunnery was not yet quite past its apogee. Dodger was tall, very thin and walked with an undertaker's gait, his erect body sloping slightly back. He was a master of the appropriate aphorism – e.g. "Cadet Middleton, there is a hole between your arm and your body through which I could drive a double-decker bus. (Long pause). I should not be able to do this." He also won great réclame for demonstrating, on the small arms range, the old cowboy's trick of rolling a cigarette with one hand whilst shooting the centre out a target with a revolver held in the other.

Mr Marchand was a paternal figure with white hair and a Churchillian face. He taught us seamanship; we gathered round the jackstay braced across his classroom to practise knots – or bends 'n' itches as they were called. His favourite opener was "Now gents, a knot behind your backs to stop a rope running though a block Go (very short pause) Stop!" We could soon manage a figure-of-eight in the dark and upside down, if the occasion arose. I got to enjoy the recondite world of knots and splices and can still manage the Turk's Head, Monkey's Fist and Square Sennet, though the Double Matthew Walker and Diamond Knots have slipped through my fingers, together with many others.

A Taxonomy of Cordage

Ropes are for land-lubbers.
Real sailors say "cordage" - and a lot more.
Forget the romance of the soaring rigging:
Cordage is technology, handed down
By horny-handed old Cape Horners.
Cordage can be laid up, hawser or cable-laid
And made of cotton, hemp, manila, sisal
Or the interlopers nylon, polypropylene.
And then the small stuff, cod and mackerel line,
Ginger string and sailmakers' twine.
Form follows function.
Massive towing hawsers, sheets and braces,
Breasts, springs and halyards, topping-lifts,
Hoists, purchases, messengers and whips,
Downhauls and dainty dhobi lines.
(For sailors too must raise their knicks aloft to dry.)
Splices can be long, short, back or cut
and there's a knot for every kind of job -
Except they're usually bends or hitches:
Bowlines, sheet bends, reef and overhand,
With timber, clove or rolling hitches.
And then there's decoration.
Turks' heads, Matthew Walkers, monkey's fists,
Pointing, square and diamond sennet, latticework.
It's said that seamen only speak in oaths.
But that ignores this rolling language of the sea.

Mr Marchand had two substantial toys. The first was a model of Robinson's Disengaging Gear, an ingenious arrangement of chains and hooks designed to drop a sea-boat into the sea perfectly level by releasing the falls at either end simultaneously. It came with numerous lurid warnings of how things could go wrong, from boats being dropped vertically from one fall, with dramatic loss of life, to the minor setbacks which involved amputation of fingers and thumbs. Blood-curdling as this was, it could not compare with the splendid 20ft. working model of a battleship's Foc's'le, equipped with perfect accuracy with all the many accoutrements required for anchoring or mooring a mighty warship. Who would have thought that such a basically simple operation would require a knowledge of such a plethora of names, words and phrases?

The Anchor, which could be Admiralty, Danforth, Stockless or CQR, was attached to cable which came in fifteen fathom lengths, joined by – yes – Lugless Joining Shackles. The cable ran up through the Hawse Pipe, and along the deck over Scotsmen. It passed round the Cable Holder and thence down the Navel Pipe to the Cable Locker where it was secured to the structure at the Bitter End. The deck was littered with methods of restraining the cable, Blake and Bottlescrew Slips, and a variety of Stoppers.

Because of the immense power of the Capstans, which drove the Cable-Holders, and because the Foc's'le Locker held a wide variety of Extra Special Flexible Steel Wire Rope Strops, Pennants and Blocks, there was virtually no end to the manoeuvres that could be carried out on the Foc's'le. Most of them were required for Mooring Ship, which involved dropping both anchors at a distance apart, and then inserting a Mooring Swivel between the anchor chains and the ship. The Foc's'le Officer's dream was to have it all set up as a cat's cradle, with lengths of cable and wire strops leading in all directions; at his command, the Chief Shipwright would knock off the Blake slip with his sledgehammer, and cables would disappear briskly through the hawse pipes in a cloud of red rust until the eventual scream of the brakes being applied by the Chief Stoker was heard. All would come to rest in perfect order.

Well, yes, on a good day. But days on the Foc's'le were seldom good. The Foc's'le Officer was young and green. The Chief Shipwright and the Chief Stoker were not the sort of sailors likely to give advice or indeed show any overt leadership. Their opinions would be exchanged later over a tot of rum. The Foc's'le was exposed to most of the weather sweeping the ship, and the foc's'lemen were probably wet and cold. Finally, and most disadvantageously, the Foc's'le was also exposed to the collective basilisk gaze of the Captain and other senior officers gathered on the bridge. They could see, all too clearly, the deployment of cable, anchors, slips, stoppers, strops and handy-billies (small purchases for heaving recalcitrant bits of cable about). They could also see every twitch of activity, or the lack of it. Since, by the time the ship was anchoring, everyone was eager to go below for a gin, a hot bath, or some breakfast, depending on the hour, the Basilisk Club on the bridge kept up a continuous and rising stream of discouragement or abuse to the Foc's'le.

"Chop-chop on the Foc's'le"

"What is the delay on the Foc's'le?"

"Foc's'le Officer, ring the bridge".

"First Lieutenant and Chief Bosun's Mate proceed to the Foc's'le at the rush".

Given this senior, unfriendly and hectoring audience, it is only surprising that more anchors and cable have not been lost overboard.

After all that *Sturm und Drang*, life in the Communications world was somewhat drab, mostly confined to teaching us reasonable proficiency in Morse and Semaphore, together with a nod to Flag Signalling, still widely used at that time. Our mentor was Chief Yeoman Bradley, always known as Sugar Mike, for reasons which elude me. A diminutive man, his lectures were always prefaced with the words, in a strong West Country burr:

"Have you got your nubux?",

a reference to the notebooks we were supposed to carry with us at all times. Sugar Mike was a great one for the written word, one of his favourite minatory statements being:

45

"Never try and memorise the meanings of flag hoists – always look them up. Otherwise you may send Nan Fox (drop a depth charge) when you mean Fox Nan (drop anchor)."

The Communications branch in the navy had always been heavily elitist. Signal Communications Officers, as they were called (Flag Lieutenants, as embodied by Nelson's Pascoe, had long since given up their signals duties), were undoubtedly the peacocks of the Wardroom, always immaculately dressed with extra-white cuffs and collars, invariably a white silk handkerchief in the breast pocket, and brilliantly polished half-wellingtons. Chief Yeomen of Signals, on the other hand, did not aspire to such popinjay appearance, but enjoyed the special position of always being at the Captain's side on the bridge at sea, advising him on every aspect of the signals world, and especially on Fleetwork, the manoeuvring of a number of ships in company by use of one of these signalling systems.

We usually practised our emergent skills at reading Morse and Semaphore before breakfast, huddled in pairs round the ramps of the parade ground. Sugar Mike would stand at the base of the mast with his hand flags, or use a Morse key to operate an intensely bright and noisy shuttered lantern half way up the mast. The noise of the shutter did not seem to correlate with the light, which made reading it more difficult. We used to confer, discreetly, but as the messages were usually taken directly from the Seamanship Manual, it was not difficult to fill in the gaps. The required standard was twelve words (of five letters each) a minute, or one letter a second; it didn't seem impossible.

The only other Chief that I recall was Jumper Collins, who taught us, in absurd detail, about the construction and systems of the Mk. 8 Torpedo. This, I was to find, was typical of RN training. The hardware was obsessively described, often with the most elaborate coloured diagrams to illustrate. None of us was ever likely to see inside a torpedo, let alone need a working knowledge of its components. But it would have been good to know:

> Why torpedoes?
> Alternative launching methods?

Role of Armament Depots?
Operational logistics?
Maintenance?
Tactical use of the weapon?
Replacement design under development?

These more strategic matters were never covered, and the answers to these questions were picked up, ad hoc, as we went along.

The Dartmouth Staff Officers were not particularly memorable, largely because they all seemed so similar. They were, to a man, smooth, very public school, charming but unoriginal or indecisive. I discovered the reason for this many years later when carrying out a study for the Second Sea Lord (he later claimed that I had exceeded my brief and suppressed its publication; a victory of sorts!). During this study I asked the Captain of Dartmouth how staff officers were selected. "Oh" he said, contentedly, " the Naval Secretary's people know the sort of people that we like." A self-perpetuating oligarchy laid bare!

My own House Officer when I arrived in Blake House was almost a parody of the type. His name was Randal von Tempsey Bernhardt Kettle, not quite British but radiating good breeding, I suppose. His wife was an attractive Sloaney girl, her blonde tresses almost always covered with a Hermes silk scarf, knotted on the point of the chin. Their golden Labrador was called Honey. There were a few officers who stood out as individuals. Boo Beattie was a rakish Beattyesque (no relation) type who drove a Triumph TR2 with great speed and aplomb; Jake Sanders and Mike Badham, submariners, were reassuringly scruffy; and John Kelly, pilot, thrilled us all with his low level strafes of the College in his Sea Venom. One pleasantly dry House Officer, Barty Tower, a Supply Officer or pusser, greeted new arrivals with the sentence:

"The Captain's name is Crawford, as in biscuit. Mine is Tower, as in Blackpool. That is all you need to know for the first day."

The Masters, on the other hand, were much more interesting. Many of them had been at the College for years, and had embellished their perceived lowly status by affecting eccentricities. They were certainly better teachers than their public school colleagues at that time. I remember many of them well.

Harry Biles, a short, plump Waugh-like man who thought that he was French.

Louis Seigne, who *was* French, and showed a marked indifference to almost everything, except the annual Novices' Boxing Competition, at which his eyes lit up in a not entirely agreeable way.

Mr Hall, scientist, whose eyes had been damaged in experiments 'at the Cavendish', and had his pupils sewn to a fixed aperture; he had several pairs of dark glasses, in various shades, to cope with the changing light through the windows of his classroom.

John Flanders Scott, mathematician, with flaming red hair, sticking out teeth and a laugh like a donkey. Strangely, he was related to Major White (Snotty Harry), who taught mechanics. White's lessons were punctuated with phlegm snorts, invariably followed by

" Excuse me, gentlemen, caught it in the Western Desert."

Brophy and Cobbold, both gents of the old school, had sons at the College whilst I was there. Geoff Cobbold had an immense hearing aid, which used to go into reverse, and play an amplified version of his chest wheezings and creakings to his delighted audience.

Joe Stork was the Headmaster, and was fondly believed by the cadets to be a Commie (= a mild interest in socialism, I expect). Poor man, he had suffered from polio, and had one leg in a brace. This clearly had its shortcomings, for it was far from rare for Joe to be discovered clinging to some wall, surrounded by the components of his brace. "Pick up my leg, Cadet", was his unusual request.

And so our first two years proceeded through a mixture of academic and naval tuition. It was always possible to see what term, from 1 — 6, any Cadet was, because we had to wear white lanyards across our lapels. These lanyards were relaxed successively to calibrated levels for each term, so that the first term wore them bar taut between the darts in the lapels, whereas the 6th term, demi-gods, sported them at navel level. Despite the best efforts of the Masters, our interest in academic work slumped consistently with our lanyards. This reflected the syllabus. The College had two Fleet Minesweepers, Jewel and Acute, Algerine Class, 900 tons and a crew of about a hundred – huge by today's standards. We started to go to sea in these vessels, mostly day running, to get experience of being in a ship at sea, living on the messdeck, keeping watches, carrying out pilotage (inshore navigation), lowering the seaboat and – oh, a few evolutions on the foc's'le. They served their purpose, but like all minesweepers they were functional rather than glamorous, and failed to meet the Cadets' expectations for swashbuckling.

Functional indeed, as I recall with special pleasure an incident concerning my friend John Coward, Cadet of the Watch on the bridge in some foul weather. The sweepers rolled, of course, like buckets, and John was overcome with nausea. Not wishing to lose face or create a scene, and with no obvious alternative, he whipped off his white plastic cap-cover and managed to contain his vomit, diced carrots and all. He secreted the odorous package under the chart-table, to be retrieved and thrown over the side at a subsequent quiet moment. Chutzpah? No wonder he became a Vice Admiral.

At some stage during our second year we learnt that the Cadet Training Ship, the cruiser Devonshire, or occasionally Triumph, a small carrier, would no longer carry out that role, and that we would stay at Dartmouth for a further eighteen months, going to sea in a new squadron of three frigates based there. This was something of a blow, although two days at sea in Triumph being shouted at had not exactly endeared the Training Ship concept to us. However, we thought that we had just achieved stasis when everything changed, a repetitive pattern of all our service lives.

So in due course we joined up with a Special Entry Term, and changed overnight from being Naval Cadets into Cadets RN. Outwardly much the same, this came with a massive pay rise, from four shillings a week to four shillings a day. There followed a period of relaxation of the irksome restrictions under which we had spent the previous two years. We were allowed to smoke - entitled to buy Blue-Liners, at miniscule prices. These execrable cigarettes, reckoned to consist of warehouse sweepings, were available to non-seagoers at the rate of 300 a month. 300 cost a few shillings. Horrible as they were, they must have been responsible for encouraging an almost 100% smoking habit among the young officers. Well done, the Admiralty!

We all had our own cabins, a pleasant change after the chest-flats in which we had slept and kept our kit up to now, and we set about equipping them with state of the art record players, usually the Dansette. I was able to indulge my growing affection for jazz with a few LPs, Jelly Roll Morton, Sidney Bechet and Humphrey Lyttelton featuring prominently, and being played into oblivion.

We were allowed our own transport, and my trusty BSA Bantam transformed into a Royal Enfield 250cc, a bike which took me on many adventures. This was OK, but there was a tendency to fall off after a few beers. Mike Tuohy was the owner, briefly, of a car, but managed, almost straight away, to have a collision with an old lady pedestrian in the town, and lost the licence that he had only just gained. Fortunately, our mutual friend Paddy Ryan had inherited a sporty little open Morris. This vehicle, bright red, registration number BRA 947, became regular transport for the three of us, for the many visits to local pubs which were now an important part of our social commitments.

The search for the perfect pint in the perfect pub took us all over South Devon. The villages where the pubs were situated often lay at the bottom of vertiginous lanes, hardly ideal for the bibulous. Fortunately, Devon lanes do tend to have ten foot high vertical banks, and these kept us on the road. This was particularly important for Andrew Pearson's car; the steering wheel had a nasty habit of coming off in the driver's hands. This led to the startled passenger being abruptly given the wheel to hold, whilst the driver tried to steer the car using the steering hub only – no easy trick.

Six of us bought an old fishing boat from Brixham for thirty pounds. They must have seen us coming! I'm not sure what grandiose plan we had for the vessel, but it was in a dreadful state, leaking at every seam and with an ancient hot-bulb engine which would only run on the petrol intended to start it. We nursed it round from Brixham to Dartmouth, baling furiously and drip-feeding the engine with petrol, but later, as the size of the repair task became clear, we rapidly ran out of funds and enthusiasm and the boat ended up, as we all do, on the beach — up Mill Creek without a paddle in fact.

During this period we all went away in groups to the Royal Naval Air Station at Brawdy in West Wales for our "Air Acquaint". We were flown around in a variety of aircraft, including the dreadful flying classroom the Sea Prince. This capacious old lady was intended to teach us a bit about air navigation. The smell of the rubber face masks, and of the disinfectant used to give them a cursory wipe, caused feelings of nausea before even leaving the runway, meaning that little navigation was learnt. We were allowed to use the Wardroom Mess, and were immediately captivated by the ancient, well-oiled aviators with their tales of derring-do. One particular character gazed round at his spellbound audience and slurred:

"I will now give you the only advice which is really worth listening to." We held our collective breath.

"Never," he said, "trust men with beards, nor women in leopardskin trousers." Quot homines, tot sententiae.

In the end, despite the blandishments and racy lifestyles of the ancient aviators, Michael and I did not volunteer for aircrew, This may, in part, have been due to the fact that we were punished, for some footling offence, by being made to run round the perimeter of the airfield. We were quite accustomed to such exercise, and took the 7.8 miles pretty well in our stride. Not so the fat Commissioned Gunner on his bicycle who had unwisely decided to oversee this event; he suffered deeply.

We went on lengthier cruises in the Dartmouth Training Squadron, Vigilant, Venus and Carron. We were probably Midshipmen by then, with the traditional white patches on the lapels, and a new height of eye which allowed us to look down on mere Cadets. The Senior Officer of the Squadron, and Captain of Vigilant, was Morgan Giles, an urbane and amiable man whom we all respected. He used to entertain us, in small groups, to lunch when at sea. Sometimes towards the end of the meal he would fall silent and withdrawn. His Secretary would explain, as he ushered us quietly away, that MG had spent time in Japanese POW camps, and had flashbacks. He was well off, and subsequently became MP for Winchester. At every port that we visited, his wife would be waiting on the jetty in the Rolls-Royce.

We visited Den Helder, a Dutch Navy port, and discovered Genever, or Bols gin. We went to Korsor, in Denmark, and I was able to meet Isse Bronnee, my Dad's salvation. She and her husband gave a drinks party before we went off to eat at the Tivoli Gardens. At the party everyone, all Danes, spoke English, and I asked why.

"Because you're here", came the simple and humbling response.

We went on to Hamburg, still quite flattened in many places by the dreadful firestorm, and busy with reconstruction. However our more dubious and inevitable destination was the Reeperbahn. We made our way through the corrugated iron entry points, reminiscent of Checkpoint Charlie, and started to view the goods on offer, much of it past its sell-by date, and deserving of a Government Health Warning. We ended up in a dingy club where we watched, with assumed nonchalance, a naked woman assault another with a large rubber dildo. When we got back to the ship we found that this weapon had mysteriously accompanied us. We inspected it minutely, from a safe distance, and then made sure that it was taken away and 'strapped down in the cells'. The next morning the Madame came onboard with a long bag to collect what she called her 'gummy prick'. As a rite of passage this episode scored highly.

Our life onboard mirrored that of young sailors quite closely. We lived on a mess-deck and slung our hammocks. These were a comfortable way of sleeping, especially in a seaway, and very economical in space. Lashed up hammocks were also handy in case of action damage, when they could be rammed into holes in the ship's side. The Admiralty almost certainly abandoned them prematurely, when all that was needed was a little modernisation. The drawback to the hammock lay in the slinging and, worse, the stowage the next morning. Simple enough evolutions if one was alone, but the spacing between hammocks was minimal and we fell over each other. In the morning the hammock had to be lashed up into a tight sausage with nine marline hitches, and its nettles tucked in, before it was stowed with the others in the netting, ready for the first shell to come through the side. A zip and an improved method of stretching it tight were all that were needed, really.

Although we were employed all over the ship to learn as much as possible, we had a standing appointment to our 'parts-of-ship', in my case the Quarterdeck. Here Petty Officer Noble, a small pugnacious man, instructed us in the ways of cleaning as an alternative religion. We scrubbed, washed and polished for our lives. Sadly, the wherewithal was severely limited – the buckets, scrubbers and deckcloths, 'pusser's hard' soap, washing soda and Brasso – we got through gallons of the stuff. The Sisyphean task would have been easier with hot, fresh water, but we usually had to make do with cold and salty. My particular bête noire, and therefore in PO Noble's eyes the job at which I should be forever employed, was the beading round the spurn-water, that part of the deck which abutted onto the ship's side. The beading was where the stokers rested their oily boots when they came up from below and, quite illegally, leant on the guard-rail to survey the horizon and enjoy a smoke. Despite my frenzied attacks, it never really passed muster.

In bad weather the Quarterdeckmen had to work in the tiller flat. This poorly ventilated spot, right aft, moved around a lot. The propellers thrummed below, whilst the swash-plate pumps of the steering gear emitted their own distinctive sound. The bulk store of pusser's rum also contributed its own puke-invoking odour. In this fetid compartment we were entrusted with 'tiddlywork'. Every guard-rail and awning stanchion, themselves quite simple and stylish, galvanised and painted white, was deemed insufficiently tiddly, and required to have a canvas gaiter sewn onto it, with a Turk's Head in hambro-line top and bottom. Talk about piling Pelion upon Ossa! When finished, this artifice was given a coat of Duresco, pronounced 'Drisco'. Totally otiose.

And so we came to the end of our time at Dartmouth. It had turned us from callow youths into young officers who would be able to fit in when we joined the Fleet. We were smart, fit, confident, decisive and reasonably well informed. Our academic education had not lived up to the skill of the Masters, and the naval paradigm had had a 1930s tinge to it. But it was not a bad start.

We embarked on the final rituals. Passing Out exams. A Passing Out Parade, attended by proud parents and dubious girl-friends. We were resplendent in the single gold ring of the Acting Sub-Lieutenant, but more than that: for the first time our uniform jackets had the side pockets that had so far been denied to us. How frightfully grown up!

CHAPTER 3

Sea Legs and the Monosex Monotech

By one of those extraordinary and unexpected strokes of which only the Appointer was capable, Michael Tuohy and I found ourselves arriving at the same ship – the destroyer Camperdown. She was a Battle class destroyer, a part of the Third Destroyer Squadron, for duties on the Home and Mediterranean stations. Rather bizarrely, her entire ship's company had just transferred, lock, stock and barrel, from St Kitts, a fellow Battle, destined for reserve. Thus for everyone the surroundings were nearly, but not quite the same. Michael and I had no such problem – it was all brand new to us.

They were handsome, well-armed ships. Two twin 4.5 inch turrets forward, two five-torpedo mountings amidships, HA/LA STAAG (pom-poms) right aft, and a scattering of Bofors round the ship. Two Squid mountings for anti-submarine work. 32 knots from two boilers and 20,000 SHP in two shafts. Good endurance. A ship's company of 220. Designed for - and just missed - the war in the Pacific.

We were delighted to join such a sexy beast, and even more so when we learnt that we were to sail, straight away, for the Home Fleet Spring Cruise to the West Indies. Devonport was at its rain-soaked worst as we left harbour, nodded to the Eddystone Light, and turned right towards the sun. It was in fact a baptism of fire for Michael and me, for we were put into two watches – four hours on, four hours off, as Second Officers of the Watch. This is a punishing routine at the best of times, but our passage across the Atlantic was through some spectacularly foul weather. If not sick, we were always tired. We did however learn very quickly.

I was slightly better off in that, due to shortage of bunks, I was sleeping in a hammock slung in the After Cabin Flat. So I slept a good deal better than the other officers, although my slumbers were interrupted by

* comings and goings of the members of the Petty Officers' Mess

* the hourly visit to the After Switchboard by a watchkeeper

* regular visits, accompanied by a strong smell of FFO (furnace fuel oil), by a member of the Double Bottoms party, come to dip the tanks.

Additionally, the flat had a panting bulkhead. This is a steel bulkhead which is slightly dished or distorted. As the ship works, it pops from side to side with a noise as if being hit with a sledgehammer. No regular pattern, just every so often. So it was with considerable relief that we arrived in the Caribbean, and started our round of island visits.

As one of the junior ships (or canteen boats) of the Fleet we were sent to the smaller, less populated islands, though in all truth the whole region was very undeveloped – the flotillas of cruise ships and cheap flights were yet to come. Syphilis was endemic, and was the subject of many earnest warnings to our sailors. We first visited Bequia, right off the beaten track, and the First Lieutenant sent half the ship's company ashore for a beach picnic, or banyan. The boys took their daily ration of two cans of beer with them. He was later less than pleased to hear that the price for a woman on the island was – two empty beer cans.

Soon after, we visited another larger island, where such an interesting and unusual incident took place that I felt bound to write it down. This is it.

The Occasion: Official Cocktail Party on the first night in.

It had been decided that the party would be held on B gundeck and the foc's'le. Immediate consternation. Fourth shackle on deck to be painted. New awnings ex-HM Dockyard Devonport to be spread. Fit: less than perfect. Result: every handy-billy in the Buffer's store employed to stretch the wrinkles out. Birdbath fitted between the cable-holders and supplied with firemain (= "Fountain"). Awning stanchions re-drisco'd. Every grating in the ship fleeted forward.

At 1700 the event started. All the lower deck, with the exception of the duty watch, had gone ashore. Their long experience told them that he who lingered on board when the Wardroom was having their 'do' was likely to grabbed, without ceremony, as part of an impromptu hook-rope party to deal with some unforeseen crisis. Plus, preceding the officers ashore gave a clear run at the local talent, such as it was.

The officers themselves had cleaned into unfamiliar ice-cream suits, still displaying the creases of their long storage. The Petty Officer Officers' Cook, PO Zammit had prepared the last of the trays of canapés and other small eats, with many an 'Alla Madonna' and not a few 'ayah seigniors'. PO Vella, the Petty Officer Steward was preparing the many jugs of gin and tonic and of rum (Mount Gay, 4/6d a bottle) and ginger. Few if any concessions were planned for teetotallers. (Vella was a taciturn Maltese of the old school, whose favourite expression was 'alora seignior, my mother she wait nine months for me, you can wait five minutes'.)

The iron deck had been given a final wash down, and the last execrable stoker had been bundled, all split overalls and oily boots, down below. The Rubik's cube of the starboard after accommodation ladder had been painstakingly assembled. The gallant little motor cutter had been lowered, its cushions had been given their white duck covers, and it had pottered inshore to collect the first guests. The brand new 3-in-1 whaler had also been designated for this duty, but had failed at the first fence. The Boats Tiff sighed and reached for his toolbox.

All doors, hatches and scuttles leading into the interior of the ship had been secured, with as many clips as possible. Under no circumstances were guests to be allowed within unless accompanied by a host. At this stage a few optimistic officers planned an intimate party in the Wardroom afterwards, followed by a personal inspection of the famed golden rivet.

By 1800 the guests were streaming on board. A capacious rust-bucket had been hired to bring most of them off. At each crunching board that it made upon the gangway, with much creaking and squeaking of rattan fenders, the Chippy, lurking in the Buffer's Caboosh, flinched and fingered his spokeshave.

The guest list had been compiled by the local British Consul, an undistinguished man in a far from pristine cream suit — real Graham Greene material. He had sedulously ignored the ship's signalled request for a contingent of attractive young women, backed by a cadre of wealthy philanthropists. The Consul had packed the list with his petit bourgeois fellow traders and merchants.

As the junior officers hung about on the quarterdeck eying the approaching boat, it was immediately clear that Plan A (attractive young woman) was probably unattainable, and that Plan B (baron strangling of wealthy philanthropist) remained the only option. Baron strangling was the demotic for using your charms on the recipient to persuade him to take you out and show you a good time.

The omens were not propitious. The guests seemed to consist, almost exclusively, of portly, middle-aged and bespectacled West Indian men, clad in anything from morning dress to a dinner jacket. If there was uniformity about the men's apparel it was that it was consistently a size too small. Strapped, triced, buttoned and crammed were the epithets that came to mind. One felt that if a consignment of extra large suits had been parachuted into the island then everyone could change up one size with advantage.

The occasional top hat shone in the evening sun.

These modest burghers were greatly outshone by their wives; substantial ladies whose avoirdupois was impressively concentrated at bosom and buttock, though with some left over. They were dressed in a truly tropical cacophony of brilliant colour and style, and these fabulous confections were almost all topped with extravagant hats and headdresses. Most wore little lacy white gloves.

There were amongst these exotic creatures a few Europeans, with the sallow skin associated with many years domicile in the Tropics. None seemed to exhibit that confident, slightly raffish, self-indulgent air which signalled to the cognoscenti a Grade A Baron, ripe for strangling. Ah well.

Half way through the party, and all was going well. The sun had set with its usual tropical thump, and most of the Chief Electrician's necklaces of bulbs had lit up to illuminate the *foc's'le. The 'Fountain' had finally been turned off, after the evening breeze had blown much of its contents over deck and guests alike. A few of the larger ladies had subsided onto the gratings, fanning themselves vigorously. By his proprietary air it looked as if the Navigator had located and identified at least a Grade B Baron, and his thumbs were inches away from the jugular. The sub-lieutenants were jockeying for position round a pretty girl with a low-cut dress.*

*At this moment the duty Signalman appeared, looking for the Officer of the Day with an Operational Immediate (- O -) signal. The OOD read it, retrieved his eyebrows from his hairline and decided that the Captain should see it. And where was **he**? Not on the foc's'le, clearly. No surprise there. The Captain was a taciturn, solitary man, well known for sloping off to odd corners of the ship at odd times. Looked like this was one of them.*

The OOD climbed the steel ladder from B gundeck to the after end of the signal deck and walked forward to the Compass Platform. Nothing. He dropped down a deck to check the Bridge, and thence down again to the Captain's Cabin. After knocking he entered the Day Cabin hesitantly, unfamiliar territory here. On his right, the curtain to the Captain's Sleeping Cabin. Still nothing. More for completeness than in any expectation, he approached the door of the Captain's Bathroom.

There were two baths in the ship, the Captain's and that situated in the Sickbay. Because of the chronic unreliability of the evaporators, fresh water was always scarce on board. It had therefore been decided that these baths should only be used in harbour. To enforce this practice, the Engineer Officer signed his name in chinagraph pencil on the bottom of each bath before the ship proceeded to sea. He checked that the signatures were still intact when they subsequently returned to harbour.

The OOD opened the Captain's Bathroom door to be confronted by the unusual sight of the Petty Officer Steward, PO Vella, in flagrante delicto with one of the large female guests, in the Captain's bath.

Whilst the essential details are firmly in place, there remain three unanswered questions:

*   *a. What was in the signal?*

* *b. Did the lady's posterior bear the imprint of the Engineer Officer's signature?*

* *c. Was she still wearing her hat?*

We had an intensely enjoyable month. The sea had never been so blue, the sand so white, the sun so – hot. Many of the lads, taking their white English bodies abroad for the first time, had nasty cases of sunburn. Working on the upper deck with no shirt on and a cooling sea-breeze was an invitation to burn, and sun-block had yet to come on the scene. When visiting Kingston, Jamaica, we lay alongside the West Indies Guard Ship, the frigate designated to spend a year or more in these Elysian waters. *They* were not sunburnt, they were deeply and evenly tanned, their whites seemed whiter and crisper than ours, and they knew all the girls and all the bars in all the ports in the Caribbean. We decided that we preferred our own less than perfect company.

All too soon we were off to Halifax, Nova Scotia, and the infamous swirling mists of the Grand Banks. By then we had settled pretty well into the somewhat eclectic Wardroom. We were all united in our dislike of the Captain, a hectoring, humourless Gunnery Officer, whose standards were so seldom achieved. I met him later and he denied all knowledge of me; absolutely typical. The first Lieutenant, Bob Reading, was a poor soul of limited ability. His single, excruciating achievement was to accompany himself on the guitar whilst singing the tunes of Paddy Roberts, very popular at the time. There were a total of twelve officers in the Wardroom, and eight played bridge, which was bad luck for those of us who didn't. The Gunnery Officer, Tansie Lee, had come up from the ranks and his parents, optimistically, had christened him Nelson Abraham Lee. His brother was a Chief Ordnance Artificer in Saintes, our 'chummy' ship, and used to accompany Tansie to officers-only parties ashore, where he assumed the identity of the Chief Constable of Waterford.

After a brief stop in Halifax, where the Canadian Navy entertained us to intense, rather cheerless drinking sessions, we were off into the North Atlantic for a major NATO exercise. This was Fleetwork writ large, and Michael and I strained to remember Sugar Mike's pearls of wisdom. There were twenty-nine ships on the Screen, surrounding and protecting the Main Body, and we were constantly rotating or reforming the screen, and exchanging positions by a technique called Rum and Coke. Our tools included the Stuart's Distance Meter and the Battenberg Disc, a contrivance of engraved Perspex discs and aluminium, intended for resolving relative velocity problems. These manoeuvres were quite complex, and we were all too well aware of what had happened to a previous Camperdown. She had collided with the flagship, Victoria, which then sank during manoeuvres in the Med in the 1890s. It was an undoubted thrill to order "Revolutions for 28 knots, Starboard 30", and even more so when the Screen Commander occasionally signalled "Manoeuvre well executed". The open bridge was bitterly cold, the naval duffle coat sported so often by Jack Hawkins being quite inadequate. I had a pair of leather sea boots which were greatly coveted by the other watchkeepers; they were much warmer than the rubber ones provided. Manoeuvres at night were even more tricky, with dimmed lights and dodgy radar – Type 293 was designed for tracking aircraft, and Decca 974 was a civilian set in its infancy.

We eventually arrived in Plymouth with some relief, and after a short break we were off for a year in the Med, a delightful prospect. Half way across the Bay of Biscay, enjoying a long lumpy swell, we had a major boiler-room fire, caused by bad insulating brick installation, which allowed heat through to the casing, which ignited the paint of the bulkhead, which fell, flaming, into the bilge, which was full of FFO which etc,etc. We rapidly ran out of electricity as the steam pressure dropped, and the only available diesel generator failed to start and emptied its HP air starting bottles. As we stood gloomily about on the upper deck , skidding on the oil which had leaked everywhere from the portable diesel fire pump, the Coxswain was surprised to see a tiny Junior Seaman, who had only recently joined, appear on deck in his No 1 uniform, raincoat and cap, carrying his naval issue green suitcase.

"Where are you going, lad?" growled the Coxswain.

"Please Sir" piped the boy " I'm ready to abandon ship."

"Get down below and clean into overalls," was the retort.

Eventually, Gerry Delaney, the Torpedo and Anti-Submarine Officer, volunteered some HP air from his torpedoes, the recalcitrant diesel was started, the fire was put out, the other boiler was flashed up, steam was raised, and we were on our way. Not a well conducted event, and we were lucky not to be towed in, or worse.

At Gibraltar I was impressed by the Commander (E), from the Dockyard, who took one look at the burnt-out boiler, and said, "Take it all down." Every brick, the three layers of firebrick, insulating brick and insulating slab was removed, about equal to that in a terraced house. New boiler casings were made and fitted, and the furnace was rebricked, whilst the boiler room was cleaned out and repainted. All done in a week – today, sadly, it would be three months. Great Britain's current, pathetic inability to complete *Grands Projets* to time and cost stems directly from our growing incompetence at these small, intensive activities, the building blocks for those larger challenges.

A first encounter with Gibraltar was bound to be dramatic. The rock hangs over all, dominating like a sub-tropical Matterhorn. The town huddles between the rock and the harbour. To the north and west, looking over the bay, can be seen the Spanish towns of La Linea and Algeciras. In the town the splendour of the Governor's Palace contrasts with the English style pubs with their offers of 'cheap doubles' and 'fish and chips'. Although the main thoroughfares run parallel to the coast, many steep lanes, often with flights of steps, lead upwards towards the rock. It seemed that there was always a local woman, clad in black, climbing these steps, and displaying the muscular calves of the rock-dweller. The monkeys, or Gibraltar rock apes, don't descend into the town, but rule the roost in the gun-emplacements half way to the top. It is true that the rock is riddled with passages, caves and caverns. One particularly splendid cavern, lit in many colours, welcomes tourists, and symphony concerts resonate amongst the stalactites. There are some historic tunnels which connected the gunners' positions for the defence of the rock, and a much greater network of military installations – not open to the public, and dreary in their under-resourced functionality. One day they will be abandoned, and people will marvel at the humdrum nature of this apparently James Bond garrison, much like the 'alternate seats of government', which turned out to be characterised by bunk-beds and obsolete telephones!

An essential feature of a visit to Gib was a Wardroom run ashore to La Linea. There was a longstanding rumour that a lady could be seen having sex with a donkey, and the prospect of this diverting spectacle was irresistible. We crammed into a taxi and transited the border, flanked by Gibraltar policemen, dressed as London Bobbies, and by Spanish Guardia, wearing those odd hats with a slanting back – ideal for leaning against a wall. The Spanish taxi-driver was typically evasive about the lady and the donkey, though he could offer plenty of ladies without. We ended up visiting a series of near-identical bodegas, where excellent sherry was on draught for next to nothing, and the national dish of tapas appeared to be going through its birth pangs. All the bars smelt of dead mice, and cockroaches crackled underfoot.

We were soon on our way to Malta, where my first task was to extract my motorbike from the funnel casing, where the Chief Stoker had kindly accommodated it, out of sight of the First Lieutenant, lower it on a torpedo davit into the ship's dghaisa, and thus transport it ashore. I went to call on the Governor, an old friend of Dad's, and he asked me to go water-skiing. There was a gang of pretty girls, very tanned and competent in the water, and I felt white and gawky. The Governor inflated some water-wings, and said "I can wear these because I'm the Governor, but you can't because you're a Sub-Lieutenant. Don't drown". *Verb. sap.* I got friendly with one of the girls, and we zoomed about Malta on the bike, before she dumped me for a classier model. I was heartbroken for a week, but we were soon off to sea again, and all was forgotten.

There are few better feelings than the anticipation with which one approaches a Mediterranean port from seawards, through a perfect Med dawn, still caressingly cool, but with a hot, cloudless day to come. The ship's arrival, always at 8 a.m., and always immaculate, was the culmination of a great deal of effort, which I tried to capture in the following piece.

The ship has been cruising quietly through the balmy night at the moderate speed of a comfortable bicycle ride. The tedious characteristics of military life at sea have been set aside; exercises are terminated, the upper deck is well lit, and a leisurely, relaxed evening meal has been followed by a stroll on deck, red-tipped cigar butts arcing over the phosphorescent wake, adorned with flying fish. There is a pleasant buzz of anticipation. Could it be that Adventure lies ahead?

But first the ship must be cleaned. The hands have been called at 0400, and the passages and flats, the gangways, ladders, lobbies, cabooshes, offices, stores and lockers - all the public places - have been washed down, swept and polished. The brass has been duly anointed. On deck, the night accumulation of soot has been hosed away, and wooden beadings and gratings scrubbed and whitened with lime. The Jack and Ensign staffs are bolted into place, and the salt-stained sea ensign is struck from the yardarm. A young bunting-tosser makes his way aft with the best harbour ensign which is soon bent on and hoisted, this time without ceremony.

At first light, the ship stops in the water, and - "crane-driver close up"- a boat is lowered.

From a jumping ladder over the side the First Lieutenant and the Buffer embark and, with much pointing and grimacing, they are driven in a circle round the ship. Every streak of rust, every flapping patch of loose paint, every tell-tale trickle of oil or worse down the side, every deposition of shite-hawk's shit, every loose rigging line, every Irish pennant is noted for immediate remedy. On the bridge, the Captain sprawls in his chair, hand clasped round the mug marked "Captain", thinking God knows what. (Actually, he's probably thinking "I wish I was in that boat. Can the Jimmy be trusted?") At the back of the bridge the Navigator is nervously re-reading the Admiralty Pilot, with its dark warnings of outlying dangers and uncharted hazards. He expects some uncharted hazards of his own - Will the gyro repeat its dreaded 'topple' at the moment critique? Will the Chmny(conspic.) that he has selected from the chart as his turning mark still be standing, still be (conspic.)? Will the tugs arrive? Will the local Pilot be sober? No wonder such men are inclined to introspection and a powerful thirst when ashore.

Upon the Jimmy's return on board, the Side Party is deployed. The ship rolls gently on the imperceptible swell, surrounded by growing patches of sudsy water from its bathroom discharges, and a thriving colony of bobbing, buoyant turds from the many heads flushing their morning receipts over the side. In the fifties the clinical days of sewage tanks, of biogest systems and oily water separators were still twenty years ahead. The limitless sea received it all, apparently, we thought, capable of total absorption. The rattle of tins and overlooked cutlery down the gash-chute was accompanied by the coloratura of the shite-hawks feasting on the buckets of kitchen waste squandered there. Good it was to be a sea-bird in those mucky, unreconstructed times! Slim pickings now in the environmentally conscious green 2000s.

The Side Party has 30 minutes to cover up the rusty depredations of the passage. Black for the boot-topping, that most corrosion-prone area 'twixt wind and water. Grey for the ship's side. Black edged with white for the pennant numbers. Red for the ship's name, and for the draught-marks. Men in blue overalls and gym-shoes - laces long since vanished - dangle from bos'n's chairs, from stages, scrambling nets and ladders. Their long-toms and rollers make swift if ephemeral work of their touch-up job, after all it doesn't have to last long. It is for the Arrival Alongside.

But this rapid painting is neither the beginning, nor certainly the end, of the matter. The conversion of a maritime killing-machine into a floating embassy, museum and night-club was, in the fifties, an extended and laborious conjuring trick. Indeed, this early morning burst of activity was but the culmination of days or, in some cases, weeks of work. Not only did the ship have to be spotless, but all the various artefacts that went to make up a formal port visit had to be mustered, cleaned, oiled, checked and rechecked. The signalmen had to be sure that, in addition to the No. 1 Jack and Ensign, the lines of flags used to dress ship overall were ready. Spare flags and pennants would also be required to embellish parts of the upper deck used for receptions or parties. Huge expanses of these decks were covered with awnings, which needed stanchions to be rigged to support them, together with a cat's cradle of wires and cordage, purchases and handy-billies to spread, slope (in case of rain), and frap (in case of high winds). Teak gratings, used to cover bollards and capstans were assembled and scrubbed, and ceremonial ladders and gangways were put together and burnished. The Chief Stoker reviewed his collection of hoses for fuel, water and lub. oil, and the various connections that he had acquired to screw into all sorts of alien sockets ashore. His opposite number, the Chief Electrician, was sorting out the snakes' wedding of the floodlighting "system", an ad hoc collection of beams and spars with their guys, terminating in biscuit boxes with large lamps inside. All this was powered from a socket on the upper deck which might or might not have been fatally corroded by seawater. Below decks the chefs changed their output from trays of figgy duff to rather brick-like canapés – nouvelle cuisine was still a couple of decades in the future. The stewards polished hundreds of glasses, and laid in the industrial quantities required of brandy and ginger ale (for horses' necks) and gin and tonic. The engineers provided the Wardroom pantry with great blocks of ice.

Finally, each man had to look to himself. White uniforms were de rigueur, bell bottoms and jumpers, ice-cream suits and white mess jackets, each with its own accompaniment of buttons, ribbons and shoulder boards. The miracle of all this is that there was any room for ammunition.

In this case, all that preparation was for a visit to Beirut. In 1958 this was a delightful city, showing its French colonial inheritance with broad tree-lined streets and smart shops and cafes. The educated Lebanese were a good looking, attractive people with pronounced mercantile abilities. On the first afternoon Michael and I stepped ashore to have a look round. In due course we found ourselves seated at a cafe in a leafy sun-dappled square. We noticed an endless stream of street urchins disappearing into the cafe's back room. "Aha," we said, cognoscenti abroad, "Fagin's den!" When we got back on board we found that Michael had lost his wallet. We were both needed onboard that night, but our friend 'Stafford' Cripps, the young Commissioned Gunner (g), went off to see what he could do. He found the cafe and went inside. There a muscled Lebanese listened to his tale, and, flinging open two large steel cabinets, said, "Black or brown?" Among the hundreds of wallets Michael's was eventually identified. Fagin thumbed through it and deftly removed the notes.

"Of course", he said, oozing charm, "your friend will understand that he cannot have the money back".

Later we had a marvellous day out with the Military Attaché, who took us through the Cedars of Lebanon, dusted with snow, to the Bekaa valley and the miraculous temples of Baalbek, at that time quite without any terrorist associations. That evening we went to a night club and saw a sheikh purchase a belly dancer, who was bundled into a Chevrolet, presumably with empty ashtrays, and driven away into the night. At the time Beirut got everybody's vote.

At this point there was quite a changeover of officers, so that Michael and I started to feel like old hands. A short, amiable bearded submariner, Philip Wood, arrived as Captain, a great relief all round after his humourless, boorish predecessor. Bob Reading was relieved by the exquisite David Hankinson, whose very young, very pretty wife Caroline was his principal and striking asset. Years later David was commissioned by the Leathersellers Livery Company to paint a portrait of Princess Diana. When it arrived the members liked it so little that it was hung in increasingly obscure parts of their Hall, ending up behind a door that was seldom closed. The bad news as far as I was concerned was that the very likeable Sandy Towers, the Engineer Officer, was replaced by Mike Usher, a clever but introverted ordnance engineer, who had apparently been a great success as a Project Manager for the Sea Slug missile system in Girdleness, the trials ship. As far as human relations were concerned, however, he never got off the ground. This hardly helped my engineering training.

We visited a few other ports — Athens, moored miles out, in company with the sizeable Med. Fleet; Marseilles, stern to in the Inner Harbour, two minutes walk from the centre of town; and Barcelona. It was in wonderful Barcelona that Stafford Cripps was transferred to the flagship, a cruiser. In the Wardroom he was ostracised and stood at a corner of the bar, sipping his gin. A flagship officer warily approached him.

"What are you here for?" he asked "Are you queer?"

"Certainly not", replied Stafford, "I'm here to be court-martialled for thumping a Petty Officer".

After this brief but telling exchange Stafford was quickly absorbed into the social life of the Wardroom. Attitudes today have changed less than they ought.

At 0700 on Christmas morning 1958 the Third Destroyer Squadron arrived at Limassol for duties as Cyprus Patrol. The Squadron consisted of ourselves, Barfleur and the leader Saintes. The Captain (D) was Otto Steiner, a cheerful man distinguished by his initials OHMS. As we swept into the low lying sandy harbour we received a signal from the Admiral ashore, the Flag Officer Middle East (FOME), Rear Admiral 'Crap' Miers.

FROM FOME

TO D3

WELCOME. FUEL IN ROTATION THEN ANCHOR INDEPENDENTLY.

Already, Steiner was on the back foot. He did not need this micro-management of his own small force.

FROM FOME

TO THIRD DS

HOLY CATHOLIC MASS WILL BE CELEBRATED AT LIMASSOL CHURCH AT 0800.

Steiner was himself a Catholic, like Miers, but the demands of fuelling from the tanker moored in the harbour meant that attendance at Mass was impossible.

FROM FOME

TO D3

THE POOR TURNOUT AT MASS BY YOUR SHIP'S COMPANIES WAS MOST DISAPPOINTING.

Now Steiner was livid. The officers of the Squadron had been invited to a barbeque Christmas lunch in his garden by FOME.

FROM D3

TO 3RD DS

OFFICERS ATTENDING FOME'S BARBEQUE TODAY ARE TO WEAR BEARDS.

It was a known fact that one of the many things that Miers detested was 'beards'. We spent the rest of the forenoon fabricating beards out of cotton wool, spunyarn, anything that came to hand, and by the time we got into the boat to take us ashore we all wore some form of dreadful bum fluff on our chins. The Admiral took one aghast look at this motley crew, and ordered Steiner to the garage. From there, as the charming Mrs Miers plied us with drinks, came the unmistakeable sounds of physical combat, a trait for which Miers was well known. Eventually the two senior officers emerged, grinning sheepishly, and showing signs of warfare.

"All right, chaps," said Steiner "off beards!" After that, we had an excellent party.

We stayed around Cyprus for about a month, ostensibly carrying out anti-smuggling patrols, boarding and searching small fishing boats full of large, cheerful Cypriots and small fish. There was plenty of time for relaxation, swimming, sailing and exploring ashore. I had recently qualified as a Shallow Water Diver. During my course in Malta I had difficulty in unscrewing some well worn connection on a diving set.

"You may have long hair like Sampson, *Sir*" (heavy irony) said the PO Diver, despairing of his amateur students, "But you've got muscles like fucking Delilah. Now shift that bastard." That was me told.

It was my duty to search the ship's bottom for limpet mines with my small team every time we left harbour, usually early in the morning. And what bliss it was. The water was warm and as clear as gin; you could see the whole way along the ship's bottom, and I remember reading the headlines of a newspaper that was lying on the bottom of the sea seventy feet below.

The long confrontation in Cyprus was just starting. Pictures of Archbishop Makarios were everywhere, together with scrawled slogans of Enosis and Eoka. The Turks and Greeks were inflaming the passions from their own respective countries, although no form of partition had yet been mooted. I landed for a week with the Durham Light Infantry and was taken under the wing of a friendly subaltern, whose first generous act was to issue me with a .45 pistol. We zoomed about the island at high speed in a Land Rover, which like all other vehicles, was fitted with a vertical length of angle iron welded to the front bumper, since the earliest guerrilla attempts had involved the stretching of piano wire across the roads, and had involved some fatalities. The little villages of the Troodos Mountains which we visited were totally unsophisticated, and the locals had little idea of what was going on. We shared foul drafts of Keo brandy with them (the VSOP was just about drinkable) and came away laden with oranges and lemons. It was a fascinating week, tinged with sadness for the simple people being dragged into a mysterious conflict by a few activists. When I got back on board, I found that the army officer whom I had swapped with had left my cabin scuttle open, and my precious and expensively laundered whites in the drawer below had been soaked and stained by sea-water. Suddenly my milk of human kindness evaporated!

After a month or so we returned to a wintry and surprisingly cold Malta, where Camperdown suffered a major engine failure. (The starboard HP turbine dummy cylinder, a complex assembly of labyrinth glands, had seized up.) The ship would be in the dockyard for a couple of months whilst this problem was investigated and remedied. I started going out with the Captain of the Dockyard's daughter. He was an Executive Officer, and was already smarting at being in a job surrounded by what he saw as a lower order of technicians and the like. The fact that his beloved daughter was in any way involved with a young engineer was too much for him, and he had a word with Otto over a gin at the Marsa Club. The next week I found myself going to sea for two months in Saintes.

When I arrived, Otto kindly asked me what I would like to do, and I said 'Ocean Navigation', as I'd never done any of that. The squadron navigator was a New Zealander called Neil Anderson, an utterly delightful man who later on became the head of the NZ Navy. He generously told me that he would be busy with navigating for the task group that we had joined, so I could do the ship's nav – the same thing really, but it made me feel great. After hours of fiddling about with a sextant, chronometer, sight reduction tables, star globes and the rest of the impedimenta, I was able proudly to tell the Captain where I thought we had been three hours ago! Otto and Neil asked me how I would take a sunsight if the horizon was obscured by mist. Remembering the handbook, I said that you could use a bucket of oil to give a false horizon. "well," they said, "You're an engineer, go and get one". So I trailed down to the engineroom, drew off a bucket of OM100 from the ready use oil tank, and carried it carefully back up to the bridge, not so easy in a gentle swell. Surprisingly, it worked rather well.

After our exercise (some sort of re-enactment of Somerville's Force H chasing the Bismarck, I think) we returned on our own to Malta. I had by now been given half a bridge watchkeeping certificate, and was thus allowed to keep watch on my own one Sunday afternoon. We bumbled along twelve and a bit miles off the coast of North Africa, all alone, in beautiful weather. Most of the crew had their heads down, including the Captain. I sprawled in his bridge chair, and competed with the signalman, about my age, in telling each other stories about our naval careers so far. At about half past two an Engineroom Artificer, in grimy overalls, came up the ladder at the back of the bridge and addressed himself to me.

"Permission to work on the sirens for half an hour?" he asked. I nodded grandly. Sometime later, he reappeared.

"Work complete, Sir", he said "Permission to test them?"

"Yes please", I replied. This was the life. The tiffy pulled on the handle, and three short blasts rang out. No other system has ever equalled the thrilling sound of destroyers' steam sirens – quite unique. The tiffy saluted and left the bridge by the aft ladder, sliding down the handrails without his feet touching the treads. But what was this? It was like a French farce. No sooner had the tiffy disappeared, than the Captain shot up like a cork out of a bottle, wearing some sort of Chinese dressing gown.

"Where's the other ship?" he shouted at me, desperately scanning the horizon. I started to realise that three short blasts signals 'I am going astern', generally used when collision with another ship is imminent. Otto gave me one of the best royal bollockings of my short life, and quite right too.

Soon after that it was time to move on again. Michael and Paddy O'Riordan, another Sub who had joined us, were off to submarine training, whereas I was going to the RN Engineering College for a three year engineering course. At the end of this, I hoped, I would no longer be a dogsbody but would become a Dogsbody. I had had an intensely interesting and amusing time. By the standards of the time Camperdown was average, but she was far from her optimum, led by a very patchy collection of officers, and would have been severely criticised a few years later when the Flag Officer Sea Training's organisation was up and running at Portland. From my point of view the 'executive' time was excellent experience; the technical training much less so. Did it matter? Not a bit!

* * * * *

The Royal Naval Engineering College Manadon was popularly known as the 'College of Knowledge', usually followed by "oh yeah?" or, more cuttingly, as a 'mono-sex, monotech'. In 1959 it was reaching the end of a long period of change. Originally the College was situated at Keyham, abutting the Naval Dockyard in Devonport. This became less and less suitable and a large site (Manadon) was eventually acquired some five miles from the centre of Plymouth. The site was green, apart from a stylish small manor house, which became the Captain's House, and an ancient Tithe Barn, which became the Chapel. As is the way with any invading administration, these two buildings were soon surrounded by huts, initially for accommodation only. The students were bussed up and down to Keyham daily to pursue their studies. Soon a large classroom and administrative block followed, accompanied by a parade ground. Extensive workshops were then built, and finally some hangars were erected to contain the large collection of engineering artefacts needed, from boilers to aircraft. If it all sounds straight out of 'Yes Minister' that's because it was.

By the time I arrived the transmogrification was almost complete. A large, very 1950s accommodation block had been completed (to replace the huts) and the only facilities still at Keyham were the Steam and Electrical Test Shops. To confer some gravitas on this expensive enterprise, a degree scheme had been started. Manadon was suddenly very cutting edge. Selection for the degree course had been made, I suppose, at Dartmouth, though I cannot recall that it was in any way a transparent process. After thirty seconds of feeling miffed at not being selected, the rest of us were delighted, since after all the initial degree course people were going to spend five years at Manadon compared to the normal three. Even three seemed too much to a twenty-one year old.

Whilst the degree stream was itself a part of the transformation of the officer corps into an organisation where 'all shall have degrees, all shall have prizes', in the early days its superiority was not always apparent. The stream had its share of "clever, useless bastards". Even the clever useful bastards were sometimes less than perfect. A good friend, Bob Hill, who later rose to the very top of naval engineering, was spoken of thus by some thoughtful contractors we were working with.

"We like the way Bob's mind works. We just don't like its conclusions".

The academic streaming we were put into had some effect on our social alignments. I found myself sharing a cabin with Jim Mills, a quiet, smiling man who eventually emigrated to New Zealand and became even quieter. John Marshall, lifetime confrère who was to be my best man, and I had both bought, in line with the RNEC ethos of the time, the remains of beautiful sports cars (his a 1938 BMW; mine a 1936 Aston-Martin) which got their fair share of admiration, and a disproportionate amount of maintenance, but could never be classified as reliable transportation. Peter Strelley, on the other hand, a sharp practitioner well versed in the swoop and glide style of ballroom dancing, had a raucous red Ford Zephyr coupe, which performed excellently and welded the three of us together as a mobile team, looking for trouble.

We, the students or OUIs (Officers Under Instruction), were destined to become either mechanical or marine engineers, or ordnance engineers or air engineers. Our first two years would consist of a common education, largely academic, followed by a final year of application in our sub-discipline. The academic work was tedious in the extreme, with mathematics, thermodynamics, fluid mechanics, strength of materials, chemistry and economics as the primary subjects. The reason they were so boring was because of the teachers. Most of them were Instructor Officers, or

Schoolies, who had presumably joined the Royal Navy to escape from teaching. Also, unlike the excellent masters at Dartmouth, they were moved on every two years by their appointer, so that they never had a chance to get good at anything. They were leavened by a few Engineer Officers, who were not much better. We suffered.

We all had our own escape routes from classroom madness. There was a particularly trying man, Instructor Commander Mount, a large, flabby individual always known as Mother Mount. I remember writing a long bit of doggerel in one of his lessons, which concluded:

> Give me a girl who is eager and willing,
>
> Give me a girl that is keen for some filling,
>
> Give me a girl to put me out for the count,
>
> But don't, *please don't* give me Mother Mount.

It is telling that I can remember this, but not the content of his lecture.

The lessons that involved some practical activity were more memorable. The Steam Test Shop at Keyham was very old-fashioned, but served its purpose. Here boilers and pumps hissed and wheezed, and many of the parameters that we had to record appeared on large polished brass gauges. The flows of various sorts of waters – feed, make up feed, condensate, cooling, auxiliary cooling and the like – were measured, not by simple flow meters, but by Leinert meters, tipping buckets which collected say 100 gallons before tipping the contents back into the system. To measure the flow in one hour you just counted the number of times the bucket tipped. By some quirk of design all the Leinert meters were mounted, in rows, in the rafters, and it was a pleasant job, if somewhat sweaty, to ascend the many ladders and quietly record the swishing, gurgling tippings whilst one's colleagues beavered away down below. It all seemed a wonderfully complex set-up for confirming, or otherwise, the Steady Flow Energy Equation, the Kyrie Eleison of Thermodynamics.

The Electrical Test Shop lacked these steamy marvels. Indeed, it had more than a whiff of Back-EMF, a mysterious electrical fluid, and the distinctive smell of ozone generated at DC commutators, but it did have two splendid human assets. Old Jock (he had been called Old Jock in Dad's days at Keyham in the '20s) was the Shop Lecturer, who described the experiments we were about to do, checked that we had wired them up correctly (an important part of the ritual) and later marked the reports we had submitted. He was an irascible Scotsman, who may or may not have had a heart of gold – probably not. He rose readily to the many torments that we devised for him. He would check miles of wiring, in and out of connection boxes, onto lamp boards, round condensers and rheostats, only to find that the cable finally ended in someone's briefcase. Cue ancient Scottish imprecations. During the time that we were busy with our experiments Jock had little to do, and would retire to his glass box of an office, light one of an endless inhalation of Gold Flakes, and settle down to do the Daily Telegraph Crossword. Vile creatures that we were, on one occasion we managed to complete that day's crossword between us on the twenty minute bus ride down from Manadon, and substitute it for his virgin copy. The reaction was all that we had hoped for.

Old Jock had an assistant called Block. Never a 'Mister', never a first name, just Block. Block was a large, silent man who had at some stage lost his right hand. In place of the normal prosthesis he had a hardwood stump, bound with a steel band. When he needed a tool he would ram its sharpened tang into a ragged hole in the stump. When he needed a hammer he just used the steel band. Deeply impressive. Block and Jock hated each other with an abiding loathing. At least, so it seemed. With the benefit of hindsight it seems quite possible that they were bound together in some ghastly symbiosis, needing to remain close and pour out contempt upon each other. Classic Sartre.

We studied, briefly and superficially (mercifully), Mechanical Drawing. Presided over by a small humourless Lieutenant Commander, this was quite useful in understanding the conventions of blueprints. However, we soon got into a downward spiral of constructing, at great length, the curves of intersection of various conical bodies. What for, you may well ask? We soon learnt that the quick, good-enough solution was to draw in freehand the approximate curve, and then surround it with false constructional lines, pin-pricks etc. Should any of us ever have become professional draughtsmen, an unlikely fate, who knows what distorted products would have flowed from our boards. However, it seemed to satisfy the Art Master.

It was the Workshops, however, that were a central and wholly enjoyable part of our life. All contained within a single large building, no expense had been spared to plan and equip a superb facility. The centrepiece was an enormous Machine Shop, with a plentiful supply of lathes, shapers, drilling machines and a variety of grinders together with benches for hand fitting. Off this space were the specialist areas – the Tool Room, where phenomenal accuracies were commonplace and micrometers could be calibrated to a tenth of a thou; the Tinsmiths, where tin-plate was cut out and fabricated; Coppersmiths, the centre of the very different art of brazing; Patternmakers, ostensibly to make patterns for casting, but in effect the Chippies too; the Welding Shop; Heavy and Light Plate Shops for rolling and cutting; the Moulders, and the Foundry which they served; and finally the Blacksmiths, where forging was carried out. Not only was it a splendidly comprehensive cathedral of the metal basher's art, but it was decently sized. There were always enough facilities for all the OUIs *plus their cars*, an absolutely vital consideration. To emphasise the importance of the Workshops in our chosen lives, they were the point of issue for mid-morning coffee, when all OUIs would foregather for gossip amongst the lathes. Admirable.

The Instructors, or high priests, were all former naval artificers, men in their 50s and 60s, invariably polite, cheerful, longsuffering and immensely competent. They wore civilian collars and ties under a brown storeman's coat. Whilst we were there an edict came out forbidding the wearing of ties by those working with rotating machinery, no doubt after some dreadful accident. It was pointed out to the instructors that they could wear clip-on ties, but to a man they all voted for properly tied double-ended bow ties, and, after sweeping like locusts through the gents' outfitters of Plymouth, they all turned out looking like professors of machinery. Distinctive, and very stylish.

During our three years at Manadon we did something like three hundred hours in the Workshops – not enough to become expert, but enough to understand how all those processes worked. It led to an instinctive understanding of the characteristics of most of the materials we were to work with in our careers, as well as increasing the bonding between ourselves and the artificers with whom we were to work. I was deeply disappointed, and saddened, many years later, to see the extensive workshop facilities at Imperial College London lying fallow, while the students convinced themselves that staring at computer screens was a way of becoming an engineer without getting your hands dirty. O tempores, o mores!

I don't think that, at the end of our time, we did much to deconstruct or analyse our course; we were too eager to get away. But from here it seems pretty clear that we were always on the back foot, receiving great wodges of knowledge without the opportunity or ability to interact or contribute. No chance of being able to say 'Surely that can't be right?' or 'Isn't it more likely that . . . .?' I hope that teaching techniques today are more participative and inclusive, but I can't be sure. If *I* was creating an engineering course now, my basic building blocks would be Design, Risk, Failure, Materials and Innovation. On these, as they say, hang all the laws of the prophets, and there is the undoubted opportunity for the student to propose and defend a view right from the outset.

If academic life at Manadon had its longueurs the same cannot be said of its sports and social activities. Naval engineers had a longstanding reputation for excellence in rugby and sailing. In the summer an eccentric body called the Friday Nighters used to play cricket of sorts (minus 6 runs for any batsman who hit one of the pint glasses scattered round the ground). They had an esoteric fixture list including the Roborough Ladies' Football Club, Stan Blowey's Gasworks XI and Saltash Sailing Club (No Boats). I spent some time shooting .303s on the range at Trevol, on the other side of the Tamar. An open air range can be one of the more unforgiving sporting venues. I also sailed, usually in Gauntlet, a nice pre-war sloop with canoe stern and a bumpkin for the standing backstay. The College had a smart boat-house down by the chain ferry across the river.

Motoring events featured strongly at the College. Our role model was the Commander, a delightful man called Tim Lees-Spalding, who had recently taken part in the equivalent of the Dakar Rally. As well as the usual rallies, speed tests and hill-climbs there was a somewhat obscure but very popular event known as Firkin Smuggling. A firkin is a nine gallon barrel of beer, weighing about ninety pounds. The object was for one team to smuggle the firkin into a nominated and defended pub, or village church. The detailed rules were rather like those for Mornington Crescent, well understood by the participants, total gibberish to everyone else. In addition, they changed for each challenge. Whatever, the contest called for novel vehicles (Manadon cars modified to hide a firkin, tractors, horse drawn carts), a lot of dressing up (nuns seemed to be a favourite), provocative behaviour by girl-friends (fishnet stockings were a powerful distraction for the defenders) and a great deal of beer drinking. In short a delicious evening's entertainment for everyone, except for those innocent travellers who were stopped and shaken down, looking for the elusive firkin.

A thin line of culture struggled to keep its head above water in this turbulent sea of cheerful philistinism. Its undoubted champion was Ted Fenner, a Schoolie Commander who, with his wife Joan (always a vision in purple), had been effectively adopted by the Degree Course, running parallel to our own. Ted's Am Dram was in almost continuous production, and I appeared in The Servant of Two Masters, a forgotten play about Christ in the garden of Gethsemane by a Czech called Fodor, a review which we wrote ourselves – Laugh Along the Dotted Line – and Treasure Island, the Pantomime.

Of course the sub-text for most of these extramural activities was Meeting Girls. We were all in our early twenties and had been inhibited by our naval training so far from more than glancing contact, as it were. We had also been pretty remote from London, where, apparently, it was all happening. I think Philip Larkin actually fixed the start of the sexual revolution as 1963, so perhaps we were the last of the *ancien régime*. At any rate, we were desperately keen to catch up. Plymouth was, not surprisingly, well equipped with a wide spectrum of female company, ranging from the cut-glass to the gor blimey. I never quite understood how the separation of 'officers' country' from the haunts of the lower deck worked, but it was an accepted fact that we should keep apart; despite the complicated demographic of the city, with ships coming and going every day, the Chinese wall seemed to operate effectively. I do remember being asked to take a very beautiful, but rather 'rough trade' girl to a party. Within minutes of arriving she was heavily enmeshed with three PTIs, all huge shoulders and rippling singlets. They bore her upstairs with practiced ease, and I was left to conclude that a scrawny Sub Lieutenant with a dodgy motor was no match for these ruthless lower-deck Lotharios.

Officers' country extended outside the town. The Moorland Links at Yelverton used to have weekend dances and the more socially adept would strut their stuff there. A favourite pub was the "Who'd Have Thought It?" in Buckland Monachorum, run by a very charming, upper crust landlord. In the bar was a handsome parrot in a cage, which we used to feed with beer mats soaked in beer. At closing time the landlord would announce:

"May I, with the very greatest regret, ask for your very last orders, Ladies and Gentlemen?"

and open the door to the parrot's cage. The bird would proceed to fly drunkenly round the bar, ricocheting off the departing drinkers.

Back in Plymouth the Brown Bear in Devonport held cult status. This was because its owners, Paul and Paula Westlake, both Polish, used to provide only one bar meal, a *sanglant* steak, with French bread and butter and fried onions, for six shillings, amazingly cheap even then, and seriously delicious. I used to drink occasionally in a little pub in a cove between two parts of the dockyard. The landlady, Mrs Johnston, was vast, and had been married to a Chief Yeoman of Signals. When warships were entering harbour they were in sight for perhaps two minutes as they passed the cove. With commendable speed Mrs J would scuttle up the stairs to her bedroom, where she had an Aldis lamp. Down below, in the bar, we could hear the clatter of her shutter as she acknowledged her friends' orders. Twenty minutes later they would arrive, to find their drinks waiting on the bar. That's what I call service!

Amongst the many and varied drinking establishments in this large city there was one Absolutely Bloody Final and that was the Plymouth Sailing School, or to give it its universal appellation The Groin Exchange or GX. A year's membership cost a quid, and it was open till midnight. Everyone ended up there and it had a *fin de siècle* feel about it. Great dramas were played out there. Encounters, fruition, breakup, despair, all were observed by the beady, if somewhat bloodshot, eyes of the regulars. Much was forgotten the next day.

By the time we were half way through our three year course we had stepped back somewhat from the frantic round of pleasure that we had started with. Could this be maturity? Unlikely, more probably exhaustion and ennui. There was a steady attrition in our ranks as a minority lapsed into long-term relationships with women, invariably with marriage in mind. Although we were all well under the age of twenty five, when the Admiralty would first pay Marriage Allowance, the national zeitgeist considered it normal and proper to marry in the early twenties. The concept of living together with no intention of permanence was, we thought, bohemian and attractive, but unattainable in our rather old-fashioned bit of society.

One day a Dartmouth friend of mine, Gavin Menzies, asked me down for a lunchtime drink in the submarine in which he was serving. (Wednesdays were a half-day, with the afternoon available for sport, sleeping – or drinking in submarines). A dozen or so of us crammed into the tiny wardroom, spilling out into the control-room beyond. I had hardly visited a submarine before, but was immediately taken with the womb-like feeling and the informal camaradie of the officers. I remember being particularly impressed that all minerals bottles could be opened, single-handed, on a valve handwheel situated in the wardroom deckhead. (It was the Guntower Inboard Drain Valve, I later learnt!)

My eyes were drawn to a strikingly attractive girl with fair hair, a generous smile and dazzling pale green eyes. Her boyfriend seemed rather possessive, and conversation à deux is seldom possible in such circumstances, but I gathered that we were both going to be at the same party that evening in another mate's ship, Tim Trounson's diving tender the Squirrel. We duly met up again in a marginally less crowded wardroom, where we were able to dance briefly, establish each other's names and backgrounds, and arrange to meet again. I wrote her name on my starched cuff with a burnt match; she always recalls this as deeply romantic, though I, soulless creature, regarded it as simple expedience. I discovered that her name was Jane Gibbs, that she was twenty years old, and was working as a nanny for Jol Waterfield, a childhood chum and Captain of Artful, the submarine in which we met. She was involved, none too happily with Gordon McBride, Artful's third hand. She lived with the Waterfields out on the moor at Crapstone. I sent her a postcard, saying "Every time I clean my teeth with Gibbs SR I think of you", and settled down to consolidate this slim alliance.

Our first subsequent meeting was not auspicious. Wearing my 'two cultures' hat, or possibly in the hope of meeting some different girls (unfulfilled), I had joined the Mutley Plain Arts Centre, a gloomy hall on the outskirts of Plymouth, and took Janey to a very alternative film possibly called 'Shadows', starring John Cassavetes; not so much black and white as grey and grey. Not designed to raise the spirits, and our subsequent tete à tete in the Fortescue Arms was glum in the extreme. Our relationship bumped along for the next few months, somewhat enlivened by the erratic actions of the egregious McBride. He took to singling out Manadon officers in pubs, and taking a swing at them. Not a winning stratagem, since they were invariably fitter and more sober than he was. The Waterfields thought it was hilarious, and gave Janey a piece of Staffordshire pottery, entitled The Rivals, and featuring a couple of rather cheesy naval types peering round trees at a milkmaid. The local submariners were mostly on McBride's side, and could not approve of one of their own being slighted in favour of a mere engineer. Some gave Janey jingoistic lectures on loyalty – advice which she neither needed nor heeded.

Came the spring and we both felt that we were not really going anywhere and it might be time to move on. We had a meal in Pedro's in the Octagon, an insalubrious extension to insalubrious Union Street. It could have been the steak, it could have been the wine, it could even have been the Italian waiter's enormous pepper-grinder, but we both suffered an undoubted, if delayed, coup de foudre – we were in love, absolutely. We never looked back.

The next few months were wonderful. Janey, with her glamorous looks and warm personality, was quickly accepted into Manadon society. In the summer of 1961 I was best man at the wedding of Peter Tyrrell, a prickly Irishman and lightning wing three quarter for the Navy, to Sarah Cartwright-Taylor, cool, composed and daughter of a prickly Commandant General Royal Marines. With weddings in the air we announced our own engagement. We picnicked in the cornfields of Tamerton Foliot, swam naked at midnight in the headwaters of the Tavy, and visited all the beaches within miles. We drove a variety of cars – my own Alvis (beautiful but fairly useless), Jim Mills' J2 MG (light to push), and Boo Beattie's fantastic D Type Jaguar. Boo had appeared at Manadon as First Lieutenant (ie doing everything that wasn't engineering) and soon made it clear to those of us who had known him at Dartmouth that we only had to ask. Hammering across Dartmoor in that divine machine on a summer night, with Janey beside me, at grossly excessive speeds, was a lyrical, and fortunately non-fatal experience. Good old Boo!

In the final year the course improved considerably, as we were now doing our specialist training – for me, marine engineering. This involved rather less of the blackboard mysteries, and more practical stuff. We learnt how to check that a boiler's tubes were clear (ball-bearings), how to clean a gas turbine compressor (crushed walnut shells), and how to check the health of a diesel cylinder (Dobbie-McInnes indicator). I wrote an extended thesis on Combination Propulsion Systems (mainly steam and something), an area I was never to work in. I spent hours freehand drawing components of a steam catapult, equipment I was never to see again. A group of us undertook our Design and Make project, which was to produce a torsion meter. The obvious solution was to stick a couple of strain gauges to a shaft, and run the electrics out through slip rings. We, perversely, decided that our device would be entirely mechanical. Our design transmitted the torque through a large spring. We had no idea how big it needed to be, so we commissioned a series of different sizes from the Dockyard. For maximum effect, we tested these in the workshop during the coffee-break, when everyone would be there. We worked our way up the sizes until we hit one that did not fracture. The regular "C-c-c-c-ranggg!" of springs disintegrating behind the protective screen of the rig became much prized entertainment for the coffee drinkers. We enjoyed ourselves but won no prizes. It was probably time to get moving.

On 31st March 1962 Janey and I got married at Aldenham Church. John Marshall was my best man, sister Netta was the chief bridesmaid, and the three Waterfield boys, aged 6, 4 and 2 were very sweet pages. It was snowing gently and when we arrived at our reception we wondered where all the guests were. Twenty minutes later they all arrived, having been listening to the Grand National on their car radios. Some kind friends of Janey's (something to do with BOAC) had given us a night in a smart London hotel and a VIP car the next morning to the airport, whence we were flying to Majorca. We drove right up to the aircraft at Heathrow, bypassing the terminal completely, and Janey was welcomed on board with a bouquet. When we got to Palma the VIP treatment had run out, and we giggled at the determination of all our fellow passengers that we should be the last out of the aircraft, as if it mattered.

As soon as we got back we settled into a modest flat in Peverell, close to the greyhound track. The flat belonged to Mrs Jewell, widow of a Chief Stoker, and she lived in the flat above, whence she would descend, every Saturday morning, to collect the weekly rent of £3 14s. 6d. This ceremony was conducted with the curtains drawn so that the neighbours should not see. It would have been chilly in the winter and the privy with the honeysuckle round the door considerably less inviting, but we loved it there.

Our first few months of married life passed in a flash, not least because of the anticipation of something completely different, which indeed it was.

CHAPTER 4

To Sea in a Darling Dinosaur

The Anticipated Event was that I was to go to HMS Lion, a Tiger Class six inch cruiser. (The convention that ships should be described by the calibre of their primary armament came to a halt with these, the last of the cruisers, and was certainly less than helpful to the uninformed.) The Corollaries were:

* i. that Lion would leave the UK for one year in November, and there would be no chance of us seeing each other during that year.

* ii. that Janey was pregnant, and would give birth in January 1963. I would not be there.

The Conclusions were that there was not much we could do about either, except grit our teeth and grin and bear it. Sympathy for a one year separation was not huge. It wasn't so long since ships had deployed to the China Station for three years at a stretch. The spirit of the age did not consider men-folk to be an important feature of childbirth. We clung together, wept and got on with it.

The Interlude was that before joining Lion there were a couple of courses to be done by our batch in the Portsmouth area. We tramped up from Plymouth, ready to take Hampshire apart. The first challenge was HMS Collingwood, the navy's electrical school. It had been decided, certainly not before time, that the Marine Engineers should take over responsibility for the high power elements of generation and distribution of electricity in HM Ships, to give the Electrical Branch more time to concentrate on the increasingly complex area of weapons and electronics. We arrived at the Wardroom full tilt, ready to take on the Greenies. We were not prepared – no-one could be – for the sight that greeted us. Round the anteroom was ranged a collection of stereotypical Electrical Officers, tangled beards, unwinking eyes magnified by thick lenses, silent, watching, like so many owls. We shrugged and had a pint. Fortunately the course was short, mainly conducted in the Ring Main Building. We met the unusually obnoxious Workshops Officer, who told us that nothing, absolutely nothing, was made in his workshops without him being aware of it. It did not take us long to suborn a couple of his Chiefs, and we made a Hero's Engine out of a copper ballcock (bought by Janey at a plumber's in Fareham). On our last day we presented it to the Wardroom, where it sat on the bar, rotating at speed with little jets of steam spurting from its jets. Some of the denizens shifted uneasily on their perches.

We spent an amazing week at Phoenix, the Damage Control School set up on some waste land at the head of Portchester Creek, north of Whale Island. In glorious weather we fought great blazing oil fires, sweating into our fearnought suits and inhaling the distinctive odour of foam reagent, which I think featured ox-blood as its principal constituent. In between, we plunged about in the Damage Control Unit, where water poured, spurted and sprayed in to simulate action damage, and we fought to quell the flow, banging in wooden wedges, securing splinter boxes and cutting and fitting shores to brace up failing bulkheads – all hopefully without getting drowned. We ended each day filthy, sodden and happy, with a roaring thirst.

Phoenix was commanded by Captain Berkeley, a Punch lookalike who had been the Engineer Officer of a frigate called Porcupine during the war. The vessel had been blown in two by enemy action, but the resourceful crew managed to keep both halves afloat until rescue arrived. The halves were inevitably known as HMS Pork and HMS Pine. I don't know which Berkeley was in, but it was a good story well told. He had a pilot-fish in the shape of small, grey, "invaluable Lt Cdr Penney". He was invaluable because he carried everywhere, like the US President's bagman, Berkeley's box of 50 Players No 3 cigarettes with him, and offered them when prompted; but also invaluable because he had attended the A-bomb tests at Monte Bello – "he was actually *there*, d'you see?" Berkeley boomed, adding verisimilitude to dry lectures on the nuclear threat. Looking back, it was all rather charmingly simple.

And so it was on to Lion, lying in Plymouth. On first encounter this was the outward and visible embodiment of sea-power. A sleek hull protected with armour belts, bristling with guns, and presenting, to the new arrival, a spotless teak quarterdeck, embellished with the traditional brass fittings. I crept aboard, slightly cowed, and remembering fondly the more human dimensions of Camperdown. There was in fact a great similarity. Both ships were at the end of long parallel evolutionary chains. In Lion's case her lineal ancestors were the Colony Class, County Class and Town Class. They were all the more the same than they were different. Nowhere was this more true than in the propulsion machinery, but goodness, there was a lot of it!

John Shepley, the senior (E) watchkeeper, took me on a grand tour. We crawled, climbed and traversed through the two boiler rooms, two engine-rooms, the notorious pipe-space, and then dropped down through mess-decks to visit a seemingly endless number of shaft passages, each containing one or two plummer blocks, main bearings for the propeller shafts. Finally we got to the stern gland spaces, damp and smelling of rust from the seawater constantly dripping in. But this was not 'finally' after all. Next we visited the steering gear, the air conditioning plant and all its heat exchange units dotted round the ship. Then there was the boats workshop, and the large upper deck crane, the laundry and the galley plus some more recondite areas that I was yet to encounter. Finally – finally – we ascended through yet another mess-deck. John, who had kept up a brilliant running commentary on everything that we had seen, spied a set of bongo drums and beat out a skilful tattoo on them. I was deeply impressed and realised that, *pace* Manadon, I had an awful lot to learn.

Soon after I joined there was an Old Lions' Day. The previous Lion had been Beatty's flagship at the battle of Jutland, and there were plenty of ancient sailors who had served in her, forty years before. A rail warrant and ten pounds was enough to lure them down to Plymouth. Admiral of the Fleet Lord Chatfield, who had been Beatty's Flag Captain, was there in full fig, back like a ramrod, though I overheard a ravaged and decrepit former Petty Officer say to his chum

"Old Chats is showing his age a bit, isn't he?"

Lord Mountbatten, a midshipman at Jutland was also there, uncharacteristically quiet. We had to look after one of the great (well, extraordinary) names of naval history, Lady Plunkett-Ernle-Erle-Drax, a grand old dame indeed. Janey told her enthusiastically about our recent wedding and modest flat in Peverell.

"Ah yes, my dear," said her Ladyship." *I* started my married life in Plymouth".

"Where did you live?" asked Janey, all wide eyed innocence.

"Oh, Admiralty House, dear", was the reply. No answer or comment needed.

All too soon it was time to sail. Janey had already moved up to her parents' house in Hertfordshire, where she would have the baby. We spent a final, miserable weekend in a dreary boarding house near the Hoe, huddled in front of a gas fire with a voracious appetite for sixpences, whilst outside it rained relentlessly.

On our way south we practised some gunnery, and I quickly learnt that the outward and visible embodiment of sea power was somewhat flawed. The mechanisms bringing the six inch shells and cartridges up from the magazines to the turrets were massive steel artefacts, operated by hydraulics, and largely controlled by micro-switches. These were flimsy and none too reliable, and when one failed it unleashed the awesome power of the hydraulics on the system, with dramatic results. Often one of these graunches took over a week to fix – three days to dismantle, two to refurbish and three to reassemble. The frequency of failure was such that every time a turret completed its planned firing the Gunnery Officer, Patrick Grotrian, opened the champagne in the mess. The three inch guns were of course that much smaller, but they were firing shells at one hundred and twenty rounds per minute, and the smallest temporal or spatial misalignment led to the same grisly end. Today we would probably use autonomous electric motors and lasers, but then the materials of the age did not meet the designer's aspirations.

I pretty soon got the hang of watchkeeping down below. The ship had been expensively modernised to be able to steam through nuclear fallout. The machinery spaces could not survive without copious amounts of fresh air, contaminated or not. Accordingly all major activities in boiler rooms and engine rooms had been equipped for remote operation from a small air-conditioned space within the citadel known as the Slit Trench. Once again the technology did not match the concept. The little air-driven pecker motors, supposed to operate various valves, were unequal to their task, and could be heard uttering pathetic phut-phut noises of frustration. In any case no sensible engineer would have left these large, power-intensive and volatile spaces unmanned without enormous incentive (ie nuclear fallout!)

At this stage we changed the Commander (E). The contrast between Hans Hamilton, the outgoing, a huge man of prodigious appetites, and the incomer, small, owlish, could not have been greater. It happened that the Wardroom had acquired a new piano, and Hans Hamilton's farewell dinner, at sea, coincided with plans to dispose of the old one. He was still playing an interminable song whose first line was "My mother's long strong black pudding. . . ." as the piano was slid over the side into the Bay of Biscay for its final float test. It did not pass.

Each watchkeeper was also a Section Officer for a portion of the machinery. I started with the forward, or Juliet Engine Room, supposedly the prestige space to show to visiting firemen on account of its broader, less cluttered appearance. This also meant that the Senior Engineer, a sour and driven man, set a standard for cleanliness and sparkle even higher than that for the rest of the Department. I was often in the dog-house. The engine room contained a wide variety of machinery but what I remember most was the proliferation of sea water cooled heat exchangers – main condensers, turbo-generator condensers, distillers for the evaporators, drain coolers, gland steam condensers, coolers for air compressors, the list seemed endless. Nearly all these leaked at some time or another, perhaps due to the ship spending a long time afloat in some particularly corrosive basin in a ship-yard. We spent hours pressure testing, plugging tubes, cutting out and changing tubes or replacing the ferrules that sealed them to the tube-plate. All to prevent sea water getting into the feed water and thence to the precious boilers.

As a result of the recent changes (and my fortnight's course) I was also in charge of Generators and Switchboards, aided by Electrical Artificer Lancashire. He had the infuriating habit of trying to complete your sentences for you, so he must have thought that I was a pretty rum chap, as I struggled to finish my instructions with words other than the obvious. Fortunately I also had deep back-up in the lanky shape of Lieutenant Fred Pointer, a Special Duties officer (ie one up from the ranks) who had lived electrics for many years. His availability was somewhat limited, however, as most of his Division of Electrical Mechanics seemed to be on charges, either of setting fire to things or of buggering each other. He was known as Lieutenant Arse 'n' Arson.

We changed round sections every six months. The Boiler Rooms were the most sought-after, because of their high potential for going disastrously wrong, but in many ways the most interesting was the ill-regarded but diverse Outside Machinery Section. Amongst its diversities was the Laundry Machinery, in continuous use by the gang of "unofficial Chinese" who ran it under direct orders from Hong Kong. They affected to speak no English, and from time to time an emissary from the Laundry would arrive, in his vest, at the Engineers' Office.

"No flucking steam," he would shriek, with a grin. We all knew that there was plenty of flucking steam, it was coming out of our ears, but on deeper investigation it became clear that this telling phrase was simply short for "There is something wrong in the Laundry. Could an engineer come and see, please?" No flucking plobrem.

A quiddity of Lion was the pneumatic message handling system between the Bridge Wireless Office, where incoming signals were received, and the Main Signal Office, from where they were distributed. Occasionally there would be a complete blockage and the Outside Machinery men with their long bamboos would be summoned. When the tubes had been cleared the offending capsules would be fallen on urgently by the signalmen, in case some urgent message had been 'lost in the post'.

The Senior Watchkeeper, John Shepley, was immune from this rotation of crops. His section was The Double Bottoms, responsible for the management of all fluids, but especially of course for the oil fuel, all 1640 tons of it, stored in 40 odd tanks about the ship. The majority of these were double-bottoms, curved tanks, two to three feet deep, lying right at the bottom of the ship. A complex network of pipework connected all these tanks, and it was the job of the DB Party to embark fuel to top up, most dramatically with high pumping rates when refuelling at sea, and to ensure that the service tanks were kept full for the thirsty boilers. The prestige held by these very specialised stokers was immense, whilst their overalls rotted on them, such is the corrosive nature of furnace fuel oil.

In due course Lion arrived in Malta for Christmas. For many of us this was our first Christmas away from home, and we celebrated in the traditional way on board. Exchange of presents in the Wardroom – none to cost more than 2/6d, and the Captain and most junior rating swapping caps and roles for rounds of the messdecks. There was a slight air of forced jollity about the whole event, exacerbated by a lot of drinking. Quick phone calls home were out of the question, and we all missed our loved ones. We were glad to slink back to work the next day, nursing our hangovers.

In the New Year we visited Taranto, a town which, in 1963, had not quite forgotten the loss of the Italian fleet at the eponymous battle, spearheaded by the brave Swordfish pilots of the Fleet Air Arm. It was, in January, a miserable spot, with flurries of snow, the outriders of the blizzards sweeping across Europe. Accordingly I was not best pleased to be appointed Officer of the Patrol on our first night in. I duly checked in at the local nick with my posse of a Petty Officer and four sailors, where we made uneasy contact with the carabinieri. As the blood wagons started to roll it soon became clear that the Old Town was a positive villains' den where our lads were being systematically jumped by the locals. Access to this area was via a bridge. With my slender resources, I decided to declare the area out of bounds and posted my men as sentries on the bridge. The flow of bloodstained sailors soon subsided to a trickle.

The next morning two things happened.

Firstly I had a telegram from Janey to say that we had a son, Toby. Born in a snowstorm after a long labour, it would be two months before England would be clear of snow, and ten months before I would see my boy for the first time. Janey and her family battled valiantly with power cuts and shortages during that hard winter, and struggled with the extreme difficulty of keeping a tiny baby at the right temperature.

Secondly I was summoned by the Commander, the suave Richard Pilkington Clayton, later to be Second Sea Lord, who told me that I had exceeded my authority by placing the Old Town out of bounds. My leave was therefore stopped. I grinned and asked him to join me and the other officers in wetting Toby's head. He agreed.

Soon afterwards we visited Istanbul, and made the statutory pilgrimage to the Blue Mosque and the Souk, both heaving with people, locals not the tourists who were to take over these famous places in years to come. Moored in the middle of the Bosphorus, we had a wonderful view of both banks – Europe and Asia. It had been agreed that we should take the ship's dghaisa with us to the Far East, and Charlie, its owner, had decided on a trip to the Souk. Abetted by a mischievous Officer of the Watch, he got the Crane Driver to lower his craft to the waterline, embarked and set off for the shore. Poor Charlie, he had never encountered any meaningful tidal flows or currents in Malta, and was certainly not prepared for the six knots sluicing out of the Black Sea. He was last seen heading for Africa, still valiantly rowing, as one of our power boats set off to rescue him.

In due course we entered the Suez Canal – sand, distant pyramids, feluccas, enormous incongruous bill-boards. A row of houseboats lined the bank. On one, a man in fez and djellaba raised his garment and waved an enormous penis derisively at us, a welcome, apparently, extended to all British warships since the Suez Crisis in 1956. I went below, chuckling, for my watch. When I was relieved, the gully-gully man was performing for the officers on the quarterdeck. Well into his routine of producing baby chicks from every orifice, he welcomed me as something slightly different, in that I was clad in sweaty overalls, and enrolled me as his stooge. After a few more chickens had been extracted from my ears, he went on bended knee to the Commander.

"Effendi, I see that you have a very fine gold ring. Can I borrow, please?"

The Commander grudgingly gave up his heavy signet ring, which was wrapped in paper and entrusted to me.

"Hold this very carefully", I was told, "and when I count to three throw it over the side".

The gully-gully man then proceeded to move a few more chickens around, and then said to me, conversationally, "OK, throw it over the side now."

Confident in his skill at substitution, I nonchalantly dropped the package into the sandy waters of the canal.

The gully-gully man appeared agitated. "Oh no," he said, "I didn't count to three!"

I went white, the Commander went red, and the audience held their breath. Of course, under the Commander's basilisk glare, the ring was eventually retrieved from my nostril, but it was a very nasty couple of minutes.

TECHNICAL SKILL: 10 TACT AND DIPLOMACY: 0

After that we embarked on a series of visits, interspersed by quite long periods at sea – the distances were huge. This routine was to everyone's taste; the gradual crescendo leading up to a port visit, excess, catharsis, regret, back to sea to regain sobriety, make up for lost sleep and restore the financial balance, and then back to the crescendo. By now everyone on board knew their job and the even tenor of life at sea was only disturbed by endless, tedious exercises. The worst were the Damage Control Exercises, which involved the whole crew, and meant that every door and every hatch had every clip on, so it took ages to move about the ship; and long periods of enforced idleness, often wearing a respirator, with partial lighting and no ventilation. The perpetrator of all this unpleasantness was John Bouchier, the Atomic, Biological and Chemical Damage Control Officer (ABCDO for short!), otherwise known as Picnic John, because of his liking for banyans, or picnics, at every opportunity. A charming man.

We paused at *Aden,* where we were entertained in the Governor's beautiful Roundhouse on Steamer Point, and where we swam tentatively behind the (allegedly) shark-proof nets.

On the long trip across the Indian Ocean we stopped daily for 'hands to bathe'. A strange and wonderful sensation to look down into blue, blue water thousands of fathoms deep, and then jump or dive in, hoping not to plunge on down forever. We splashed happily about under the bored gaze of two sailors with loaded rifles, hoping to spot a man-eating shark and take a pot-shot at it. We climbed back on board via a scrambling net, a painful and exhausting heave that left us as hot and bothered as when we started. Still worth it, though.

After an exercise with local forces we entered *Trincomalee*, the superb natural harbour in Ceylon, as it then was. The naval base, long since turned over to India, was dilapidated, and in the process of being reclaimed by nature. Monkeys played where once Gunnery Instructors drilled parades of British sailors. We saw an elephant swim steadily across the harbour.

I had agreed to put on a weekly jazz programme on the ship's radio, which gave me an excuse to buy more records. I used to sit, happily sweating in some minute windowless compartment full of electronic cabinets, playing a dodgy turntable and burbling on. I never got any requests, nor indeed any recognition that anyone had heard any of the programmes; maybe I was just playing to myself. An early Cannonball Adderley bossa nova called Clouds was my signature tune.

We arrived in *Singapore*, the first of several visits, but seldom for long enough to do more than drink Tiger by the pool at the Officers' Club and enjoy the immaculate surroundings of the base. The end of the Raj was going out in style. Two years later I'd be back, with wife and family in tow, with much more opportunity to explore.

We visited *Saigon*, a long way up a narrow, silted river to discover:

*   a. some of the most beautiful girls in South East Asia,   and

*   b. that the President's wife, a major power in the land, had just started a morality campaign.

Bars were strictly controlled, and all the many dance halls had been summarily shut down. The message, not for the first or last time, was: "You should have been here last month!"

We dropped into **Hong Kong**, which was still intensely British, despite the huge Chinese majority. We had curry lunch, washed down with silver tankards of ice-cold San Mig, with the hospitable Ghurkhas on the Gin-Drinkers' Line, the final redoubt of the locals in their (unsuccessful) rebuff of the Japanese invasion. I went ashore with the Surgeon Commander, a large and cheerful man called Mallows. Sporting a flapping white suit and an enormous panama, he guided me to a favourite bar. He was warmly greeted by the Mama-san, who said,

"How many girls you want, Master?"

He replied, "Great white master requires several girls, but first, a glass of gin."

'But first a glass of gin' became a family saying. It usually seemed to work.

Whilst at Hong Kong I paid a visit to **Macau**, the former Portuguese territory and Chinese gambling Mecca. This involved a passage in a distinctly bumpy hydrofoil, packed with Chinese – and me. It was clearly a loss of face to be seasick, but they could not prevent their faces from slowly changing from yellow to green, like so many lemons ripening in reverse. The casinos themselves were enormous wooden structures, with gambling taking place on a number of floors. An impressive central well, or atrium, ran from top to bottom, and was useful for a multitude of baskets on strings, carrying money and chips up and down.

An official visit to **Japan** was unusual. We went to **Osaka** – home of Mitsubishi - and **Nagasaki** – home of, er, the Atom Bomb. Osaka was a belching industrial city, but Nagasaki, despite its dreadful history, was more accessible. We were puzzled to see the cherry trees in the Main Street covered in blossom as late as June, but soon realised that it was all plastic. The local people seemed to have a great need to become extremely drunk, every evening; the older they were, the greater the need, and the effect. As they veered and ricocheted down Plastic Blossom Street, we called it the 'Naggers Staggers' and attributed it to the effects of radiation. But of course in reality this obsessive behaviour may have been an attempt to obliterate their terrible memories. In the Peace Park there had been built, right at the epi-centre, a huge stone statue of a Japanese warrior in the traditional pose for peace, cross legged, one hand vertically aloft, the other outstretched. "Don't drop it here," said Jack, ever the black humorist, "drop it over there."

We had a formal, official and ceremonial duty. We took the Governor of *Sabah* off, on the country achieving its independence. We put in to *Jesselton*, the tiny capital, not much more than a large village with, nevertheless, an imposing Government House. At the top of its game, the United Kingdom had no shortage of style, even if our colonial ambitions turned to ashes. If all the colonial nations round the world had waited another hundred years before pulling out, the world would be a better place, but sadly it is too late for that.

The saluting guns were red hot by the time all the proper salutes had been fired, and the Gunner was hoarse from repeating to himself:

"If-I-wasn't-a-Gunner-I-wouldn't-be-here-Fire-One!" the age old mantra to time the interval between shots. The Commander-in-Chief's Royal Marine Band, immaculate as ever, and specially embarked for the occasion, went ashore and started a two day round of music and marching. Their repertoire would include Beating Retreat, Ceremonial Sunset, Last Post and Reveille, and a number of more arcane ceremonies, probably invented by the Bandmaster. Our own Royal Marine contingent provided the Drums, and a Division of sailors was landed to march about.

"Oh my good Gawd," sighed Frank Trickey, the Lieutenant (G)(g). "Marching sailors, what a debacle".

Meanwhile the rest of us ventured short distances into the jungle, or *ulu*. We were paddled in dug-out canoes along muddy rivers in 100% humidity, hoping to see the wildlife, most of which seemed intent on eating us. In vain we swatted away the huge mosquitoes that zoned in on us out of nowhere, and cautiously kept our fingers from trailing in the water 'just in case'!

At last the great moment came. The Governor appeared, aquiline, serious, composed, patrician, a thing of austere beauty in pressed white sharkskin and ostrich feathers. The final elements of the ceremony unfolded. The Governor inspected the Guard, in company with his successor, Prince, President, Prime Minister? No-one quite seemed to know. The Band played on. The Union Flag was lowered, folded and presented to the Governor. The Band played on. Another, unfamiliar flag, presumably that of independent Sabah, was hauled aloft. The Governor shook hands with the new man and stepped into the Captain's Barge. The Band played on. Sailors and Royal Marines were gradually retrieved on board. There was one last round of 'If-I-wasn't-a-Gunner. . . .' As we steamed away the former Governor waved at his former fiefdom from the bridge. Then the Captain led him below to his cabin, where the Captain's Steward served him the largest, and the most earnestly desired, gin and tonic of his entire life.

After returning HE to Singapore we set off for **Fremantle** in western Australia, a long way for a few days there and nowhere else in Australia, but a new continent and a chance to get out of the soupy South China Sea. Everyone was, by now, well accustomed to working in a hot climate, but life down below and in some of the poorly ventilated operational spaces, stuffed with primitive electronics, thermionic valves and rheostats, was definitely wearing. The Outside Machinery boys provided huge chunks of ice all round the ship which sat in mess fannies full of limejuice to which all had access. The limers arrived as green crystals in a tin, which were then diluted with water.

Down below the watchkeepers took a salt tablet a day, and I heard that oatmeal was reckoned to be a good specific against heat exhaustion, but I never saw it used, and have no idea how it was prepared. The worst scourge of the high temperatures and humidity was prickly heat, which affected everyone a bit, and some poor souls dreadfully. The more you scratched the more you itched. Severe sufferers had to be repatriated.

On the way south we crossed the Equator, and a majority of the crew were novices to King Neptune's kingdom. The Master-at-Arms presided, and his helpers shaved the initiates with great wooden razors, before dumping them in the birdbath, a canvas bath rigged up on deck, and kept full with a fire hose.

Fremantle made very little impression on me, a pleasant port ten miles from Perth. What was singular was the Western Australians' feeling of isolation from the rest of their country, and their paranoia about invasion by the 'Yellow Peril'. We were welcomed as a shield against this eventuality, which fortunately was not put to the test.

As we set off for home, I learnt that Toby was to have a minor operation for a hernia. Even a minor operation is quite major for such a mite, and I drafted a telegram to Janey which started "Balls to Mr Bangelstein. . . .". The Chief Tel. rang me to say that 'Balls' could not be transmitted. Even here the Morality Police were vigilant! Thinking of Churchill, I substituted 'Round objects'. The telegram winged on its way. (Churchill, when he received such a telegram, asked "Who is Mr Round and to what does he object?")

Shortly afterwards we paused at *Diego Garcia*, in the middle of the Indian Ocean. It would have been a classical tropical atoll, had it not been defaced by an airstrip and the unmistakable signs of military infrastructure. The story of how we, the Brits, ousted the lawful residents, the Chagos, so that we could lease the facilities to the USA is not one of our proudest achievements. Keeping the Chagos away to this day has compounded the felony. It is said that, when the large aircraft carrier design of the 60s was under consideration in the Ministry of Defence, the Royal Air Force "moved" Diego Garcia so that they could show that all the Indian Ocean could be covered by land-based aircraft, thus obviating the need for a carrier. Well, we never got it!

We wriggled our way homewards. Through the Canal, gully-gully men again, but I kept well clear of the Commander and his ring. Past the Egyptian with the big penis, still waving it. Through the Med., where various flag Officers came and went; they loved us as a flagship: there was an Admiral's bridge, and a huge cabin under the quarterdeck.

Eventually, a week before we were due home, we secured in Gib. We were surrounded by most of the Home and Med. Fleets and there was a lot of ship visiting and catching up with old friends. After my success in Taranto, the time had come round again for me to be the Officer of the Patrol. This time the differences were:

* 1. Instead of 400 there were 8000 libertymen ashore.

* 2. The Gibraltar police were entirely used to dealing with most known situations involving sailors, and did not need the assistance of one Lieutenant (E) plus four.

Need us or not, we duly reported to the Central Police Station and had not been there for long when we heard the shocking news, over the police transistor radio, that President Kennedy had been fatally shot in Dallas. As we digested this sombre report I was summoned to attend a "disturbance, at the Winter Gardens". When I got there the nature of the disturbance was clear. The Winter Gardens was a large pub-cum-music hall on Main Street. On the stage, addressing about 600 sailors, was a Regulating Petty Officer from Lion. His message, delivered in best parade ground manner was:

" President Kennedy has been assassinated. World War three is therefore imminent. All leave is cancelled. Return to your ships."

It took me very little time to explain to the RPO that if anyone was going to cancel leave it would be me, not him, and that in any case his authority was severely prejudiced by the enormous pink teddy bear that he clutched to him throughout. My message, relayed to the audience by the Petty Officer of the Patrol, was received with delight since it was still early and there was a lot of beer to be consumed. I left discreetly before the mood changed, and glimpsed the RPO wandering disconsolately back to Lion, to prepare for World War Three alone, apart from the pink teddy bear.

Janey and I approached our impending reunion with similar feelings: after six months marriage and twelve months apart, would we still get on together? Perhaps even recognise each other? We needn't have bothered. Five minutes after clapping eyes on this beautiful, slender blonde and her blonder baby boy it was as if we'd never been apart. Amid the euphoria of reunion we embraced and sped away to Alverstoke where our new home awaited us.

Number 18A, Broderick Avenue, was an Edwardian semi in a leafy Edwardian avenue. It had every advantage save two: it wasn't ours and the heating was dreadful. The latter was the fault of the boiler, a plucky little cast iron stove called, with some optimism, the White Rose Mk 0. Whether subsequent Mks were better I don't know, but our model spent weeks on end sulking, with only the occasional blast of white-hot heat to keep hope springing eternal. We were however perfectly happy and celebrated Christmas together with love and enthusiasm.

Lion remained alongside in Portsmouth Dockyard during January, and I travelled to work daily on the draughty Gosport Ferry, in plain clothes, as was the custom. On chilly days I replaced my cloth cap with a fur hat bought from Gieves. I noticed that each time I wore the hat I was stopped and interrogated by the dockyard Police on the Main Gate. Eventually I said to them:

"Look, you surely don't think that I'm a Russian spy because I'm wearing the fur hat?"

"Of course not, Sir," came the courteous reply, "but we *would* look silly if it turned out that we *had* let a Russian spy in, wearing a Russian hat."

In due course duty called, and we had to lever Lion off the wall and back to sea. These elderly, complex steam ships took a lot of effort to get going, rather like an old person. After a great heave-ho to get them on their feet, they can potter along quite happily for ages. Thus Lion. Once steam had been laboriously raised, and a few systems had been tested, it was time to dispense with the huge black cables of electrical shore supply (EA Lancashire to the fore), and to disconnect the two coal fired donkey boilers on the jetty which had been providing us with shore steam for heating and the galley. It was always difficult to remember to order the coal for these beasts, and occasionally only frantic messages from the Leading Stoker in charge to the Engineers' Office allayed a stock-out situation. In the preceding week every form of fluid had been embarked to make sure that we sailed with all supplies at 100%. Simultaneously the Supply Department had been embarking victualling and naval stores, and the gunners had been topping up with ammunition. We sank visibly in the water. At last, with the comfortable assumption that all these things had been done, the Command team tripped on board, let go a few ropes and springs, and took the old girl to sea.

We had a short exercise with some Dutch ships in a lumpy North Sea, the sand coloured waves seeming to come from every direction, and were relieved to put into the Firth of Forth. After a few gun-salutes we anchored. The great thing about these salutes is that they have no-one's name on them, so any number of VIPs can imagine that the salute is for them. We had come to attend the Opening of the Forth Road Bridge, a few hundred yards upstream of the famous Rail Bridge. We secured directly below the Road Bridge. The locals, in an uncharacteristic gesture, possibly propitiating some ancient Celtic god, threw their small change, or bawbees, off the new bridge, and some of it ended up embedded in the Commander's prized teak quarterdeck. He was not amused.

When the time came for us to leave a sea-mist had descended, and a frigate, radar no doubt confused by the two bridges, managed to crash into our bows whilst we were still at anchor. The damage was extraordinary. The frigate impinged on the starboard side, whereas we were secured by the port anchor. The shank of the starboard anchor was snapped clean in two, and the hawse-pipe, a massive casting some twenty feet long, two feet in diameter and fashioned from steel two inches thick, was similarly shattered. The cells, paint shop and Chinese shoemaker (the Snob) were all hastily evacuated and we proceeded gingerly back to Pompey, whilst the chippies banged some shores in to support the rest of the structure.

When we got back to Portsmouth the class spare hawse-pipe and the class spare anchor were sitting on two railway wagons, waiting for us. This generous ranging and scaling of naval stores has long since been cut back, but it was mighty impressive to see it work so well.

Come the spring and we were back off to the Med, for a shorter spell this time, and with the possibility that Janey could come out. By now I considered myself a competent watchkeeper and fairly all about on most engineering matters in the ship, so it was a shock to have my leave stopped twice, within a month, for engineering reasons. The circumstances of both stoppages were so unusual that I jotted them down at the time, and have dined out on them since. Here they are.

We lay at anchor in Argostoli Bay, where the Mediterranean Fleet had gathered for a Regatta. After two days of pulling, sailing, crash-cuttering and the like, interspersed with banyans and visits to one's chums in other ships, the last race had been keenly fought and the celebrations were concluded by a massive Sods' Opera held ashore under acres of flapping canvas redolent with the aroma of canned beer and hot-dogs. At times, this finale looked more like a Disaster Exercise than a theatrical performance, but such role-confusion was not uncommon.

Before the Fleet weighed and proceeded the next morning it was the very pleasant duty of the Commander-in-Chief to present the prizes on Lion's quarterdeck, the awning having been struck at both watches in anticipation of our departure. At the same time it was my considerably less pleasant duty, albeit self-imposed, to attempt to fine-tune the boiler controls in the after (Kilo) boiler-room. The opportunity of having both boilers flashed up in this unit with, for the time being, nowhere to go was too good to miss. There was an irritating little hunt in the system that it should be simple enough to tune out.

Pneumatic boiler controls were in their infancy at that time, and the available courses were either absurdly academic (Nyquist's stability criteria remain lodged in the memory, unfortunately) or totally elementary. We gained our experience on the hoof, which is, of course, the only place to get it. So when ERA Thompson and I selected our thinnest screwdrivers and advanced towards the master Sunvic controller, we enjoyed that frisson of excitement that presages a voyage into the unknown. It was a short but eventful voyage. The first tweak of my screwdriver, a marginal adjustment of the proportional action, we had agreed, immediately provoked a dramatic onset of the phenomenon known as "panting". This is a massive dynamic instability within the boiler furnace, where the flame changes rapidly in intensity, causing the boiler casings to resonate vigorously. Whilst observing this reaction with enormous professional interest, we remained happily ignorant of the scene unfolding above us.

On the quarterdeck, all was serene as the C-in-C, dressed in gleaming white samite and gold, presented the prizes to all those sort of people who habitually win them. His staff, mingled with a bevy of smooth and ambitious officers, struck elegant attitudes and clapped softly from time to time, somehow managing to give the impression that they were applauding the C-in-C himself rather than the prize winners. The sun shone upon the wine-dark sea. The birds, at least those birds that had been spared by the Greek hunters, sang. A shimmer of heat emerged from the after funnel (**my** funnel) to the accompaniment of the well-modulated hum of the forced-draught blowers. It was a scene as tranquil as any vicarage tea party.

The combustion instability initiated by the little tweak of my screwdriver caused rapid changes in the pressure in the boiler uptakes. The control system sensed this and tried to correct it by changing the supply of steam to the blowers so that they sped up and slowed down as rapidly as they, great lumbering fans overfull of momentum, could manage. This had the interesting effect of producing alternating bands of black and white smoke from the funnel. The rhythmic sighing of these great beasts, accompanied by the occulting obscuration of the sun by black and white smoke alerted the quarterdeck party, not usually much interested in the Stygian workings beneath their feet. Lifting their eyes reluctantly from their beloved leader, they were in time to see an enormous pancake of soot detach itself, as a result of all this unusual activity, from its roosting place inside the funnel, and ascend vertically upwards. It hovered for a moment, like a UFO determining its next resting place, and then, caught by the Ionian zephyr, descended as straight as a die upon the C-in-C.

ERA Thompson and I were by now congratulating ourselves on stopping the panting before anything much had fallen off the boilers, and on having cured the hunt that we had set out to do. We left the boiler-room thankfully, ERA Thompson to enjoy a well-earned pint in his mess, and me to have my leave stopped, for "blowing soot upon the Commander-in-Chief". I don't think I ever knew his name, and thankfully I am pretty sure he never knew mine. Now, in the hope of time's healing balm, all is revealed.

* * * * *

The ship lay to bow and stern moorings in the unrivalled surroundings of The Grand Harbour, Malta GC. Place of my birth - the King George V Hospital for Seamen (pronounced carefully) looked across the water to its companion and rival, the Royal Naval Hospital at Bighi. On a good day, and this was such a one, the harbour, surrounded by tier upon tier of golden stone buildings, mostly in some combination of military and religious styles, gave rise to feelings of comfort and security. This was a Sunday, and thus the island of bells and smells was noticeably more tintinabulous than usual and, because it followed a Saturday night, probably smellier too.

The sun beamed down upon the historic scene, and the first dghaisamen started to creep out upon the water, propelling their craft in the unique Maltese fashion of standing up to their oars, facing ahead and pushing the boat through the water. Deep in the bowels of HMS Lion, the engineer officers gathered in their Office. Sunday was a time for review and anticipation, and, fuelled by the execrable coffee provided by ME Widger - "Straight off the boiler front sir," he proudly proclaimed - we shared briefly some of the highlights of the previous evening's entertainment before moving on to more earnest matters. What was the state of the machinery? What work needed to be done today? Would all be ready for our departure the following morning?

The consensus was that overall we were in good shape though my old enemy, the after evaporators were still not making good water, good enough that is for the notoriously fastidious boilers - the men on the other hand were more easily satisfied. It was time to plan our personal endeavours. It transpired that the Senior Engineer, a man of anorexic construction weighed down by the permanent disappointment that attends on a perfectionist at large in an imperfect world, was going to delight us all by spending the day underground in some deep pothole. From there he could not make our lives a misery on board, but he could on the other hand attract further kudos in his alternate role as Secretary of the British Speleological Society. We rather felt that they deserved each other.

The senior watchkeeper, who also rejoiced in the title of Double Bottoms Officer, intended to inspect one of his Reserve Feed Water Tanks, which had been opened for cleaning, before attending Church ashore. This would be followed (for such was his wont) by a gathering of the Officers' Christian Union, a fierce but mercifully impotent mafia, much given to internal strife. Bill was proceeding to the next stage of his long (and ultimately unsuccessful) siege upon a Nursing Sister with a flat in Sliema, a perennial saga of Wagnerian proportions. Ricky was going to have lunch with "someone in the Dockyard", an enterprise that we understood would entail the painful consumption of a great deal of gin and Marsovin; but would in some obscure way give us much future leverage when it came to getting work done by the Dockyard. Dennis was going on that most innocent, but most portentous of naval diversions, a Postcard Run. Henry was spending the day writing to his wife. And I, I was duty, and I would, it was agreed:

* a) Sort out the After Evaps;

* b) Top up all round with feed and fresh water;

* c) Do rounds and check that all was prepared for tomorrow's sailing; and

* d) Tune the Sirens.

Everyone who has enjoyed the films "The Cruel Sea" and "In Which We Serve" knows exactly what a naval siren sounds like - a crisp, rising, thrilling sound, evocative of bustling efficiency and war preparedness. HMS Lion's sounded like wet farts. As such they did little for navigational safety, and still less for the Captain's machismo. Those few officers senior enough to be on informal terms with such a demi-god made his life unbearable with their snide references to his flatulence, and his choleric displeasure was in turn visited upon the denizens of the Engineer's Office.

The sirens' lamentable performance was not amenable to simple remedy. They were mounted high up in the forward funnel, in the space between the inner and outer skins, looking hopefully outward through apertures cut for their bell mouths. The steam supply for them ran vertically upwards from the wrong steam main. This soggy, saturated steam, a second class version of the crisp, dry, vibrant superheated steam used elsewhere in the ship, had usually turned to water by the time it had ascended the eighty feet of poorly drained, inadequately lagged pipework between the main and the sirens. They never stood a chance. Nevertheless, it was possible to improve their lamentable performance, if only marginally, by giving them a rather loosely described bollocking known as "Tuning". It was in any case necessary to carry out a futile *gesture, if only to give the Commander (E)'s handwringing the next day some substance. I was to be the instrument of that futility.*

So, later that morning, I found myself incarcerated in the hot, dark confines of the forward funnel, in the company of Mechanician Elkins. We had drained down, we had bypassed the traps, we had warmed through, we had opened up and now we were ready for the Tuning itself. Each siren consisted of a large circular phosphor-bronze plate, clamped at the edge, against whose centre a steam nozzle was set. Adjustment of a mighty nut (by a similarly mighty spanner) moved the nozzle position relative to the plate and had some effect on the quality of the fart. I, the Officer, would adjudicate on the preferred characteristics of the resultant sound. Elkins would wield the mighty spanner. Our humble task was not made simple by the fact that the sirens, when activated, resonated the entire structure on which they were mounted, and this general level of commotion, coupled with the rushing of the steam, the clanking of the traps and the gurgling of the drains created a cacophony through which it was scarcely possible to pick out the reedy voice of the sirens themselves. Clearly this was why an Officer was required.

At about this time the Commander-in-Chief, my former inadvertent target, was embarking in his barge at Customs House Steps to go to church in the Flagship, moored ahead of us. He was, as ever, exquisite in his ice-cream suit, and his wife who accompanied him was similarly the very acme of burnished fragrancy. The barge, a large green motorboat, always known as the Green Parrot, was also of surpassing beauty, being richly polished, decorated with chromed dolphins, and with the seats dressed in white duck covers with blue piping. The Maltese boat's crew were immaculate; even their boat hooks were decorated with perfect, white Turk's Heads and Square Sennet. In the circumstances, the layman might have been surprised that the barge had displayed near its bows a red disc, which was the naval code (rock of ages stuff, this) for "this is an informal occasion. Only the normal marks of respect are to be paid."

This meant, to the Officer of the Day, betelescoped upon the Quarterdeck, that it was not necessary to parade a Lieutenant's Guard of forty-two men with bayonets fixed, accompanied by a Royal Marine Band, which would have been the case had the Commander-in-Chief's barge sported the white disc indicative of a Formal Occasion. This welcome relaxation came as no surprise to the Officer of the Day, nor indeed to anyone else, since the Commander-in-Chief's movements and state of informality had already been promulgated by signal to the Fleet, and were now firmly clipped to the Officer of the Day's sheaf of daily business.

Accordingly, as the Officer of the Day prepared to salute the passing Green Parrot, he was accompanied only by the Duty Lieutenant Commander, who had emerged from the Wardroom to ensure that all went well and to work up a bit of a thirst, the Quartermaster, the Boatswain's Mate and the Royal Marine Bugler. The Commander popped out from his cabin at the last moment (glad to have a short respite from the thankless task of writing Daily Orders - no sooner published than overtaken by events) to remind the Duty Lieutenant Commander to tell the Officer of the Day to order the Quartermaster to get the Boatswain's Mate to pipe:

"Men out of the Dress of the Day Clear off the Upper deck." And then, as an afterthought:

"In Wind Scoops"

By this intelligence not only would the Commander-in-Chief and of course his Lady set eyes only on a ship which appeared to be almost totally devoid of life, certainly of the common vested or overalled variety, but they would also see a ship completely stripped of the curious curved tubes that normally stuck out of every scuttle or porthole whenever the ship was in harbour to catch whatever zephyr of wind was passing and so introduce a measure of fresh air into the foetid messes within. The Commander-in-Chief and his Lady therefore believed that all ships existed permanently in this emasculated and unnatural state.

The Green Parrot drew abreast the Quarterdeck, the Commander-in-Chief's eagle eyes raking the ship for signs of the tiniest imperfection, and the Royal Marine Bugler sounded the Alert; the Quartermaster piped the Still, and the Boatswain's Mate broadcast over the Tannoy:

"Attention on the Upper Deck. Face to Starboard. Commander-in-Chief Mediterranean."

The Officer of the Day stood proudly on the stage at the top of the starboard after gangway, and saluted. The Commander and the Duty Lieutenant Commander lurked under the shadow of the awning also saluting, with a barely perceptible increase in languor appropriate to increasing rank.

It was at this precise moment that Elkins and I, lost in a steamy world of our own, and happily oblivious of the great drama unfolding outside it, decided that the time had come to 'give them a blast', the mighty spanner having been used to turn the mighty nut half a turn. Elkins obligingly swung off on the lanyard that opened the steam up to the sirens. Perhaps the mighty nut had been turned the wrong way. Perhaps some disturbance had taken place far below; a chef may have loaded a new tray of figgy duff into the ovens, drawing off more saturated steam and allowing a slug of water to pass up the main to the sirens. Whatever the cause the effect was that HMS Lion farted like a thunderclappe at the Commander-in-Chief and his Lady, and I suffered the consequential penalty of having my leave stopped for the second time in as many months. Elkins was bought a beer by the Chief Engine Room Artificer when he had regained the power of speech.

Fortunately all this nonsense was behind us by the time Janey and Toby came out to Malta to visit. I picked them up from the airport after dark, and we got a taxi to our rented flat, overlooking Grand Harbour. She still talks of the moment she drew the curtains the next morning to see that wonderful panorama bathed in golden light – talk about coup de foudre! We had a great time exploring the island together, Toby in a 'colonel's' sun-hat and riding in a strange rented pushchair which sprang shut like an umbrella to enter a bus. In the flat was a paraffin fridge, completely useless at a time when we really needed it. I decided to clean it, partly to show Janey the manifold skills of an engineer! Paraffin soot is one of the blackest and most clinging substances known to man, and whilst the fridge thereafter worked splendidly ("you see, darling"), I spent days trying to get clean and avoid contaminating my white uniforms.

The flat had been found for us by a local estate agent, an Egyptian called Joe Busitil, a charming if amorous man, who was keen to do everything for us, or more particularly for Janey. It was through him that Toby went off for the day with a Maltese family, who, in common with most of the island's inhabitants, loved all babies but especially blonde ones! We waited up patiently, but with increasing concern, until at about 10 pm Toby was returned, face like a boiled orange, eyes out on stalks, stinking of garlic, totally hyper. We subsequently discovered that he had been taken to a football match, returned home with the family, met all the members of the extended family in various bars round the island, and feasted on a variety of pasta dishes. It took him days to return to earth.

The flat was in Gunlayer Square, a name so compelling that, having decoked the fridge and de-garlic'd Toby, we felt that we should try for another baby, an entirely successful stratagem. Eventually Janey and Toby flew back to England and I repaired to my duties.

The last event that I was to attend in Lion was the Malta Independence Day ceremony. In keeping with the Maltese immemorial and total love of fireworks, the culmination of the ceremonial was a massive firework display over Grand Harbour. Soon after sunset I came up from my rounds, secured a whisky and soda from my friend Leading Steward Davy through the wardroom scuttle, and stood in awe on the quarterdeck, whilst quite the most stupendous display I have ever seen burst, fizzled and crackled in the darkening sky, whilst massive explosions reverberated off the ancient flood-lit forts ringing the harbour. A spectacle sans pareil.

It was almost time for me to leave Lion, and my Chief ERA paid me the supreme compliment. He took me to the ERAs' Club on Crucifix Hill. This handsome building had been well endowed over the years, and was decorated by all manner of artefacts constructed by the skilled tradesmen of hundreds of ships. I was taken to meet the Chief ERA of the Mediterranean Fleet, who sat enthroned like a Buddha surrounded by his intimate friends. He offered me the soft handshake which strangely so often seems to be the greeting by the horny handed sons of toil, and a few pleasantries. I had the feeling that he habitually had Lieutenants (E) for breakfast. I was led away and filled with beer.

I had been selected for submarine training at HMS Dolphin. I would like to say that I reviewed my past two years before I left, but in fact I had a few drinks with my pals, packed and went home. We flew in a Comet, and my neighbour was a frightfully well bred, not very bright, Signals Officer. He was in a bit of a state because a Comet had recently crashed into the Med, with the loss of all on board. I explained to him that we had round windows, not the square ones suspected of causing the crash. As I waffled on to him about sharp corners being stress raisers his eyelids drooped, and I felt that perhaps I had helped him in some way.

Forty years on I *can* look back and say that this dear dinosaur provided excellent training and enjoyable employment for many of the enormous ship's company. The artificers liked her because 'you could fix things, even if you had to make them.' She was great for giving parties (lots of room) and for disaster relief (lots of men). Operationally she was severely limited. She consumed huge quantities of (cheap) fuel, and discharged every sort of pollution in gay profusion. Like most ships I've served in, we illogically loved her to death, warts and all. In war-fighting terms it was probably not until the arrival of the Type 42s some years later that we had a surface combatant, apart from our carriers, appropriate to the Cold War. Ironically *Lion* and her siblings probably trained most of the sailors for the new wave coming up behind them.

CHAPTER 5

Introduction to the Trade

"To shine as an engineer, go to a place where there are no other engineers." Verb sap, quoted by Dad in one of his lighter moments. That was one of the reasons for volunteering for what was still called, by old hands, of which there were many, The Trade. Other reasons were a wish to be cock of my own roost as soon as possible, and a desire to serve in a ship where the engineering was undeniably and inescapably integrated into the organisation, rather than pushed out of sight below decks.

So I was delighted to start my submarine training at HMS Dolphin, also known as Fort Blockhouse due to its strategic position right at the mouth of Portsmouth harbour. Plus it was just a couple of miles from our house in Alverstoke. Dolphin was a curious hotch-potch of buildings and activities. The Flag Officer Submarines and his staff squatted in the middle of the complex, many of them being housed in 'The Bungalow'. The First Submarine Squadron was based there, generally about eight boats, with all their supporting impedimenta, including the premier periscope workshop. Accordingly very long, unmanoeuvrable lorries were constantly coming and going on their way to Plymouth, Glasgow, Faslane and Rosyth, to the chagrin of drivers up and down the country. Dolphin also provided all forms of submarine training, including Submarine Escape, which required the landmark Tank, a steel tube twenty feet in diameter and one hundred feet high, and visible for miles around across the flat south Hampshire countryside. Dolphin had been the alma mater of the submarine service since the beginning and was permeated with the spirit and artefacts of our illustrious predecessors, much of it on display in the panelled Wardroom, full of lovely Wylie pictures. Right from the beginning we felt that we were joining a very special and privileged tribe.

The auguries were not great: neither the training staff nor the candidates (us!) seemed of the highest quality, so 'special and privileged' could well be a problem. My Dartmouth seaman contemporaries, Coward, Pitt, Milne Home, Innes and Tuohy, had joined years ago, and were now Third Hands in various boats round the flotilla. My Manadon contemporaries, Hill, Wixon, Pulvertaft, Marshall and Young had also preceded me and were installed as Engineer Officers here and there. The contents of our own training class (OTC 158) called to mind the expression 'rag, tag and bobtail'. Never mind, it was not for long, and at the end of each action-packed day I could go home to Janey and Toby.

Once again the instruction was based on knowledge rather than principle, and we spent hours copying out and memorising some of the more vital systems in a submarine, HP Air, Telemotor, Trim, Ballast, Fresh Water, Slop Drain and Sewage, and various kinds of electrics. Since we might move on to one of four classes of submarine we studied the Typical Submarine, which turned out to be roughly similar to all four, but the same as none. So when we got to our boats we would have to start again!

One of the most interesting aspects of our time at Dolphin was the Escape training. Opinion has always been divided on its merits, for most of the world's oceans are much deeper than the crushing depth of any submarine. Nevertheless, enough submarine accidents had occurred in shallow waters to justify the training, which was thought to pacify politicians and families alike.

The principle was simple. Within the stricken submarine a small compartment was brought up to the pressure of the water outside by admitting seawater and discharging HP air into the space. It was then possible to open the hatch, take a deep breath, and rise upwards to the surface. On the way you had to "breathe out all the way to the top", a ritual phrase. If you did not, the expanding air in your lungs would burst them. You went up because you had an inflated life-jacket on. (Otherwise you would stay put – the human body becomes negatively buoyant below about fifty feet.)

It was felt necessary to practise this process, and we started with a few runs from the thirty and sixty feet locks - blisters on the side of the tank - before the "real thing" from bottom to top. It was quite alarming for the first time or two, but the worst thing was often the excruciating pain in the ears as the pressure came on fast. The Escape Coxswains, hairy men in their thirties with skin-tight yellow swimming trunks, were able to swim from top to bottom of the tank at will and were constant guides and mentors. On one occasion I was in the thirty foot lock with an exceptionally fastidious electrical officer, who was having ear problems. Despite the coxswain's hoarse exhortations to "keep ahead of the pressure, Sir, clear your ears!" his discomfort grew worse. As a last resort the Coxswain rummaged in his trunks and produced, from the general region of his testicles, a Vick inhaler. "Here you are, Sir, shove this up your shonk and breathe deep." The ghastly dilemma was etched indelibly, perhaps permanently, on the recipient's face.

When you emerged and started swimming upwards the Coxswains would thump you on the chest if you were not breathing out, and redirect you with playful tweaks and nudges if you veered off at a tangent. Eventually, in a euphoric explosion of bubbles, you surfaced, under the watchful eye of the Tank Officer. Unique experience.

In amongst our many lectures and short outings in the training submarine, which together with the Tank gave us inconspicuous screening for claustrophobia (much feared, seldom experienced), we went on a couple of industrial visits. The first of these was to Chloride Ltd, who made the main batteries for all RN submarines. A submarine battery is enormous – 220 cells, each cell four feet high and eighteen inches square. Stowed in the capacious battery tanks under the main deck, these were coupled together to provide 8000 ampere hours at 440/220 volts – a formidable amount of power. Hopefully the battery sections would remain in situ throughout the commission for it was a difficult and tiresome job to change them. The odd "sick cell" that developed would be shorted out. The batteries were carefully nurtured – they were a submarine's lifeblood. The Chief Electrician fussed over them, and his mechanics were forever crawling over the tops of the cells, topping up, checking specific gravity of the electrolyte, looking at the cleanliness, cooling and ventilation. This last was particularly important to stop build up of hydrogen, and if ever you see someone checking a bathroom fan by holding a piece of loo-paper to it the chances are that he is a submariner. All tools used in the battery compartments had to be specially insulated – there was a legendary tale of someone dropping a spanner which shorted out two terminals and disappeared in a puff of vaporised steel!

Chlorides took us through all this at a brisk canter, because the real point of the day was a serious drinking session in a Manchester hotel, followed by a visit to a theatre featuring Scantily Clad Girls, followed by return to the hotel for more drinks, perhaps to be joined by some of the SCGs. We were somewhat rocked to hear that on this occasion the SCGs were off, and we would be seeing a couple of young male comedians instead. They were extremely funny and joined us afterwards – Morecombe and Wise in their very early days.

Our other memorable visit was to Barr & Stroud in Glasgow, an altogether more austere affair. B&S were world leaders in periscopes, only being rivalled by Kollmorgen, a US firm. We discovered that every single piece of a B&S periscope was made on the premises, down to the smallest screw. No wonder they were so expensive! Submarine COs loved these periscopes with unbridled passion, and in the '80s defended them vigorously over the optronic mast of the future, which did not penetrate the hull and used miniature television cameras instead of direct vision. The latter were preferred by engineers, for obvious reasons, and eventually prevailed. The old guard were amazed to find that they could now look at much better pictures on a monitor in their cabin, without having to push the tube, dripping with telemotor oil, round and round in a darkened control room. But their exclusive view was compromised, and a bit of the old magic had died.

Throughout my training class Janey had been getting steadily bigger, for the Gunlayer stratagem had paid off. One early morning in February I was duty engineer officer in Dolphin when Mr Hawkins, the delightful, paternalistic Hall Porter, stuck his head into my room and said, "Better get off home, sir, your wife has started". In some disarray I quickly got dressed and went along to see the Senior Engineer, Mike Phelp, who lived on board. He was sitting up in bed with a cup of tea when I burst in.

"Can I go home?" I said, "My wife's having a baby".

Aware that this seemed a rather bald assertion, I added lamely "she's been expecting it for some time". He waved me away.

Having missed Toby's birth by a farmer's mile, I was thrilled to be on the spot for this one, and raced home in a lather of excitement. Here all was calm. Dr Raperport had visited, immaculate as always in stiff collar and a dark suit. Janey was pottering about, unable to settle. The midwife turned up, not as I had expected a whiskery, Dickensian matron, but a smiling young girl. Indeed much of my expectation of this moment must have been based on Dickens, for I had laid in large stocks of Guinness and fresh towels. I was somewhat taken aback when all she asked for was a cup of tea and some newspapers. She soon had Janey in bed, taking the odd guff of gas and air from her portable kit. The male elements of the family, me, Toby and our little dachshund, loitered, eyes out on stalks, wondering what our role was in all this. (Answer: none.) Isobel was born at about three o'clock on a sunny February afternoon, a perfect home delivery. We were all overjoyed. She would soon be known as Wizzy or Wiz for evermore. I made a start on drinking my way through the Guinness.

Our course ended soon afterwards, and I was surprised to be awarded the Max Horton prize, a nice silver tankard. It transpired that Management preferred to award it to seaman officers, but this component of our course had already left before anyone remembered about it. We heard with some excitement that I was to go to be Engineer Officer of HMS Ambush in the Far East, but would have to spend three months as Spare Crew Engineer in the depot ship Adamant first.

Adamant was an old-fashioned Depot ship, 13000 tons displacement, with plenty of room for workshops, magazines, stores and accommodation. As Spare Crew, we also had to man the depot ship, and, after a year or two in some greyhounds of the ocean, I found that this lumbering leviathan was very different. I learnt a few tricks about watchkeeping down below from Fred Lovejoy, a fat and elderly SD lieutenant who spent his days crammed into a corner of the Engineers' Office, smoking continuously and grudgingly dispensing advice, usually after the event. ("What you *should* have done. . . .") He was not a pretty sight, his overalls, open to the waist, were a size or two too small, and revealed a string vest, strained over his large white stomach. At the time this garment was known as 'a Brown Hatter's Scrambling Net', though not, I fancy, in this case.

On one occasion I was shutting down to one boiler auxiliary. When all was done below I came to get some tea in the office. Suddenly there was an anguished wail from the boiler room:

"I've got all my burners on but the steam pressure's dropping!"

Funny, I thought, I've never run out of steam before. Fred shifted on his stool and said:

"If you've got the evaps on whilst the capstan's running she won't hold it"

I shut down the evaps and simultaneously the foc's'le must have finished with the capstan. Minutes later the main safety valve lifted, with its distinctive thump, followed by the shriek of escaping steam. Fred sucked his teeth and lit another Benson and Hedges.

The engine-rooms sat side by side, separated by a fore and aft bulkhead. If you needed to communicate with the other engine-room there was a six inch brass scuttle set into the bulkhead, and you had to give it a tap with a wheel spanner. Moments later a face would appear: "You wanted something?" Each engine-room contained a single main propulsion turbine about the size of a sofa. Amongst the usual auxiliaries there were no air ejectors, but a delicate reciprocating Weir's Paragon air-pump. This used to jog along for a while and then quietly stop, causing the vacuum to drift slowly back. A smart knock with the aforesaid wheel spanner was enough to shock it into action again, and there was no problem knowing where to hit it, for it bore witness by its many scars.

These tiny engines meant that Adamant's performance at sea was less than startling;

we visited Hamburg (no sign of the gummy prick this time) and Charlie Hammer, the Captain S/M, refused to take tugs in coming alongside. This is a common conceit amongst Commanding Officers, and I have seen many expensive bangs and dents as a result of this desire not to lose face. Charlie was very short and a sailor was detailed off on the bridge to move a box around for him to stand on. The river flowed briskly past the jetty and Charlie took three hours to get us alongside. We had been greeted by the Hamburg Town Band in full oompah mode, but eventually they ran out of time and packed up their instruments. The British Consul cut a lonely figure as other members of the welcoming party melted away.

By June of 1965 I'd finished with Adamant and went home to pack up and take the family to Singapore. A real adventure. Fortunately, we didn't have too much in the way of goods and chattels and packing was easy. When, if ever, would we see our precious bits and pieces again? Fond goodbyes to Mums and Dads, and off we went. We travelled in a trooping flight, a charter Britannia, stuffed with all ranks of the services plus families, assorted. Assorted, mostly young, and quite soon rather damp. An immaculate young Guards Captain had been appointed Officer Commanding Flight, though commanding that lot would always have been questionable. It became a bit of a game amongst the girls who were travelling with families to meet their husbands to go up to the OC Flight, and dump their moist and odorous offspring on his knee whilst making some futile complaint about something. The more hot and bothered he became, the more discoloured his tailored linen suit grew. A cruel jest, but universally enjoyed! Toby, at 2½, was above such mischief, and Wizzy, 3 months, had been given a sky-cot, a sort of beer crate which clipped to the luggage rack, and in which she slept peacefully for most o f the long, hot trip.

We paused at Bombay, wonderful rows of shining new wash-basins, none of them plumbed in, and then plunged on to Singapore. Humid, hot, bright, satisfyingly foreign. We were met by friends and installed in the Government Rest House in Johore Bahru, the traditional staging post whilst we found a house.

These Rest Houses reeked of the old colonial administration, probably having been set up as ports of call for the itinerant District Commissioners. Even in the 60s their ambience was curiously old-fashioned, and tea, antimacassars and steak and chips meals were very much in evidence. Nevertheless they were clean, welcoming and incredibly good value. I would happily have spent several days there with the family, but to my surprise I was booked on a flight to Bangkok the next day to join Ambush there.

In the best traditions of the Submarine Service all hands were accommodated ashore, officers and senior ratings in one hotel, junior ratings in another. People only went 'down the boat', moored between buoys on the river near the Floating Market, if they had work to do or were duty on board. This was a Rest and Recreation period, after some months of hard work around Indonesia, and I was startled at how few of the ship's company seemed to be in evidence. So, after a superficial saunter through the boat to observe the salient points, Dick Swithenbank, whom I was taking over from, and I sat opposite each other on twin beds under a lazy fan, San Migs in one hand, notebooks in the other, whilst he told me all he knew. After a bit of this we shook hands and he left to fly home. I was now It, but there did not seem to be anyone to tell.

During the rest of our stay there I was greatly tickled by the following episode, and felt it was worth recording.

HMS Ambush had had a busy period confronting Dr Sukarno. The battery temperature had never dropped below 98F, and the pool at Terror had seemed impossibly remote. It was time for some R&R, decided Cdr (S/M) 7.

Right on the second count if not the first. The trusty lads of the Bush had a long overdue agenda for the visit to Bangkok, and Rest would have to wait until their more immediate and pressing Recreational needs had been satisfied.

A period of duty is often considered a welcome break in the progress of a five-day visit. A chance to veer off the unending motorway of pleasure and find quiet reflection in a lay-by. An opportunity to allow the wasted tissues some attempt at recovery, to attend to those irritating but necessary items of personal maintenance (like a square meal), and to indulge in some practical and theoretical personal dhobi. Above all, to get some zzzzzs.

The Second Coxswain was made of sterner stuff. He regarded his day of duty on Day Four of the visit to be an unwarranted direct attack on him by an unfeeling Creator — and of course by the Coxswain, who drew up the Watch bill. It was with far from good grace that he jabbed his long tom into a tin of black low sheen Pocoptic and proceeded, with his winger, to adorn the inside of the after casing with this witches' brew.

It was therefore a matter of great relief to him when a pretty young girl - not exactly a novelty in that city — drew up alongside in her little boat with some bananas for sale. It was, similarly, quite a surprise for her to find herself instantly helped aboard across the ballast tanks and hurried, bananaless, down to the fore-ends mess, to be plied with cans of Courage sparklers and assaulted with the fullest charm offensive in the Second Coxswain's repertoire.

Sometime later, they swayed off in search of a little privacy. Unfortunately the CO's cabin, that little boiler drum half way up the ladder to the bridge, which would have been ideal, was ruled out by the presence in the Control Room of the Duty Officer, doing something pointless with a chart. They moved on to the Second's natural habitat - the casing — and, noticing blearily that a casing hatch was open, slipped inside.

Soon afterwards the OOD was enjoying a breath of fresh air on the after casing and observing the busy river activities when the Second Coxswain and his new friend emerged from the casing hatch. It was difficult not to notice that both were liberally coated in black low sheen Pocoptic. It seemed so long, doubtless, since that very spot had been the object of the Second's attentions.

It was also difficult not to notice that, as the Second handed the banana girl back down into her boat, he slipped a large and quite heavy box into her bilges, at which she smiled fetchingly and cast off. The OOD, sensing some irregularity with Naval Stores, urgently enquired, "What was in the box?" The Second, smiling his charming, if low sheen smile, replied, "Oh that Sir, that was a case of that tinned beetroot that's been on board for months. The Coxswain says there's always a market somewhere".

Eventually we set off for a surface passage back to Singapore. As we went to Harbour Stations I stood in the Control Room, wondering vaguely what to do, whilst the wraiths of the undead, the well R and R'd ship's company, completed their tasks with all the joy and spontaneity of automatons. I then levered myself with care into the miniscule wardroom, where some of the officers were toying with a cup of coffee, reluctantly wet by the killick steward. I had a feeling of enormous pride, albeit laced with a little foreboding, when there came a knock at the curtain and a voice asking for "The Engineer" – ie me!

It turned out to be the Chief Engine Room Artificer, name sadly forgotten, who had seen Engineers come and go, and took the rough with the smooth. Which was I? I've no idea but we seemed to get on well enough. He was a natural artificer, who slightly resented the enforced transition from hands-on tradesman to middle management. He was always preceded by a heady aroma of Swarfega and Rosalex, the unguents favoured for removing ingrained oil and grease, and enjoyed an easy tolerance of all sorts of machinery, however recalcitrant. He spoke of the two Vickers A Diesels, clattering away in the 'Donk Shop', with the wry tones of a fond father.

After we'd left the mouth of the river a brief discussion with the Captain, Charles Baker, always known as Charlie Bun, revealed that I had kept a few bridge watches in surface warships. I promptly found myself on the bridge, facing into the South China Sea, with just a lookout for company, and a helmsman and Petty Officer on watch in the Control Room below. It transpired that the Wardroom was nearing the end of some massive game of cards that had been running for weeks, and my watch on the bridge gave them the chance to edge towards its final climax. I was perfectly happy. It was hot and sunny, the sea was slight, and there was very little shipping around. The surface muffler exhausts from the engines burbled away, half in and half out of the water as we rolled gently. Through the voice-pipe I could hear snatches of chat from the Control Room. The odd flying fish planed across the azure sea. Not many birds sang. Most of the Ambushes spent most of the time in their bunks, desperately catching up on their sleep.

I was on watch again as we made our way up the channel between Singapore and Malaya. It was low featureless country on either side, with thick vegetation coming right down to the water's edge, and occasional withies marking fishing grounds. The odd little bamboo house stood on stilts near the shore. The water was treacly brown.

As the banks slowly closed in I kept reporting progress to the Wardroom, expecting to be relieved by someone who knew the channel. Not a bit of it! The long-running card game had entered some crucial phase, and my reports were met with some asperity. "Just keep to the buoyed channel, Chief", came the message. Eventually, there was some sign of habitation, a warship alongside, and, right ahead, a road right across the channel – the Johore Bahru Causeway. "Stop together", I said, "Group up, half astern together." (The diesels propelled ahead only. For going astern, and manoeuvring, battery drive was selected, 'group up' to put the main battery sections in parallel, 'group down' in series.) I told the Wardroom that I could do no more and soon afterwards a distinctly grumpy Captain and Navigator appeared on the bridge to take her alongside. Another fortnight and I'd probably be expected to do that too. Brilliant really, but unexpected.

I got ashore to be welcomed by Janey, bronzed and beautiful, and by two blonde, brown faced children. Actually, their hair was greeny-blonde, due to the chemicals in the pool. In the few days that I was away Janey had found a house, a car, an amah and kebun (gardener), arranged rentals on furniture and fans, and an account with the Johore Bahru Cold Store, universally known as the Colly Stolly. What were husbands for, I wondered?

48U3 Jalan Non Chik was our bungalow, quietly situated away from the fashion and bustle of the Scudai and Jalan Waterworks. (It was said that the Malay language only had about 400 words in common usage. This, and the colonial past, probably explained why there were so many English words embedded in the demotic.) The bungalow was modest, and neat, tiled floors throughout, three bedrooms, a single large sitting/dining room, kitchen and amah's quarters. A simple grassed compound ringed by the ubiquitous monsoon drains. The rented furniture was mostly rattan, the fans essential to stir up some air in the humid afternoons and evenings. The girls were invited to put their fur coats (if they had them!) into cold storage to avoid them becoming mildewed. Once a month we used to visit one of the few fiercely air-conditioned bars in Singapore, identifiable by a plume of condensation pouring from the outlet onto the street, just to remember what life below 75F was like.

We all drove wrecks, passed on through the years. No need for heating, ventilation or indeed much bodywork. Essentials: good tyres and brakes, a strident horn and a rattan insert to stop being burnt by the sun-scorched leatherette. I soon added my nice new Honda motorbike to the family Ford Zephyr. We lived a simple, sybaritic existence when not at sea. Working Tropical Routine, I finished work by one o'clock, and met Janey and the children for lunch at the superb Officers' Club, where life rotated round the pool, the bar (run by Mr. Tan, delightful man) and later in the day the tennis courts, the nine hole golf course and the skittles alley. The club laid on evening film shows and dances. It was a time of bonding and the beginning of many enduring friendships.

But it wasn't all lotus eating. There was work to be done and before long Ambush was working up for our next excursion into Indonesian waters. We used to creep about during the day, observing the movements of naval and merchant ships, and recording 'interesting' buildings on the littoral. Some 'sneaky beakies', specialised secret communications ratings, were embarked with us and spent hours listening to and recording local VHF traffic. At night we snorted to recharge the batteries. This was quite demanding. In the area where we snorted, off Jakarta, there could be anything up to 300 fishermen out each night in their little boats. Small, poorly lit, erratic in course and speed, it was impossible to keep track of them, and only the periscope watch stood between us and collision. I don't think that we ever hit one, but it must sometimes have been very close. As a primitive fisherman it must have been terrifying to see and hear the snort induction mast go sluicing past, followed by the chuffing fumes of the exhaust. Dragons be here indeed!

We were interested in the doings of Bung Sokarno, but of much greater daily concern to all of us were the living conditions. Heat and humidity were the true enemies. The presence of the main battery underfoot meant that underfloor heating was continuous. The batteries heated up if they were discharging, and when they were being charged; they were always doing one or the other. There were a few little air-conditioners, but they returned their extracted heat to the submarine atmosphere; they were thus only spot coolers, adding to the total heat inventory. When snorting there was a welcome flow of relatively cool, very humid air, but this was at the expense of a great guff of heat coming forward from the diesels after we had stopped snorting. We all wore shorts or sarongs and a rag around the neck, and were permanently beaded in sweat. We got used to it, which is more than could be said for the rather primitive electronics of the time, which kept its maintainers, the EA and the LREM, permanently fighting a losing battle.

We were always short of fresh water. The tank was relatively small and the Type D distiller (what happened to the Types A, B and C?) was deemed useless, as the watchkeeper needed more than its output to replace his additional sweat. A gallon per man per day including that used for cooking was the ration and, as the engineer, I was in charge. Monitoring was easy enough, a dip of the tank. Regulation was more tricky; we just turned off the supply for hours on end. Sticky times!

Things went pretty smoothly on that patrol, save for one small drama. In common with most submarines at the time, Ambush had under-designed snort exhaust pipework. This was made of very flimsy material, because it only had to withstand a differential pressure of about 15psi. When the boat went deep the pipework flooded i.e. no differential pressure. But if the pressure requirement was minimal, the exposure to corrosion was enormous. Alternating blasts of cold salt water and hot, wet exhaust gases could hardly be bettered, and the pipework never lasted long. When it perforated the submarine was unable to snort, as the diesels were exposed to too much back pressure. Unless we could effect a repair, we would be forced to withdraw many miles from our area of operations.

So the Chief ERA and I went out to fix it. It was dark, of course and Charlie Bun told us that when he blew a whistle on the bridge we had three minutes to get below before he dived the boat. We squeezed dubiously under the casing. Here, because we had been dived for a month or so, was a worrying proliferation of marine life, some scuttling, some squidgy; I'm sure I saw a phosphorescent something wink at me. We were uncomfortably aware of the venomous sea snakes said to abound in those waters. Eventually we managed to strap a crude covering of steel sheet over the hole, secured with jubilee clips. We edged back on board, stinking like a rotten fish-market, apparently. The fix was good enough.

When we got back to base we were 'de-indoctrinated', one of many dreadful words invented by the Ministry of Defence. For this exercise a tired looking man in a yellow shirt interviewed me. He was from MOD (Security) I think.

"Now that the Operation is over", he said portentously, "I want you to forget that you have ever heard the following Codewords – Biscuit, Tophat and Salamander".

"Until you mentioned them just now, I never have," I replied. This seemed to terminate the interview. I was entirely truthful; all these secret things were confined to the Captain and the Navigator.

On a much lighter note, we spent a lot of time practising operations with the Special Boat Service (SBS). These many activities all featured variations on the same theme – large Royal Marines getting out of the boat, with or without canoes, going ashore, blowing something up, and returning to Mother. All collectively called Goldfish. All great fun.

Great fun, not least because of the personalities involved. Charlie Bun had been relieved by Frank Grenier, a charming and most capable man, full of humour and humanity. Bill Coles, the taciturn and monosyllabic First Lieutenant, had given way to Norman Dingemans, less taciturn but equally monosyllabic. The leader of the SBS was Major Pat Troy, a grizzled old hand, but most of his work was done by his energetic Lieutenants, Hugh Clifford and Paddy Ashdown. Whilst in Singapore Hugh had built his own junk, named Slo-Mo-Shun, which he sailed home, single-handed, to the UK. On one occasion, as we anchored off one of the local islands, Hugh came up to the bridge to ask the Captain's permission to go ashore – a conventional courtesy. As Frank nodded his approval Hugh stepped up to the top of the bridge and did a perfect swallow dive into the water 25' below, narrowly missing the ballast tanks, which in an A boat jutted out quite widely. Style! Paddy was a delightful unaffected companion, but that was before he entered politics.

One of the problems in operating with the SBS was recovering them after their dastardly deeds ashore. The principle was that that the six swimmers would line up, joined by a line. The outer two would emit a sound underwater. In the submarine the Sound Room took bearings of both noises and bisected the angle. We would then steam slowly down the bearing until the line snagged on the fin and the swimmers ended up on the after casing.

The noise was made by something called a 'bongle', a sort of underwater rattle. It made a lot of unwanted noise, was difficult to operate, and was cumbersome. The weapons workshop ashore made some electronic replacements – 'trongles'. We went to sea to try them out. Paddy, who had been testing one in a bucket of water, came bursting into the wardroom.

"Bloody things aren't watertight!" he exploded. I investigated. Design defect. Could only be rectified by enclosing them in thin rubber sheaths.

The Coxswain was the keeper of the boat's supply of french letters, issued to the lads on request. He looked at me strangely, tinged with awe, when I asked him for a couple of dozen. As I spent the afternoon at the wardroom table forcing the trongles into two french letters each, double knotted, I reflected on the years of education and training that had brought me to this point.

After one of these Goldfish sessions the boat stayed at Pulau Tioman, one of the prettier islands up the east coast of Malaya, for a couple of days. Norman Dingemans called for volunteers for a banyan (ie picnic) ashore. When the party got ashore, they noted with alarm the absence of the usual mountain of beer and corned beef sandwiches which accompanied these events. Norman smiled: "if you are thirsty we will drink the river water; if you are hungry we will catch a snake and cook it. Next question?" The word 'banyan' was never again mentioned in Ambush.

One of the key features in all Goldfish operations was the ability to proceed at dead slow or stopped, without losing trim; that is to say without losing depth, whilst remaining broadly horizontal. Without the help of the hydroplanes (fore for depthkeeping, aft for attitude) this could only be done by pumping or flooding small quantities of water in and out of the trim and compensating tanks. This became my special skill as Action Officer of the Watch, one of which I was rather proud.

Life in submarines was addictive, entirely due to the comradeship and shared discomfort. The crew was small enough for everyone to know everyone, and to know their unique contribution, however modest. One of the axiomatic characters in any boat was the Outside Wrecker, a role so misunderstood that many years later I felt the need to describe it:

If the engineering heart of a submarine was the donk-shop, then its arteries sinews and tentacles extended to every extremity of the boat.

The former was the purview of the Chief Tiff, assisted by the Donk-Shop Horse, the Baby Tiff and the SPO. A formidable team to keep two large diesels and a handful of auxiliaries going.

Outside, that is to say outside the Engine-Room, was the Wrecker's empire. This comprised just about every mechanical artefact that you could think of, and several that you couldn't. As well as the high-end systems of HP Air and Hydraulics, and the surfacing, diving and steering arrangements, the Wrecker had a grubby finger in every pie from atmosphere control (ha!) to escape, and from oven doors to sewage tanks.

The Wrecker was nominally responsible to the Chief Tiff, who seldom acknowledged such an arrangement. In practice, if the Wrecker was beholden to anyone, it was, with a grudging nod, to the Engineer. This relationship required a degree of tact and forbearance from both participants, qualities not generally uppermost in either.

The Wrecker was, typically, an unprepossessing creature, greasy and unkempt, an oil-soaked cigarette pinned behind his ear. His stock in trade was his enormous collection of sectionals, stilsons, wheel spanners, adjustables and shifters, together with a formidable array of 'eavy 'ammers. All stowed in a large box bolted down by the diving panel. The REA's thin screwdrivers and snipe-nosed pliers were entirely foreign to the Wrecker.

The Wrecker and his fellow watchkeepers on the panel, the Chief Stoker and the POLTO, constituted an unwelcome and critical corps of observers of the Command Scene. Seldom actually vocal, their body language and general demeanour provided a vivid commentary on the affairs of state. If more intervention was needed, the periscope rams, raising operations and the roundabout provided a ready agenda for Wrecker initiatives. Should he feel the need to extend his area of operations, various aspects of the slop drain and sewage systems could easily be deployed to raise his game. The blowing of the sewage tank, and the subsequent use of the inboard vent to unleash a surge of dragon's breath into the boat was an evolution from which he gained special pleasure.

Whilst the story that an Outside Wrecker installed a small loudspeaker in one of the traps so that, when visited by a lady guest during a cocktail party, he could say at a crucial moment "watch out lady, I'm working down here" is probably apocryphal, the Wrecker did have considerable presence in this particular part of his realm.

The Wrecker's tolerance for his fellows within the boat was severely limited; his views on those inboard were less equivocal. The Engineer found himself in the unwelcome role of apologist for this substantial sector of society, comprising as it did the shipbuilder, design authority, refitting dockyard, squadron staff, FMG, OAs and Periscope Tiffs. Each worth a paragraph in a longer piece.

The genesis of the Wrecker was in conventional submarines, but it was surprising how the breed transferred, unchanged, to the nuclear world. I well remember ERA Gower, a saturnine and scrawny man, with a distinct odour of non-floaters. Despite his dissolute appearance he was immensely strong and gained some reclame from swinging off on a recalcitrant LP Master Blow with such enthusiasm that the whole assembly fell apart. He was known, throughout the boat, as Hercules Uncottered.

Sometime later we went off to Hong Kong, where we did all right, this time without the guidance of Surgeon Commander Mallows. We lay alongside an American guppy (conventional submarine) and socialised in the traditional UK/US way – their steaks for our whisky. I learnt that because I was an engineering specialist I would be dubbed, in American parlance, Super Snipe. I rather liked this, and used 'SNIPE' as my pseudonym in later years when writing for the Naval Review. Eventually Toby and Wiz pointed out that this was an anagram for 'PENIS', after which I never felt quite the same about it, and reverted to using my own name. I expect there's a rude anagram for that too, but they haven't told me yet.

Whilst in Hong Kong I bought a battery driven cockerel as a present for Wiz. On the way back I put it through its paces on the deck just outside the Wardroom and POs' Mess. It ran along, flapped its wings, and made a cock-crow so much like the diving klaxon that everyone started rushing to Diving Stations. Wiz took one look and burst into tears.

Another great character in Ambush was John Thomas, the Chief Stoker. I couldn't resist the following:

Amongst the least salubrious of the many insalubrious nooks and crannies of HMS Ambush, the port after corner of the Control Room stood out. It was effectively an outpost of the Diving Panel, but the high profile HP air manifolds for blowing the main ballast tanks and Q tank, and the hydraulic systems for operating main vents had tapered off and the port after corner held a collection of lesser pipes and valves delegated there by the Olympic system of shipbuilding.[1] This corner also held a variety of valves associated with snorting, from the massive Snort Induction Hull Valve and Flap Valve to the proliferation of valves for draining the system, Snort Drain One and Two, the Intermediate Flood and Drain Valve, all terminating in the Visible Tundish.

The corner was also the home of the Trim Pump, a substantial motor driving a diminutive pump whose principal and undemanding duty was to pump small quantities of water from forward to aft and vice versa to maintain a fore-and-aft trim. If one man (mean effective displacement 15 gallons) walked from forward to aft, this should theoretically have been followed by the order "trim 15 gallons from aft to forward". Sometimes it was. The Trim Pump itself tended to get very stiff when not in use, and though the motor would bumble along nicely when running its starting torque was disappointing. The Panel Watchkeeper frequently had to assist it by heaving on the Ferodo belts between the pump and motor — a hazardous and unpleasant task usually accompanied by muffled curses.

---

[1] In this legendary method of construction, all the trades involved with fitting out the ship lined up on the dockside. When the Foreman blew his whistle they all raced for the ship. The first fitter there could have a straight run of his pipework, whilst successors had to work round him – and each other! It often seemed that the order of arrival had been in inverse proportion to the diameter of the pipework. Ie fat pipes squirmed, Laocoon-like round thin bits of wire.

Additional characteristics of this unloved corner were an almost total lack of illumination and ventilation. Even under the airiest of conditions, when running diesels on the surface with the Conning-Tower hatch open, when a cyclone of fresh air raced aft through the Control Room towards the voracious engines, the corner remained an eddy of fetidity, still managing to retain the grace notes of last week's curry.

The corner seemed to have a special resistance to light. Even the beam from a trusty Pusser's torch seemed to be completely absorbed without any resultant illumination. It was, truly, a place where the sun don't shine.

With its motley collection of pipes, valves, pumps and subsystems, the port after corner was the natural purview of the Panel Watchkeepers. This band consisted of:

The Outside Wrecker

The Baby Wrecker — makee-learn to the above.

The PO Electrician — POLTO (the Torpedoman roots still showing).

and The Chief Stoker — of whom more anon.

The Panel Watchkeepers were tolerated — no more — in the Control Room, but their presence was especially resented when the Attack Team closed up. These oily denizens of the Auxiliary Machinery Space, redolent of their duties with Slop Drain and Sewage Tanks, added little tone to the elite warriors who, collectively, were there to achieve a Firing Solution, with a little help — but not much — from the Fruit Machine. It certainly would not do, in a surface ship, to harbour such alien beings in the Ops Room.

However the Panel Watchkeepers had the last word because amongst their other duties was the raising and lowering of the periscopes. A twitch on the operating lever was quite sufficient to remove the eyebrows from whoever was looking out — very often the Captain. Thus a relationship of neutrality prevailed. The Panel Watchkeepers regarded themselves as critical and sardonic observers of the Attack Team in action, displaying disapproval by a refined body language, and *regaling the rest of the crew afterwards with what had transpired. Had they been aware of the as yet unheard of expression "Team Players" the Panel Watchkeepers would have allowed themselves a collective smirk.*

Now seems the appropriate moment to introduce the hero of this piece — Chief Stoker John Thomas (it would seem that his parents, Glaswegian nonconformists, were ignorant of the works of DH Lawrence, or else were the possessors of a very peculiar sense of humour). John Thomas did not greatly enjoy his name, but then he did not enjoy anything very much. His disapproval was legion, and many were the targets of his scorn. He spoke, unsurprisingly, with a strong Glaswegian accent, and his conversation often degenerated into a fearsome recitative of Gorbals patois.

JT was quite one of the smartest submariners I have ever met (selected from a fairly short list). His harbour uniform was immaculate, and so perfectly pressed that I sometimes suspected him of having one of his stokers tucked away, iron forever on the go. Even at sea when the heat and the humidity drove the rest of us to don the most disgusting rags as 'steaming rig', he stood out, pristine, from the piratical crew.

Soon after I joined the boat JT approached me.

"Engineer, Sir," he said, "Could you see Stoker Evans? His wife's being trapped by this lesbian in Singapore."

With a barely contained gulp I, poor innocent, agreed to talk to Evans, and we had a chat on the only private place onboard, to wit the after casing — the submarine being alongside and on the surface at the time. Evans confirmed JT's report, with much rolling of eyes and heavy sighing. I said, with an optimism that I certainly did not feel, that I would 'sort something out'.

Fortunately, I had an old shipmate in Regulating Petty Officer Dunstan, now working for the Naval Provost Marshal ashore in HMS Terror, the barracks. Dunstan believed that he 'owed me one', as a result of an incident some years previously when I had been the Officer of the Patrol in Gibraltar. I unburdened myself to him over the phone, and was very much relieved by his answer.

"No problem, Sir, I'll put the fear of God into both the young ladies."

Dunstan was clearly as good as his word, for when I asked JT a week later how things stood with Evans he told me that 'the wee problem was sorted'. I felt, by the amelioration of his attitude towards me, that I had been set some sort of test and had perhaps passed.

JT had a special enemy on board, the Snort Mast Locking Pin. Early snort masts were hinged at the base, and in repose lay back horizontally in a depression in the casing. The mast was raised by a hydraulic ram, and locked in the raised position by a pin, screwed manually into place via some rod gearing that terminated at a handwheel in the port after corner of the Control Room. A pleasant touch was that the position of the snort mast (usually up or down) was indicated by a tiny aluminium replica of the mast itself, driven by a Bowden cable (think bike brakes). Snorting could not start until the locking pin was in; the mast could not be lowered until the pin was out.

The pin was a billet of steel two inches square and two feet long; its operating mechanism was sized accordingly. Despite being anointed with 'non-floaters' grease every now and then by the Wrecker's Mate the assembly was undoubtedly stiff. The Wrecker, who affected a rather dégagé attitude to his duties, had agreed to have a look when he got round to it.

It seemed that it was always on the blackest of nights, with the Control Room therefore in 'black' lighting, that JT was on watch on the panel when the order came to standby to snort. At the right time in the drill, once the mast had been raised, he would launch himself over the Trim Pump armed with a large wheel spanner. The progress of his epic battle with his old enemy could only be judged by the vigour and incomprehensibility of the Scottish oaths that poured forth, interleaved by the sounds of tortured metal.

On one occasion, after a longer than usual recital of curses and grunts, silence suddenly ensued. JT emerged from the port after corner clutching the handwheel and a length of shafting.

"Snort Mast Locking Pin is — broken," he reported with a ghastly grin. He had finally won.

The Captain was delighted. No pin meant no snorting meant no more pointless exercise.

"No 1, get on the roof, 420, and up homers", he cried, leaving the First Lieutenant and Navigator to arrange things.

The next day, as we approached the base, I asked the Wrecker how the Locking Pin job was going.

"All fixed", he replied, "it wasn't broken — just a cotter pin had fallen out".

"I don't think", I said, "that we'll tell JT".

"Nor the Captain", answered the Wrecker. And we never did.

We returned to more Goldfish exercises. It was lucky it was so warm, because there was salt water *everywhere*. The gun-tower hatch was a favourite underwater access point for the Royals, directly above the Wardroom. Despite all the built in drains, when the lower lid was opened half a ton of water descended. All kinds of save-alls were deployed to catch and direct this water — there was a "bird-bath", a canvas abomination in the Wardroom itself, and elsewhere an "elephant's trunk", but the fact was that we were never going to catch and control the deluge. How dreary all this would have been in a Scottish loch in winter — or in summer for that matter!

By the autumn of 1966 it was time for refit. We had spent months writing Defect Lists — an entirely pointless exercise I later discovered, since every part of the submarine was removed, dismantled and refurbished. To my delight Michael Tuohy arrived to take over as First Lieutenant. Once the refit had started he and I would be the only two officers to remain. Refits are often considered the nadir of naval life, but this was quite the opposite. The Chinese were wonderful craftsmen, apparently entirely bereft of the English habit of being permanently at war with different trades. The submarine refit, taking a year, was the largest individual bit of work undertaken by Singapore Dockyard, and was therefore the prestige project, getting all the resources it needed lavished upon it. Many similar boats had been refitted there over the years so there were few surprises. I and my artificers were always welcomed in the shops where our equipment was being rebuilt. Finally there was no Ship's Staff Work List, an undisputed blessing. This product of a puritan mind-set represented less than 1% of the total work package, was out of the hands of the

Dockyard Officers and caused the Ship's Staff considerable grief: game not worth the candle.

Once we were fully settled into refit I had a chance to reflect on what I'd seen of the Submarine Service so far, at Dolphin, Adamant and now Ambush and SM7. Whether I did reflect or not, I don't know; perhaps I'm only thinking now what I should have thought then! It's quite likely that the sense of comradeship, of exclusivity and of fun blinded us to the black clouds rolling in upon the submarine service. Despite a brilliant war record, things were hardly moving on, although the new P and O boats were an improvement on their predecessors, the Ss, Ts and As. The service was dangerously small, and ill-suited to the peacetime activities of flag waving and social tittery. If the mechanisms for cost attribution had been in place the submarine service would have been seen as unduly expensive for what it offered. The Mk 8** heavyweight torpedo had been a great sinker of shipping but badly needed a makeover or replacement, which it was not going to get for another 25 years. The Mk 23 antisubmarine torpedo was frankly pathetic. Improvement time about the same. Only in the field of sonar was any real progress being made, due to some very bright boys at the Admiralty Under Water Establishment at Portland. No wonder the Soviet spy apparatus targeted it so successfully.

Nor was all entirely well on the Officer front. Senior submariners had not been very successful in challenging the primacy of the gunnery and signals specialists at the top of the navy. Some Commanding Officers suppressed their ambition and lived for the day, often imitating their perception of the wartime heroes. Inevitably this involved alcohol. There was an awful lot of it about. There were also some rather dodgy beliefs and practices. It was often held that every member of a submarine crew knew the whereabouts of every valve and starter box in the boat. Even if this had been true it would have been downright dangerous. Knowing where something is not the same as understanding the implications of operating it. Hrmph! There were also several emergency operating procedures which, designed to avoid catastrophe, were likely to take one closer to the brink.

All this was about to be changed by the advent of nuclear powered submarines, commanded by commanders, often part of, or in support of the Deterrent. This revolution caused beneficial changes in every part of the submarine service, and raised it to a central, high profile position within the navy, which rightly treated it as a salvation for the whole service, and dubbed the Polaris boats the new Capital Ships. Just in time, I reckon.

From my more parochial engineering point of view I was appalled to see how much maintenance was carried out regardless of condition. Apart from making some desultory comments to the SM7 Engineer, Brian Hall, which were dealt with in similar fashion, I decided to bottle it up till later: I shall return to it (he said ominously).

Everything was going swimmingly until the middle of January, when Janey and I took off up country for the weekend on the Honda, leaving the children in Eng's very capable hands. We were pootling back on the Sunday morning when Crash! Bang! Wallop! – motor smash. This is how I wrote it up soon afterwards.

My submarine had completed a series of busy patrols round Dr Soekarno's Indonesia, and had collapsed thankfully into refit in the dockyard in Singapore. After an initial flurry of activity, life became leisurely, and Janey and I had some time to observe the gentle sinking of the colonial sun over one of the last bastions of the British Raj. We had discovered that the best vantage point was beside the pool at the Officers' Club, HMS Terror, surveying the scene over a glass of ice-cold Tiger Tops. But such lotus-eating quickly palls and we decided that it was time for a short break - get up country, meet the natives etc.

On the Saturday morning then, we asked the amah to slam in the lamb for Sunday lunch when we would be back, kissed the kids good-bye, and leapt into the saddle of my trusty Honda CB72 motorbike - the first generation derivative of the seminal Honda Dream, when the bikes were better than their names. Revelling in the rush of relatively cool air, we dodged our way past potholes and timber-lorries, pirate taxis and the odd comatose python, on the long haul up the east coast of Malaya to Mersing.

Probably now a glittering tourist paradise, the Mersing of the mid-sixties consisted of a small fishing village with a few little shops, a lone monkey-seller, a crumbling cottage hospital and - most importantly - a Government Rest House. Despite their daunting title, these were excellent small hotels set up round the country in the colonial days, probably principally for the benefit of roving District Commissioners and their entourages. They provided an approximation to unsophisticated English fare, and were particularly strong on bacon and eggs, steak and chips and huge quantities of tea. This one had the additional advantage of a breath-taking view across the beach and the South China Sea to the romantic heights of Pulau Tioman, an island that I was already familiar with as a venue for a variety of unusual submarine / Special Boat Service operations.

We enjoyed a long romantic evening, retiring to our room - open-topped like a squash court - to be lulled to sleep by the susurrus of Malay gentlemen enjoying the favours of their paramours. In the morning we poured buckets of water into the header tank for the geyser and ate the obligatory bacon and eggs before setting off back to Johore Bahru.

Some ten miles back along the deserted road we bimbled along relishing the morning air and green scenery. The Chinaman had probably driven straight out onto the main road without stopping every Sunday for the past twenty years. This morning we were in his way. The Landrover struck us broadside on and in a second we were sprawled on the road in a cloud of dust, blood and broken bike. In that appalling moment of first assessment it became clear that we both had compound fractures of the left leg; we were also unpleasantly mindful of the local lore that if you saved someone's life you were responsible for them and their families forever after, and of how people were often left to die as a consequence. Fortunately, the villagers ignored this theory and handed us, none too carefully, into a passing taxi which took us joltingly back to the little hospital at Mersing. Here we were installed in separate open wards surrounded by the entire population of the village, for whom such excitements were a rare treat. We were given a jab of some rather dodgy looking morphine, probably left over from Japanese days, which had no noticeable effect. I asked the nurse to phone the duty officer in the submarine depot ship, as a prolonged stay in Mersing did not seem the best solution. She could only do this if I gave her 20 cents for the call, which luckily I had.

Time passed, and to our considerable relief an Army helicopter arrived, complete with MO. One at a time we were levered into the tiny back seat , our legs immobilised in some ancient iron splint. The two trips to BMH in Singapore were long, uncomfortable, but enormously reassuring. When we had been separately trundled through the theatre for cleaning up and the first of many plaster casts, I asked the redoubtable Matron, Miss Gottschalk, if we could have a ward together.

"*Certainly not,*" *she bristled,* "*we don't want any of your filthy naval habits here.*" *So I ended up in some style and comfort in the Officers' Ward, whilst Janey was banished to the Women's Ward, mainly filled with Ghurkha ladies giving birth, and preparing their own aromatic meals on charcoal braziers on the veranda.*

In due course our life was re-established with our children and friends coming to see us, and Janey being brought down in a wheelchair to see me. We spent some weeks in the Hospital under the tender care of Colonel Payne and Major Sharpe; then Janey went home and I was allowed out to visit her occasionally. We made love under the lazy fan in our bedroom, our twin casts crashing noisily together like amorous tortoises, whilst the amah and our children tittered outside the door. We attended various submarine parties, being carried into the confines by sweating stokers, markedly more friendly to Janey than to me, I'm glad to say.

Our short holiday continued on for some months and we were eventually evacuated back to the UK. As we relaxed in our local, still on sticks, an old boy lent over to Janey and asked:

"*Was it a break or a fracture?*" *There was really no answer to that.*

Some repetition there but you get the drift. I can add a few remarks in amplification. The difference between our wards could not have been greater, and we were lucky that a girl, who possibly fancied Janey, pushed her down to see me regularly, in a decidedly wonky wheelchair. Since nothing much had happened to either of us in the interminable routine of the hospital we had difficulty, for the first and only time, in having a conversation. We learnt to welcome visitors who were busy, pressed for time and had lots to say. Our friends were wonderful and we were overwhelmed with kindness. Michael Tuohy and his wife Janet had scooped up Toby and Wiz, and were looking after them at their house. They were always a bit disorganised, and dear Eng decided that the children were not being appropriately looked after. Courageously, she took them back to our house, where the 'scrambled egg would be properly made'.

Janey soon escaped, but I was kept in for much longer, as my broken bones could not be plated until the surface wounds had healed, a slow process in the humid tropics. Apart from the leg I felt fine, and fretted at the enforced inactivity. A doctor got me to translate, laboriously, a whole stack of French papers on the tropical disease 'meliodosis'. Talk about sweated labour! I was allowed out for parties and other functions. I usually got back to the hospital quite drunk and extremely late, to the icy displeasure of the beautiful Chinese Night Sister. In the meantime, I had been relieved by David Goldson, a man of decidedly sombre countenance, and Chris Wood (a much cheerier chap!) had joined as the Captain for the new commission of Ambush, which, sadly, I should not be part of.

Eventually, some six months after the accident, all the surgery was complete, and Colonel Payne discharged me, saying airily,

"Off you go, don't play rugger on it for a bit."

As if! I had no muscles left in the leg and couldn't put it to the ground. After one last party we were casevaced home – which involved being flown in a RAF plane fitted with bunks. Janey and I got one each and the children had seats nearby. Poor Toby had a dreadful attack of the runs, but was perfectly looked after by an RAF medic with the largest moustaches I have ever seen. On arrival, the RAF lackadaisically sorted us out: Janey and the children went home to Mum, and I went down to Haslar.

Whilst waiting to see the consultant, I fell into conversation with an ancient naval officer, well into his 70s, who was also in the queue. He said that he was at Osborne House, the Officers' Convalescent Home on the Isle of Wight. When he arrived, he said, he was asked to be Sports Officer. Wasn't he rather old for that, I asked. Not at all, came the stern response; his arrival had lowered the average age by several years. Armed with this intelligence it was not difficult to answer the question later put to me by the quack. 'Would I prefer to go to Osborne, or some RAF place near Leatherhead called Headley Court?' Neither he nor I knew anything about the latter, so I jumped (or rather hopped) at it. It was an incredibly fortunate decision.

Headley Court was absolutely brilliant. It was set in an old manor house, with its own extensive and manicured grounds. It had formerly been owned by a Chairman of the GWR with a penchant for panelling, which he had secured from half the great houses in England that were being dismantled during the '30s. It had a friendly bar, excellent cuisine, but most of all an impressive collection of medics, PT instructors, remedial gymnasts and physiotherapists. A rigorous work schedule meant that we were hard at it for eight hours every day, Monday to Friday, with a great deal of one-to-one attention. The change was phenomenal. In five weeks I went from only standing on one leg (classified Early Legs Class) to running faster than I ever had in my life (Intermediate Class). The only down side was an awful lot of piped Herb Alpert. The professionalism of the staff was superb, and the unquenchable human spirit was very evident in the more severely injured. An uplifting experience, and in sharp distinction to the National Orthopaedic Hospital which happened to be close to Janey's parents' home. Fortunately I was able to pass on a few of the tips I had learnt about how to walk proper!

All in all, after a rather difficult interlude, we were up and running (literally!) by the autumn, in time for us to move to Greenwich so that I could learn something about nuclear engineering.

CHAPTER 6

Gone fission

> **The Borough of Greenwich is a Nuclear Free Zone**

So declaimed the notices on the lamp-posts along the Woolwich Road, which cuts between the Maritime Museum and the Royal Naval College. Twenty yards from this road, in the basement of the King Edward Building, lurked Jason, the Navy's very own zero-energy reactor. Jason was in all things modest: not quite zero-energy, it could squeeze a magisterial ten watts, not enough for the dimmest of light bulbs. Jason satisfied the amour propre of the Admiralty and of the Admiral President of the College, whilst justifying the post of Professor and Deputy Prof. It was intended to focus the training on reactor dynamics and to facilitate various experiments. In practice most of its functions could have been provided by a less prestigious (and considerably cheaper) simulator. It had, however, one unique function. The spent fuel cartridges were kept in a small pool to keep them from overheating. This was in no way similar to the famous Swimming Pool Reactors, which were illuminated by the renowned Cerenkov glow of radiation. Dramatic, but spooky. Eric, one of the reactor operators, and a keen gardener, had kept some tomato seeds in a plastic bag in the pool, secured by a piece of string. He admitted, rather sheepishly, that since doing this he had won many prizes for his tomatoes.

It was weird to be studying such a contemporary subject in such historic surroundings. The buildings reeked of antiquity, especially the exquisite Chapel, and the Painted Hall, where randy young officers sat down to dine beneath the 173½ pairs of female breasts in Thornhill's masterpiece. Antiquity also extended to some denizens: many of the mess servants were beyond old age and moved with the deliberation of Galapagos tortoises. The Senior Officers' War Course, a collection of senior Captains, seemed almost equally ancient. They didn't mix much.

Our course was also a mixture of the old and the young – or, seen from here, the young and the slightly older. The younger element had come straight from Manadon, and had heads bulging with mathematical formulae, but did not know one end of a submarine from the other. We, on the other hand, the wrinkled old retainers (average age 30), had forgotten most of the Manadon nonsense but had gained some valued experience at sea. The academics running the course discounted the valued experience and decided that we needed a refresher course – the Nuclear Preparatory Course.

Near the West Gate was a utilities area of compost heaps, of compounds full of mowers, and of the headquarters of Navy Works, who strived to look after the College. In this workaday place, remote from the grand and beautiful parts of the College, was a collection of wooden huts, known as Zulu Village. It was here that the Nuclear Preparatory Course had its being.

The backbone of the course was mathematics, in conformity with the widely held view that engineers needed to be good mathematicians. No longer true, a good grasp of arithmetic is all that is necessary for all save a few. We laboured our way through the swamps of differential equations, and even struggled, briefly, to the heights of Bessel Functions. But, like a chocolate teapot, they had no staying power. The day after the exam they had melted away. The redeeming feature of our maths course was that it was taken by a pleasant, lackadaisical man called Dr Pepper. His real interest was the history of mathematics, and we deviated several times into how Napier invented logarithms – not exactly riveting stuff, but a big improvement on differential equations – believe me.

We also did a bit of metallurgy, closer to the point since a naval reactor contained several novel materials; even conventional materials changed their properties when irradiated. The metallurgy department had some labs in King William Building, and therein dwelt its secret weapon. We trooped eagerly into our lectures there because there was an extraordinarily shapely and attractive red haired female lab assistant. We had decided, improbably but for our own gratification, that she wore nothing under her white lab-coat, and many a happy hour was spent dreaming of this in preference to the carbon steel nil ductility temperature radiation shift that we were supposedly studying.

There was however a downside to this lusty atmosphere, in the person of Professor Dowson. He was pedantic, dry and opinionated, and did not endear himself to his students i.e. us. He particularly did not endear himself to me, for we had a couple of minor confrontations early on in the course. We spent the rest of the time in a state of barbed neutrality. At the end of the course there was a cocktail party, at which, to my chagrin, I found myself talking to my old adversary. Well, not talking, but being talked at, for he was in full academic cry. As he droned on I became so comatose that my wineglass slipped from my hand, and shattered on the carpet at his feet. I scrabbled around picking up the pieces of glass whilst he addressed me:

"And now, Middleton," came his infuriating voice, "are you at last able to distinguish between brittleness and fragility?" I could have ground the shards into his ankle!

As a family we were living in a rented house a couple of miles away. It was a newish house in a cluster of fourteen and the residents were properly house-proud. They insisted that this was a Close in Blackheath, and claimed this as their address. Since it was in fact a small estate in Lewisham, considerably less smart as an address, they got their mail twenty four hours later than us. There was an interesting mix of residents there, the law, local government, and the rag trade being represented, as well as a couple of Thames lightermen. The collective fruit of the loins careered up and down the central runway between the houses, and Wizzy, who was one of the smallest, objected to being dubbed The Baby, and pushed vigorously in someone else's pram. Our dachshund, Punch, thought it was heaven, and crapped regularly on the communal lawn. His droppings were returned to us by a stone-faced old biddy. The day of the pooper-scooper was in its infancy. Behind our little square of garden there was a wall, on the far side of which ran a steep hill. It was used as the practice place for learner drivers doing their hill-starts. The Ford Anglia was the car of choice, and its starter motor had a distinctive sound like a strangling cockerel. We were serenaded by the mating cry of the Ford Anglia from first thing in the morning till late at night, so desperate were the learners to have a crack at our hill.

Back at the College we moved on to the Naval Reactor Course proper, where we united with the junior division. We plunged into atomic and nuclear physics, fascinating because we started to see, rather dimly, the convergence with our future business. It does, however, remain difficult to keep the life cycle of the fast neutron, measured in hundredths of a second, in mind when, at sea, you are confronted with a large steam leak and the lights are going out.

It was exciting, too, to be studying, however superficially, such a modern branch of science and engineering. Enrico Fermi had built the first nuclear "pile" less than 25 years earlier, as part of the Manhattan Project, which finally spawned the A-bomb. At its initial criticality he stood on top of the pile with a bucket of boron (a neutron absorber) in case it ran away with itself. He obviously didn't know about the life cycle of the fast - or even the thermal - neutron. The boron would have arrived too late, but fortunately was not required, or history would have been different, and Fermi would have been fermé.

As the course went on it became steadily less comprehensible (though we all remembered Heisenberg's Uncertainty Principle with pleasure) and we were relieved when a few lectures of a more practical turn started to appear. To those of us well-versed in the mysteries of the Closed Feed System from our surface ship days it all seemed pretty simple – the reactor had replaced the boilers. Even the method of testing the feed water for purity was the same – a drop of silver nitrate in a test-tube. The difference was that, because of the sensitivity of the steam generator tubes to corrosion, the limits for purity were so demanding that the methods of measurement and analysis were quite inadequate. Water chemistry, together with the purity of the air in the submarine, were to be two of our principal preoccupations in our forthcoming sea-jobs.

Despite all this heavy technical stuff, we had a very good time, enjoying our proximity to London and the local attractions. Janey and I made good friends with Mary and Tubes Maclachlan, who we were to see a lot of over the years. They were the greatest of fun and it was tragic to see Tubes die unreasonably early. We also met Rob and Christina Walmsley. He, being extremely bright, was doing the Nuclear Advanced Course, and no doubt juggling Bessel's Functions with an adroit flick of the wrist. We were close friends for many years, until he finally became stratospheric, as the Chief of Defence Procurement, and transferred his friendship to his stratospheric buddies, none of whom I would have touched with a barge-pole!

One of the little entertainments that we enjoyed was a trip to the Waterman's Arms on the Isle of Dogs, right across the Thames from the College. There was a pedestrian tunnel which started near the Cutty Sark and came out in some gardens on the far side. The stairs to the tunnel were housed in rather beautiful cupolas. The tunnel itself sloped sharply towards the middle, and fear of a cave-in and watery catastrophe was only averted by running at full pelt, whilst shouting or screaming loudly. By the time that we got to the Waterman's we were in fine voice for the East End sing-song that was always in progress.

Towards the end of our year came the great set-piece College Summer Ball. Whilst ruinously expensive it was a 'must do' event, and worth every penny. On a perfect June night we sauntered through the floodlit colonnades, glass in hand, whilst to the south the Royal Observatory, the Queen's house and the Maritime Museum all complemented the College's extraordinary beauty. The Thames slipped by like black silk to the north. It was a time of rare enchantment, and many an eye was damp.

Eyes were far from damp, however, when we got our next appointments. Rob Walmsley and I were to join HMS Churchill, third of the class, building at Barrow-in-Furness, wherever that was. We were to follow the normal pattern of going to Dounreay in the very north of Scotland, to learn some practicalities on the Submarine Prototype that had been built there, before joining Churchill. However the Engineer Officer already standing by Churchill decided that the boat was being built so fast that there was no time for delay and we should go to Barrow immediately. Christina and Janey went off by train to find places to live. When they came back Janey was unusually uncommunicative about what she had found.

I finished at the College. Toby, who had enjoyed a year at his first Primary School, the John Ball School, was extracted. During this year Wiz had tried a number of nursery schools without much enthusiasm; she particularly disliked one where the poor woman who ran it had no nose. The packers came and went. We rammed ourselves, plus Punch, plus everything else left behind, into our slightly wonky red Volkswagen, and headed north. Another opportunity to sing.

* * * * *

The M1 was a pleasant, almost empty novelty along which we hummed till we met the old A5, a markedly inferior road. Eventually, however, we entered Cumberland and turned off for Barrow. "Nearly there," we cried, but no, it was another long hour along an increasingly windy road. Wearily we finally reached Barrow, and struck out in search of – Roa Island. At last we found this extraordinary little place, at the end of a half-mile causeway.

No wonder Janey had been somewhat coy with her description of the place ("I didn't know if you'd like it," she said later). Not like it? It was love at first sight. We were to live in the top of a small Victorian mansion built on the island by the German ironmaster Schneider. He added a tower to the structure so that he could keep an eye on the ships bringing iron ore - which he suspected of short-changing him. It is said that he brought his German bride there one November night, when the island was swept by a rain-drenched south-westerly gale.

"I will nevair spend a night in zat house," she cried after one look, and hotfooted it back to civilisation. She missed a treat.

The house overlooked the sea – in fact there were fabulous views from all sides – south to Morecombe Bay, west towards the Isle of Man, north to Black Combe, glowering over the Duddon estuary, and east across the Lake District. The huddled community of seventy souls supported a corner shop run by Mrs Pennington, a woman of uncertain age and elaborate hairdos, and the Roa Island Hotel (prop: Jack Cochrane), a watering hole of the very last resort. The 'snug' bar, a misnomer if ever there was one, had a perpetually smouldering coal fire which produced no heat, but volumes of oily, greenish smoke.

In our flat, by contrast, we had a fire in the kitchen which consumed coal by the hundredweight, whilst it glowed white-hot. It was indeed a windy spot – we had to block up the overflow grill in the bath with plasticine to stop an icy blast at head height when you were in it. The worn carpet in the sitting room tended to hover disconcertingly a foot above the floorboards when the wind was from the southwest, which it usually was. The tower seemed to rock a bit in the wind, but the children, whose bunk beds were there, loved it.

The house was owned by Laurie Allan, former Town Clerk of Barrow, who lived in the bottom half with his wife who he always referred to as Mummy. His abiding preoccupation was his care of his three Karmann Ghia Volkswagens, in various stages of disrepair. His work was frequently interrupted by islanders stopping for a chat, for his garage was open to the street. One of the most frequent was Uncle Eb, an ancient Cape Horner; his choice of headgear foretold the approaching weather with startling accuracy, and we all watched him with great interest. He would spend hours in the bus-shelter chatting to Wiz, keeping an eye on the horizon, and no doubt wondering if he ought to go home and change his hat. A lovely man.

All too soon I was off to work in Vickers Shipbuilders yard in Barrow. The town itself was small and plain, but in no way unpleasant. The Ironworks was in the final stages of decrepitude, and Vickers was easily the largest employer. Shipbuilding is a clean enough activity, so that the town, although it consisted, like so many northern towns, of apparently endless brick terraces, was not blackened by the usual effluent of the smokestack industries.

In 1968 Vickers was a thoroughly old-fashioned company turning out cutting edge contemporary products – nuclear submarines. The first thing to strike you as you entered the main Gate was a large notice which read:

> # No throwing of orange peel.
> # PENALTY: INSTANT DISMISSAL

What a way to engage the loyalty of a highly skilled and valued workforce! The Directors drove around in a fleet of matching powder-blue Jaguars. Management all gathered for lunch in the Company Dining Room and at 1 pm, as the works hooter sounded, all fell silent, to listen to the Home Service news on a crackling public address system.

The pecking order was entirely feudal. Top of the heap were the steel-bashers – the constructive trades that designed the hull and put it together. These were followed by the mechanical engineers, by virtue of historical precedent and sheer weight of machinery. Electrical engineers, although responsible for thousands of miles of cables, assorted, were regarded as a necessary, lately arrived evil. Weapons specialists were undoubtedly beyond the pale, however vital their contribution.

The Managing Director of Vickers at the time was Sir Leonard Redshaw, a steel-basher through and through, who had recently acquired his K, probably after Resolution, the first Polaris boat, was commissioned. Lady Redshaw had persuaded Sir Len that his elevation needed some embellishment and they bought a large house in Abbey Road, complete with peacocks in the extensive gardens. One day Sir Len was chairing an important meeting when his secretary came bustling in.

"Sorry to disturb you, Sir Len, but Lady Redshaw needs to speak to you on the telephone. She says it's very urgent."

"Nonsense, tell her to call back later."

The secretary soon returned, carrying a telephone on a long length of cable.

"She says it's vital that she speaks to you now."

"Very well, what is it dear?"

"Oh Len, such a disaster. One of the peacocks has got into the drawing room."

"Is that all? Well, shoot the bugger."

He returned to his meeting. That evening, so the story goes, when he returned home, it was clear that she had used both barrels of his Purdey on the unfortunate bird. Blood, feathers and scorch marks had rendered the drawing room a shambles. "Well, shoot the bugger" became a familiar cry round Barrow.

Coincident with Rob's and my urgent arrival the fitters went on strike for what turned out to be several months. Fitters are absolutely the key trade, and whilst others did what they could without them it was lackadaisical work, and key dates started to slip. HMS Churchill was still just a Yard Number – 1076, which was sprayed, stamped, etched and engraved on pretty well everything. This was important as there was Repulse and Courageous building at the same time, and the two Firsts of Class, Resolution and Valiant, to be supported. 1076 was a series of hoops on the slip, in the process of being end-loaded with equipment and then welded together into a watertight submarine hull. It was an old-fashioned method, an open, west-facing slip poorly protected by adhoc sheds and acres of flapping canvas. Later an expensive assembly hall together with a ship-lift was built and launches were never the same again. Being lowered in to the water on a very deliberate lift is not at all like the drama of the boat gaining speed sliding down the well-greased ways with a scraping rumble and clouds of rust from the massive braking chains as she hits the water. (And beyond sometimes. Repulse shot across the creek and embedded herself in the soft mud on the far side to roars of applause from everyone except the Vickers VIPs.)

Despite the lack of progress on the fitter front we settled down to work in what were called the Sub Dock offices, a row of north facing portakabins overlooking a stagnant lake, on which some swans swam by, looking mournfully in on us looking mournfully out. We were trying to understand the submarine that Vickers were building for us, how it was going to work, where everything was. In due course we would be involved in the endless testing of units, subsystems, systems and eventually the whole boat. In theory at least, Vickers would build the boat; we, the Ship's Staff, would operate it through every permutation and combination known to man; and the Principal Naval Overseer would accept it on behalf of the Admiralty. In practice it was much more of a team effort, and involved a stream of visitors from sub-contractors, MOD sponsor sections, and, occasionally, some gilded soul from the Naval Staff.

We had an enormous aid to our endeavours to understand the topography of the boat. These submarines had been considered to be so complicated, with such a packing density of equipment, that a full-scale mock-up, in wood and cardboard, had been built. The idea was that when the layout in an area had been confirmed and was accurately represented in wood, the pipe-shop boys would come in, bend a wire to conform to the shape in the mock-up, and then go back to the shop to fabricate the real thing in steel, cupronickel or whatever. Nice concept, and I suppose that it worked quite a lot of the time, but there were still plenty of reworks, when things in the real boat didn't quite fit.

The whole mock-up project was the joint purview of the several separate drawing offices, who had never worked in such an inter-disciplinary way before. Though it was effective it was ridiculously expensive, and was vulnerable to the clumping boots of all who visited it. The lower reaches of the structure were like a forest floor, strewn with broken bits. The next class processed to a fifth scale model in Perspex. It was said that the scale had been chosen because it was the scale of Actionmen, popular children's toys of the period. Certainly there were plenty of them, with realistic hair and beards, scattered through the model. In cutting edge fashion, all the pipework could be tracked in three dimensions by collimated telescopes, and the coordinates passed direct to the pipe shop. It was still an infinitely time consuming system, and has of course now been replaced by all manner of wonderful computers.

One amusing feature of the mock-up was the proliferation of graffiti, mainly, as is normal, of a sexual nature. I nearly wrote "suggestive", but the Barrovian sense of humour did not feature such subtleties. The graffiti were usually directed at the gang of female cleaners who had the strange job of cleaning the mock-up in the small hours when there was no-one else around. So a torpedo stowage would be crudely labelled "Brenda's Shagging Couch" and the many faintly phallic artefacts were invariably chalked up as "Tracy's Dildo" or similar. None of these adornments got translated into the boat itself.

If life was somewhat tedious in the yard, it was quite the opposite at home. The children had started school, Wiz in an infants' school 'over the Co-op', and Toby at Roose Primary. After a couple of days he came home and told us with a grin:

"We don't have books in our school." Cue wild eye rolling from fond parents, imagining some Dotheboys scenario with slates and frequent floggings.

"No, we have boooks!" Both of them soon mastered the local patois, reserving the received Oxford demotic for the home. They could potter all day on the stony beach round Roa Island, and there was always someone keeping an eye out for them, often Uncle Eb. In the winter a flock of sheep came down from the Lake District high pastures, and were ferried across to Piel Island, assisted by all the Roa children. Janey had a friend's pony called Roger to stay for a few days, and he was immediately the centre of attention, with old men manoeuvring their buckets under his backside. A little boy, showing his maritime upbringing, gazed at Roger's bridle in amazement.

"Eeh, missus," he asked Janey, " is that to keep his beak shut?"

We all loved exploring the deserted west side of the Lake District, the Duddon estuary, and the little roads leading up through Broughton to Ulpha. Rob and I walked up a few modest peaks, including the Old Man of Coniston. Idyllic.

1076 was launched, and became HMS Churchill to us if not to Vickers, who retained the yard number. One of the by-products of a launch off the slip was a huge amount of timber, shores, spars and the like, which had propped up the vessel on the slip. This all floated down the Walney Channel, until, despite stern warnings of illegality in the local press, it was scooped up by the canny Roa Islanders. Many fires burnt green that winter from the salt, and gardens bulged with serviceable lengths of wood awaiting future projects.

My sojourn in Churchill was cut short abruptly by an appointment to Warspite, already in commission. Frank Turvey, who had been about to take over as the Engineer, fell sick with respiratory problems, and needed an immediate replacement. To be truthful, apart from being parted from my family and the wonderful surroundings, I was not sorry. Nigel Buckley, the large, bland Commanding Officer of Churchill, was not really my cup of tea, and Chris Ward, the newly arrived First Lieutenant, seemed dangerously intense. Brian King and Mike Tanner, the two senior engineers, were worthy rather than inspiring. Besides, I did not want to be an assistant to *anyone*. With a smile, I left.

* * * * *

Faslane sunshine aka driving westerly rain was established as I stepped over the brow to HMS Warspite to be greeted rather truculently (as is the custom) by the Trot Sentry, a sailor immersed in foulweather gear with his cap rammed down over his ears. Things seemed brighter and drier down below where I warily accepted a gin and tonic in the Wardroom. Warily because I remembered the tale of the submarine in which the wine caterer observed the first drink of newcomers, and then provided them with a bottle of e.g. gin every morning thereafter – to drink or to throw away. He said it made the accounting easier.

But this was the new submarine Navy, where the drinking was decidedly moderate, everyone wore passable uniforms, and there was a general air of serious endeavour, some distance from the cheery piracy of the past. The boat showed it too, for a two year old she was definitely worn, clean but not sparkling, an assessment equally applicable to the crew. I learnt that Warspite had been employed on 'sneaky' trips to the Ribachiy peninsula, where the Soviet bases were. She had recently been involved in an underwater collision with a Soviet submarine, a terrifying moment that took a big chunk out of the fin, but otherwise caused no injury or damage. The boat withdrew to Lerwick, in the Shetland Isles, for a temporary patch-up, and then to Barrow for a full repair. The cover story was that she had been hit by an iceberg. A Vickers lad said, drily, " first iceberg I've heard of with antifouling". Some of the crew were naturally still a bit jumpy when I arrived.

The Captain was an interesting man called John Hervey. He was a born raconteur and kept us in stitches for hours over his stories, some of which we heard several times. He had no hair on his head nor any eyebrows. When we were at sea he used to wear a black roll-neck sweater and, because the oil dripping from the periscope rams ran unimpeded into his eyes, a turban of mutton-cloth. He looked just like the Grand Vizier in this kit. His father had been a victim of the Geddes Axe, when the navy was drastically reduced in the 1920s, and John still fulminated about it bitterly.

I, and Ian Anderson who had joined about the same time, spent the first couple of months qualifying "back aft", working and being examined, in all the ten watchkeeping positions. Eventually, after having passed the final Board, I had my licence to go solo. For the first time I sat, unsupervised, in the Engineer Officer of the Watch's seat in the Manoeuvring Room, with a Chief of the Watch to my left and three panel watchkeepers in front of me, and 900 visual and audible alarms wrapped round the space. My mind raced with all the things that could possibly go wrong, and what my reaction should be. After an hour of acute angst I could see that either I could remain like this, on the edge of my seat, awaiting doom, or I could relax, and deal with problems as they arose. I took the latter course, and started enjoying myself.

Soon Ian and I were installed as Heads of our Departments, he Weapons Engineer and myself as Marine Engineer. In addition he was the Senior Technical Officer, a bastard title which thankfully did not last long, but was invented by some clever greenies to indicate supremacy over the Reactor Plant. We agreed that there needed to be some changes. As is not uncommon with a new build, our predecessors had been hyperactive, to the extent that they carried shifting spanners with them at all times, so that they could operate the Reactor System valves, whilst the Chief

Artificers looked on with interest. We decided that we should be looking on with interest, gave the spanners to the Chiefs, and replaced them with torches, A symbol of "look, don't touch". This worked well and the Chiefs soon delegated downwards to the proper level in the hierarchy. If only all management was so simple.

Warspite was not unusual in having a number of nicknames, some of them memorable. When Sandy Woodward arrived as the new Commanding Officer he was soon dubbed Mr Spock, a tribute to his all round competence as much as to his slightly pointy ears. John Coward, a term-mate of mine, appeared soon afterwards as the First Lieutenant, and became the White Tornado, on account of his rushing round at high speed, insisting on exceptional standards of cleanliness. Ian Anderson, a large Ulsterman, was naturally Big Murphs, and his Assistant, Fred Scourse, also large but with a shining bald dome, was christened Fred the Egg. This was in contradistinction to a killick stoker called Febbrarro, who turned into Fred Bravo. I've already mentioned Hercules Uncottered, but my favourite of them all was Steward Newberry who translated into Nude Strawberry.

Sandy Woodward was an interesting man, clearly destined to go far (which he did!) and a master of the attacker's art – how to visualise the position of ships on the surface and their movement, when it was safe to put up a periscope, and what to expect to see. He was sometimes described as an exceptional mathematician, but the skills required were mental arithmetic and the ability to solve time-speed-distance problems in your head. No requirement for Bessel's Functions. When he first arrived he gave me an unpromising greeting.

"I've spent six months in Skipjack (an American SSN) so I know more about nuclear engineering than you do. If anything goes wrong you are to give me a full briefing before you do anything."

The next time something went bump in the night the Chief ERA and I fronted up to Sandy's cabin. We had with us Atomic Books, Confidential Books, Books of Reference, Drawings, Parts Lists, and the defective Widget and its Replacement. After ten minutes of thumbing through this lot Sandy gave me a long look and said:

"Take this all away and never bother me like this again." For me, a small but important victory.

He was, basically, a very shy man. He disguised this with a gruff manner which became publicly evident during the Falklands campaign. I remember a day in the SW Approaches, doing 'Angles and Dangles'. This was a routine exercise in which the boat was put through its paces, diving, rising, twisting and turning at alarming angles. He controlled the exercise with superb precision and icy calm. Apart from testing out the boat it gave great comfort to those still twitching from the 'iceberg' incident. It was a bravura performance. We then went into Cardiff for a visit. That evening, as we awaited the local worthies for a cocktail party on board, I went to Sandy's cabin to report that 'the beast is back in its cage', ie that the reactor was shut down. He was shaking.

"Reaction from the angle and dangles?" I asked, sympathetically.

"Certainly not," he replied, "it's the thought of having to meet all these bloody guests this evening."

John Coward was also highly capable and gave Sandy the operational support that he needed. He was quite different from his predecessor who ran a 'total war machine' type of submarine. John had a feel for the finer things; the mess silver was retrieved from store and displayed, and elegant titbits started to accompany the wardroom meals. On one occasion after a longish patrol we arrived at Faslane and moved swiftly to the Wardroom for that first reviving drink after weeks of abstinence. The bar was locked. The Nude Strawberry explained that the Petty Officer Steward had been sent ashore by the Jimmy (John) to buy flowers for the Wardroom and had the bar keys with him. A fairly universal sense of humour failure ensued. John did his best to civilise us, and in return that period was called 'the Year of the Boudoir.'

Before the family moved up from Barrow they came up to Faslane for a long weekend. We borrowed a large wooden shed called 'The Bothy' from our friends the Fosters, in an idyllic position on the shores of Loch Long. It was well equipped with beds, sofas and other furniture, grouped round a large open fire. The Bothy was however uninsulated., and during the cold weather when we were there we had to set the alarm-clock for 2.30 am to get up and pile the fire high with coal to avoid freezing in our sleep. When we finally moved from Roa Island we held a party for the community. Every member came, like locusts over Egypt. Every scrap of food and drink was consumed, including the half bottle I'd hidden in the bookcase for emergencies. It was however judged to be a proper Roa Island party – praise indeed.

We moved up to a pleasant flat in the suburbs of fragrant Helensburgh. Janey drove up with the children, dog, cat and everything else in the (not very faithful) Beetle. We eventually discovered that this was a 'cut-and-shut', two half-cars welded together. This accounted for the fact that, every so often, as some concealed weldment flexed, the steering wheel became almost impossible to turn. Challenging! It did not account for the appalling headlights. In desperation I took the car to a man in Barrow, who pronounced:

"T' trouble wi' these lamp-glasses is they're more door than window." Picturesque artisan-speak indeed. Janey drove up on January 1st, and when she had arrived and disembarked her sick-smelling cargo asked if there had been an outbreak of nuclear war. Startled, I asked why. She said that, as she drove along Sauchiehall Street in Glasgow, the pavements were littered with recumbent bodies.

There were many friends, old and new, at Faslane, and during the all too brief periods that I was not at sea we had a very busy social life. It does rain a lot there, but the trick is to get some good oilskins and go out anyway, otherwise you might spend months with noses pressed against the windows. Unlike the east of the country, the sun usually shines, albeit briefly, once a day. Ted Gibson, a buddy from Singapore days, arrived and asked me to show him round the boat – he hadn't seen a nuclear before. This is what I wrote:

I first met Ted Gibson in Singapore, when he was Commanding Officer of HMS Oberon. He had earned the soubriquet 'Tinhead' after a nasty incident, which involved him moving from the bridge to the control room in the inverted position. He used to rattle the airport metal detectors.

153

Ted had the smallest inter-ocular distance of any submarine CO at the time. Search periscopes were always to be left with the CO's settings applied. All Oberon's officers were identifiable by having no skin on their noses — the result of lunging at the search periscope in black lighting and coming up all standing wedged between the eye-pieces.

We met again in Faslane where I was the Marine Engineer Officer of Warspite, still pretty new if not exactly shiny, and Ted had just arrived as the Deputy Support Manager, a crucial job in waterfront assistance to submarines alongside.

Ted asked for a look around the Back End, the engineering spaces which formed about 50% of the submarine. By chance we were flashed up and doing some endless trials, which involved varying the load on the reactor by dumping steam into the main condensers.

After a cup of coffee in the Wardroom, we changed into overalls — mine a well-worn off-white, bearing the signs of many bruising encounters with oily machinery, Ted's pristine white and belted.

On our way aft we paused in the Tunnel to peer through the heavy glass scuttles into the Reactor Compartment. A bit of an anticlimax, no Cerenkov radiation glow, no green fuming vapours; just a collection of pipes, valves and pressure vessels rendered unremarkable by their heavy lagging.

We paused to savour the aroma, so horrible, so evocative, so typical. Hot steel, wet steam, lub. oil, the particularly unpleasant sweetish whiff of burning Houghtosafe 271, a hydraulic system additive which went straight to the eyes. Oh, and an overlay of cigarette smoke. This was the 70s, remember.

We checked in at Manoeuvring, and observed the 900 alarms which plastered the bulkheads, the hot dusty boxes housing the reactor protection and control circuitry, the large tattoos that adorned the Electrical Panel Operator's forearms. And then down we plunged.

Down through the Diesel Generator Room, stuffed with two large diesel generators, the ultimate get you home if the reactor opted out, and with a lot of bulky switchgear, parcelling out the 4MW of generated power to its many destinations.

On down to the TG Room, dominated by the two WH Allen turbo generators, with a strong supporting cast of feed pumps, distillers, air conditioning plants and a host of extras, all screeching, whirring, hissing, grunting or moaning. Even so Ted managed a few penetrating questions and I a similar number of slightly dismissive answers.

Back to the Motor Room. Nothing much to see there except for one enormous main motor driving the shaft which disappeared out of the back end of the Back End. There was also a trainable thruster, handy for manoeuvring and propulsion when the main shaft was unavailable, and called the Eggbeater.

We finished in the Engine Room, or Donk Shop to its denizens. There wasn't much room here for anything more than the main engines themselves, linked together through their gearbox, and a few more extraction and lub. oil pumps. Any remaining space was occupied by two Foster-Wheeler steam-vac air conditioning plants, monsters that had the power to create ice in the chilled water system, and as quickly to turn it into steam.

Finally we concluded our tour in Steam Drains Alley, both seated rather uncomfortably on bubbling Yarway traps: a sensation much like sitting on a very hot bicycle saddle. It was a horrid little spot of which no-one could be proud, yet it had its humble but essential purpose.

We sat facing each other with a wild surmise (in Keats' words). We had discussed, during the tour, what each lump of machinery did, how they were interconnected, what happened when they failed, how we measured and controlled feed water purity (answers: patchily, and with difficulty), a few words on basic nuclear physics, atmosphere control, maintenance procedures and ergonomics.

"Well, Ted," I asked: "Any last questions? You've seen it all."

Ted fixed me with his brilliant blue (and close together) eyes, and I fancied I could hear the smooth tumblers of the executive mind clicking into place.

"One question," he said, ominously.

I flinched in anticipation.

"Tell me", he said, "Does your wife know that you come here?"

Our principal, overwhelming and abiding activity was the Cold War. We trained for it, we practised it, we added equipment to make us better at it, and we fought it. There was a constant stream of expensive little men in vans fitting some 'special fit' or another. Often this arrived accompanied by its inventor, of the wild-haired kind, who sometimes had little idea of the practicalities of installing or operating his precious baby. Sandy imported a young electronics expert, Lieutenant Harry Atkinson, who was good with such things, and spent much of his time knocking up bits of electrical circuitry in a biscuit tin to provide new capabilities, usually linked to the sonar. The 2001 Sonar, a large bow array, had been designed primarily as an active set, pinging away to locate and track the enemy. This mode was now verboten for obvious reasons (more of a beacon than a detector) and the emphasis was on passive detection i.e. listening only. The array together with other, flank arrays was excellent, but the signal processing was pathetic by comparison. The computer age had hardly started. We were the proud, if slightly baffled, owners of a device called DCB, which was supposed to integrate all sonar inputs and provide a firing solution. It was an enormous computer, about the size of a small car. It sat in its own air-conditioned room, attended constantly by its own Electrical Artificer. Poor thing, it never had a chance. It had 64 KB of computing power, a lot less than today's mobile phone. So the boat was littered with the old analogue devices which had evolved over the years, the General and Local Operations Plots, Time-Bearing Plots drawn on Perspex, the Battenberg disc, a variety of patent slide-rules and, to record everything imaginable, the Graphic Format, or Phallic Doormat as it was invariably called. It all seemed a bit of a step back from the Fruit Machine which lurked in the Control Room of Ambush, and its lineal predecessor the Is-Was. Progress is a vector quantity, not always forward.

The marine engineering contribution to the sonar world was to make sure that Warspite was extre-e-mely quiet. This involved checking that all the rotating machinery was in balance and sitting on its rubber mountings so that no noise was transmitted to the hull, and onwards. No easy task. Despite rubber or flexible pipework, machinery sitting on springy rafts and endless examination, it was all too possible for a bucket to slip down in some cloacal corner and short out the insulation. To see how we were doing we went to the Static Noise Range in Loch Fyne. Here the submarine was secured fore and aft to large buoys and then lowered to a depth of several hundred feet where it was surrounded by hydrophones connected to a solitary boffin in a hut ashore (much of the west coast of Scotland was inhabited by solitary boffins in huts at the time). We then ran all sorts of machinery in different combinations to see the result. A noisy pump could blank our own sonar, and provide a beacon for the enemy; distinctive combinations of frequencies, unique to Warspite, could make a powerful and unwelcome identifier.

One evening, as we were preparing to dive on the buoys, a rubber dinghy appeared with three men and some more special fit equipment – they'd had to leave their van behind. As they were making the hazardous transfer from dinghy to submarine casing, exacerbated by the usual Scottish rain, one of the men fell in and promptly disappeared from sight, leaving only a trail of bubbles. We peered gloomily down into the black water for what seemed like an eternity. Eventually, with some more bubbles, the man re-appeared. As he was manhandled on board his leader said:

"What kept you so long, Jock?"

Jock replied, in his strong Glaswegian accent "Weel, I wasna goin' tae leave my wee toolbox doon there," gesturing at the hefty box that had been down and up with him.

Once all this tweaking and preening and more besides was complete we were ready to go. Our job was either trailing elements of the Soviet Fleet, or intelligence gathering up north. The first was a directed task at short notice. There were now three nuclear 'hunter killers', or SSNs in commission, Dreadnought, Valiant and us. One of us would be scrambled. The brief was to shadow a Soviet Task Group or submarine transitting north or south, often at high speed. The notice was short, so we bundled out of Faslane whilst the ink was still wet on the Op Order. We barrelled out past the Cumbraes, diving as soon as possible, which was often a relief. A nasty sea could develop in the approaches to the Clyde, and submarines roll like the devil. A collective sigh of appreciation would run round the boat as the pipe was made 'Diving now, diving now,' and the roar of the main ballast tank air exiting via the main vents could be heard. Soon we were rolling gently in a pleasant, soporific motion.

When we arrived in the Irish Sea we sat and waited, as in a lay-by, for our target to trundle past. The Soviet surface units made a terrific noise and could be heard for miles. Their submarines were quieter, but still noisier than we were, so trailing them was not too taxing. Once we were locked in astern our business was to keep in contact and record everything we heard. The Soviet units often cracked on at a terrific pace, and we found that we were at full power for hours on end, apart from occasional pauses to 'clear stern arcs', ie to see that no-one, in their turn, was following us. John Le Carre steps into a doorway.

These high speed runs were exhilarating. The boat thrummed with excitement and with the water whooshing past. We were dead level, only the smallest angle on the planes was needed to keep depth, and the machinery all seemed well matched at what was, after all, its design condition. The only downside was that if something did go wrong it would go wrong a lot more quickly, and more profoundly, so we were all kept on our toes. The Command team were all metaphorically peering ahead, trying to keep their eyes, well their ears actually, on the quarry.

If these high speed trails were exhilarating, then our intelligence gathering patrols were exciting in a different way. These were meticulously planned as extended periods at sea, together with up to a dozen 'riders', the specialists who would gather and analyse our 'take', the intelligence we obtained. These riders were collectively known by the Warspites as 'the Sneaky Beakies'. Food was a limiting factor, and we started the trip with a false deck, so called, whereby the Accommodation Space passages all had a carpet of cardboard boxes containing tinned food. We thus started the patrol perpetually stooping as we moved around, straightening up as we ate our way through the carpet.

Once we were in position off the Soviet littoral our primary concern, like the Polaris boats, was to remain undetected. This meant creeping about at two or three knots, keeping quiet, and occasionally withdrawing from the patrol area to conduct our noisy, but essential evolutions, like blowing our sewage and slop drain (dirty water) tanks overboard, and perhaps blowing down the precious steam generators, to reduce the accumulated level of impurities they had collected. There was always a running battle between the communications specialists and their sonar opposite numbers, the former wanting us to be at periscope depth with their aerials poking above the sea surface, the sonar boys wanting us to be deep with our ears flapping. Tempers sometimes ran hot in Sandy's daily planning meeting. Occasionally we thought that the opposition had got a sniff of us, and moved delicately to avoid any questing Soviet, eager to flush us out. No more iceberg incidents, we determined!

The engineering bits of the submarine usually worked well; machinery thrives on steady running without too much stopping and starting. Nevertheless there was always plenty to be done. The primary, or reactor, plant had been well designed and carefully constructed out of the proper high grade materials, doubtless with an eye to nuclear safety criteria. The secondary plant, the so called 'steam—swallowing end', had suffered some fatal economies and mistakes during its design. In particular the aggressive nature of saturated (cf superheated) steam, blasting its entrained water droplets at every surface had been badly underestimated. Ian and I quietly crossed our fingers; if anything serious went wrong we'd be in for a three day passage to the nearest Norwegian port, relying on our not very reliable diesels to get us home.

Domestic life on board trundled quietly on. Everyone on board was watchkeeping, mostly one in three, which doesn't give you much time for anything else. Each mess watched two films a week, bulky 16mm reel-to-reel movies projected on the faithful Bell & Howell. The ratings' entitlement of alcohol was two cans of beer per day, but the Wardroom abstained, limiting themselves to a Bandmaster (ie a wineglass) of sherry before Sunday lunch. This meal was also embellished by some modest extra luxury, and to this day I can't look a smoked mussel in the eye without harking back.

Eventually it was time to set off for home, to a feeling of relief all round. The length of the patrol meant that we had often missed a complete season, and it was a little sad to leave home in the spring and return in the autumn, having spent the entire summer locked in our black tube. We were about to be exposed to the unusual sight of natural daylight and objects more than a few metres away. We were also about to breathe fresh air, although the atmosphere we painstakingly created in the boat was generally of better quality. In the old days, when boats ran with an elevated level of CO_2 for weeks on end, the crew were often nauseous when at last faced with fresh air. This was called the Off Effect.

When we got back, and secured alongside at Faslane it was time to go home. Walking along the jetty with one backward glance at the rusty tube that had been our unwavering focus for three months, and then casting one's eyes up to the majestic, often snow-capped hills across the loch, there was a powerful feeling of "Is that *all* it was?" a feeling rapidly blanked out by the excitement of reunion with the family. Happily Janey and I always found ourselves 'on song' within a few minutes of meeting again. We were soon clattering away as if we'd never been apart. Some sailors found that their efficient wives had embraced all the family duties, as indeed they had to, and the lads felt unsure as to what was left for them in terms of making a contribution.

There were interludes in our entwinement with the Cold War. Warspite visited Kiel, steaming sedately through the Kiel Canal, escorted by two, fortunately superfluous, safety tugs. In Kiel we were looked after by the renascent German Navy, who were efficiently friendly. It was however something of a shock when, during a stilted conversation about the twinning of ships to towns, an Oberlieutnant said:

"Ah yes, we too have such arrangements."

"And what town is this ship twinned with?"

"Ravensbrück." Follow that.

We also visited Gibraltar, and stayed ashore in the Bristol Hotel. Warspite was berthed right at the very end of the very long mole. One evening Ian and I were strolling on the Rock, with wonderful views of the last of the day over Gibraltar Bay and Algeciras beyond. Warspite was clearly visible, bedecked with outline lighting.

I remarked to Ian how good his lighting looked, and what an unusual effect it was that they went on and off at irregular intervals.

"Oh Christ," he said, "they're not supposed to do that." Down we went to discover what was wrong. Was it a coded message of distress? No, just a sticky relay.

The next night I went along to the Casino with Sandy. He studied the roulette wheel for some minutes, applying his fine arithmetical brain, and said

"The wheel is fixed; I'll prove it by winning £50 in the next ten minutes," which he proceeded to do. It so happened that Chief ERA Maxwell was also in the vicinity. Maxie never travelled anywhere without his torch, and he soon dived under the roulette wheel to see how it was fixed. Soon after the management asked Sandy and Maxie to leave. On the way out I noticed a rather feeble fountain playing in the foyer. I found a nearby cupboard gratifyingly full of valves which I started to turn, hoping to tune the fountain. Moments later I too was ejected, and joined the other two on the steps.

The end of our commission was in sight, not least because we were running out of fuel. How much useful fuel remains in a reactor core is a moot and complex point, necessitating many more expensive visits from men in vans, this time physicists from Rolls-Royce and Associates at Derby. The limiting feature tends to be not so much the reduction in Uranium 235, which is miniscule, but the increasing presence within the core of poisons, long half-life fission products which absorb neutrons. We knew that we were near the end when, during one of these tests, we sat sub-critical looking at all the control rods 100% withdrawn. The Rolls-Royce men kept tapping their instruments in disbelief. We had some interesting strategies for dealing with the shorter term transients whilst we were at sea, known as operating in Xenon-Iodine space, but the fact was, our time was up. We steamed gently round to Chatham, and entered Her Majesty's Dockyard.

We locked into the graving dock where Warspite would be refitted. The caisson was put in place, and, before the water was pumped out, we embarked on one final set of physics tests, dumping steam into the main condensers until the dock water was steaming in its turn at 85 degrees, in a November afternoon. Ian had now left and I was undisputedly in charge. I shut the reactor down for the last time and went home for tea.

Looking back, we'd had a great time despite a punishing schedule which left the families forlornly on the jetty for too long. Still, a stimulating environment, interesting operational tasking, sharp colleagues, a huge sense of community and some amusing toys to play with — who could ask for more? If I made a personal contribution, apart from what I hope was a cheery presence in the Wardroom, it was to shift the emphasis of my department away from the novel reactor plant, simple, rugged, well designed and constructed, and towards the other equally pressing hazards around the boat, which had few of these advantages. My delightful assistants during this time, John Holl, Mike Taylor, John Bullard and Johnnie Clayden all got the point and made it happen.

So, was all this clandestine activity worth it? Impossible to say from the point of view of the value of the 'take'. However the fact that we were doing it alongside the Americans obviously weighed heavily with them in the maintenance of the often debated 'Special Relationship.' Recently, rather strangely, the US Navy has created a Garden of Remembrance for the Cold War. The centrepiece is an SSN surfacing through a flower bed! Curiouser and curiouser. Our contribution has been recognised by a glass slab engraved by Frank Grenier, so they must have rated us. At a more parochial level, the operating experience was excellent training and allowed us to develop advanced techniques of ship handling and sonar operation far in excess of what would otherwise have been possible.

We moved down to a fascinating house on the banks of the Medway, directly opposite Nuclear Towers, where I worked. It was a six mile drive from Upper Upnor through congested Rochester and Chatham streets to the Dockyard, so I bought a little dinghy to make the four hundred yard crossing instead. I kept the boat at the Sappers' landing on the Upnor side, known as Engineers' Hard (a phrase which caused some amusement amongst the other engineers' wives), and crossed over to Thunderbolt Pier within the Dockyard, the tiny outboard screaming away throughout. On a good day it was the best possible way to travel to and from work, though disdained by the dockyard mateys who considered a Ford Cortina as the proper transport for my pay grade. But there were some less good days, when the Medway was full of fog, or when the wind and tide threatened to overwhelm me. All good fun! On one occasion, returning from the Dockyard, I came across a marine saga: my friend Sergeant Cattermole from the Engineers' Hard was under way in a Mexiflote, a sort of tennis court with an engine at each corner, used for landing army vehicles across a beach. He was pursuing a large catamaran which had broken adrift and was being blown all over the river to the public danger. I managed to scramble on board and secure some lines and the job was done. From then on we had a shared bond of maritime rescue, though we never got a drink out of it, at least I didn't!

Meanwhile work was getting underway in the yard, where Tubes Maclachlan was already installed, officiating at the little wardroom bar we had on the top floor, spicing up standard pizzas with additions of anchovies and extra cheese. Because the nuclear disciplines of Test Groups, Test Procedures and Test Forms had been adopted for all parts of the boat, we were much more involved with the refit than had been the practice in the past, but, though the concept was excellent, the bureaucracy was an invitation to many jobsworths to grind exceeding small and make us exceeding cross! The preparations for removing the highly active reactor core and replace it with a new one was heart surgery on a grand scale, and the combination of careful thought, meticulous procedures and heavy work by the craftsmen was engineering at its best.

After three and a half years in Warspite it was time for me to move, with some regret. Shortly before we left, we attended that most hazardous of activities, the Ship's Company Dance. In a flag bedecked hall we met, often for the first time, the wives and girl friends of our close knit community. At some point on the evening there was a lull in the uproar, and the distinctively reedy voice of the Outside Wrecker's Mate, who had taken rather a shine to Janey, was heard quite clearly all round:"Have another Pernodd, Jane". Definitely time to be off!

CHAPTER 7

Office Jobs, and Tubby's Flagship

Anything would have been an anticlimax after Warspite, but we were happy enough to go back to Faslane where the action (and our friends) were. We were less happy to leave Upper Upnor, an amazing village. At some stage it had been a bit of a Greater London overspill, and there were many grass widows whose husbands were "on holiday" for months, if not years. Whilst we were there there were two murders, plus one attempted, next door to us. We lived next door, on the non-murdering side, to an old boy who styled himself as the Harbourmaster of Upper Upnor; he spent all day in his car, peering out across the Medway. Mr Curd, for that was his name, lived in some squalor in a modest bungalow with quite a large garden. Because of its position it was considered a development opportunity, so much so that he had a large painted notice on his front door: -

> ## NOT FOR SALE OR PARTIAL LET
>
> ## KINDLY RESPECT OWNER'S PRIVACY BY NOT ASKING

Back up to Scotland then, this time to live on the married patch, drily rather than romantically called Moon City. When this estate was scheduled to be built, as part of the massive expansion of the Faslane complex, the local authority specified that the roofs of the houses should not be visible from the loch. The architect's way of accommodating to this constraint was to build all the houses where he originally intended, but with single roofs sloping back from the loch aspect. They looked a bit one-dimensional, like those on the Main Street of a Western movie.

The ratings' patch was similar, though much larger and pretty soulless as a result. For young wives left on their own for long periods it could be a lonely place. The Chaplain introduced a scheme whereby a red fish (provided by him to every household) displayed at a window signalled "I am in need of company". Unfortunately one or two girls used the fish to indicate "I am in need of sex." Gangs of Glasgow youths were soon roaming the place, looking for the famous Red Fish Club. The Chaplain hastily withdrew his fish.

I was appointed to the staff of Captain SM 10, the Squadron responsible for the four Polaris Submarines. It was strange to stand on the jetty and wave goodbye to the boat, instead of being on the inside looking out. It was stranger to welcome them back. The jetty in question was at the Armament Depot in Coulport on Loch Long. Peering into the loch's black depths through the icy rain, it seemed very close to the edge of the world. The boats returning to this god-forsaken spot, must have wondered, like the submariners in 'On the Beach', if they had come home to an empty world devastated by nuclear war. On a warm, sunny day though, it could be austerely beautiful.

It took a bit of time to get used to the 'Bomber' ethos. The two crew thing for a start. Not really an engineer's ideal. A bit like sharing your car with your best friend: you may love him, trust him, respect him etc., but what does he do with it when he gets round the corner? The two crews only really met during the maintenance period between successive patrols. The concept of maximum effort over a short period was fine, but 300 men swarming over a boat plus the usual collection of contractors was quite unwieldy. Sometimes the strain between port and starboard crews showed a bit. The incomers, unsurprisingly, wanted to get off on leave with the family. The new crew wanted to be left alone to get on with it.

The whole ambience, the zeitgeist of the bomber community, was different to that of the SSNs, the hunter-killers. It started with the objectives. The primary patrol objective was 'to remain undetected', which meant that the boats crept about on patrol at 2-3 knots, shying away from any potential contact, and maintaining high standards of silence throughout. This in turn engendered a thoughtful, mature approach, a far cry from the tatterdemalion Jolly Roger behaviour of the rest of the submarine flotilla. No doubt the knowledge that they carried the means to send us all to oblivion in the twinkling of an eye had something to do with it too.

The role of the Squadron Staff was not particularly inspiring, particularly in dealing with these large submarines manned by senior, competent people. We spent quite a lot of time 'sea-riding' their boats to provide an objective eye for their own training. This frequently meant clambering aboard the boat at sea, sometimes lowered from a helicopter. In rough weather this was no joke, with the casing awash as sailors, clipped on with their safety harnesses, tried to grab the descending staff officer. Opportunity for much ribald comment:

"Ooh er, nearly lost you then, Sir, oh well never mind" etc.

I was involved in a couple of interesting engineering problems. The first concerned hydraulic oil, not in itself exactly fascinating. However it seemed that a batch had been incorrectly formulated. As a result the oil circulating through its many pipes, pumps actuators and valves became steadily waxier and waxier. There was a fear that it would finally set solid, immobilising the system and proving impossible to remove, rather like the cooking fat incautiously emptied down the sink which solidifies in the drain. Quite legitimate cries of 'fuck'. The potential for the nation's deterrent to grind to a halt was real and present, and I spent many hours on the phone to the Admiralty Oils Laboratory in Cobham before an emissary arrived and set up his mobile lab. In the meantime we arranged massive hydraulic oil changes, with thousands of gallons being jettisoned, no doubt to the delight of a railway arch merchant somewhere in Glasgow. Eventually the moment passed and all was well.

We (well, I) had another flurry of activity over the rather arcane matter of main turbine blade shields. Because of the soggy steam conditions the turbine blades had been protected by little cupro-nickel shields, about the size of a fingernail, being brazed onto the blades themselves. Brazing such an insubstantial lamina to a curved blade is not easy, and before long they were coming off in handfuls.

Would this unbalance the turbines?

Would it allow the now unprotected blades to erode rapidly?

Would the shields pierce the condenser tubes, allowing the dreaded seawater to gush in?

After hours of consultation with the Turbine Section in Bath, the Admiralty Materials Laboratory at Holton Heath, and the manufacturers English Electric at Rugby, we decided that the answers to these three questions were No, No, and No. The 'problem' went away as quickly as it had arisen, leaving nothing but a delicate little pile of fingernails in each condenser sump.

In addition to these class events, each boat brought back a regular crop of failures, breakdowns and other defects from patrol. Due to the presence of a large, skilled, navally manned Technical Department within the base, backed up by Vickers, most of these were fixed without Squadron involvement. The Shipbuilder had a resident engineer, Arthur Roberts or John Wild, who lived a spartan life in the smoke-filled Vickers Caravan. They were frequently rung up by young sailors asking to be married.

If the job was somewhat mundane, we had a very good time socially. Whilst Wiz was happy enough at the local school, Toby found it harder to settle, and he went off to a Quaker boarding school in Yorkshire called Wennington Hall. It was quite progressive, not very academic, and creaking at the seams financially, but Toby learnt a lot about life if not much else there! We camped on the Mull of Kintyre, where we had a beach to ourselves and a colony of seals, but were eventually driven home by the insatiable Scottish midge – never to be underestimated. We had a great cruise in one of the base yachts, culminating in a romping sail back from Arran averaging seven knots over the fifty miles, mostly because the stern wind had blown up too quickly for us to reduce sail safely. Our faces glowed like beacons for days afterwards.

Into this scene of family domesticity arrived a small bombshell; I was to be promoted to Commander and go to a job in Bath. Apart from the natural feelings of relief (I deserved it!), surprise (but didn't think that *they* agreed!), and delight (onwards and upwards is always nice!) this was a very welcome development. We were keen to buy a house, and had already cast envious eyes over Pru and Barry Wallace's brownstone terraced house in Craigendoran, which we couldn't quite afford. We couldn't afford much in Bath either, but found a charming Georgian artisan's house in the not-so-smart part of Bath around the London Road. This house had been gutted after the demise of its owner, one Fishy Edwards, and cheaply renovated. We could move straight in. We started to buy some furniture from the second-hand shops in Dumbarton and prepared for yet another move. At the time of our departure there was a horrendous gale. As we drove down the A6 over Shap the roadside was littered with vans blown over on their sides, and we got stiff necks trying to read if one of them was our removal van.

As we drove south I had a chance to reflect on the past year (between manic games of I Spy and regular enquiries "Are we nearly there?"). There was no doubt about the dedication, competence and commitment of the crews of the Polaris Squadron. If they had been ordered to do so, I am certain that they would have fired their deadly payload. For boats in their first commission it was difficult to be sanguine about the chances of a seamless deterrent for the next twenty five years. Much of the design was too complicated, skimping on suitable materials, and too reliant on outmoded technology. The 19th Century secondary plant, the 'steam swallowing' bit, was the worst culprit. It would need an awful lot of work and expense over the years to keep it all going. (And of course it got it. As the boats got older, piecemeal improvement of the most vulnerable systems started to pay off, but, inevitably, weaknesses in the reactor systems themselves, and in the nickel-aluminium-bronze castings that carried seawater in and out of the boat, started to become the most worrying aspects. However, the investment paid off and the class eventually retired having maintained that deterrent strand throughout, though not without a few close calls.)

The change in the social milieu from Moon City to urban Bath was considerable. Bath was still a very architecturally distinguished city, despite the so-called Rape of Bath, which had taken place a few years earlier. The Council, zealous for modernity, had bulldozed many lesser Georgian streets to make way for horrific 60s' shopping centre and housing developments. They had not appreciated, or had not cared, that the appeal of the city was not based on individual high points like the Royal Crescent or the Circus, but was on the buildings being all of one piece, from the grandest to the humblest. But the rape had been going on for years. In our own road, Brunswick Street, the west side was a delightful row of Georgian terraced houses, perhaps built as quarters for the artisans who built the grander structures. On the east side was a terrace of undistinguished Edwardian bay-windowed houses, no doubt cutting edge in their day.

The principal activity in Bath was tourism, and in the summer the humid, airless centre of the city was flooded with coach-loads of tourists. The locals enjoyed the financial rewards they brought in, but felt that tourism was somehow demeaning, like the attitude of a prostitute to her profession (sometimes!). This resulted in a lack of community spirit. I used to infuriate the odiously smug Bathonians by suggesting that a steelworks in the middle of the city would be a powerful unifying factor. Anyway, tourism allowed Janey to get a job as the Chef in the County Hotel, where all the kitchen staff were Ecuadorian and in love with each other, regardless of gender. She used to come home exhausted, after trying to untangle their affiliations in between cooking industrial quantities of Shepherds' Pie and Apple Crumble.

At the bottom of our street was a pleasant town pub called the Porterbutt. It was altogether delightful to stroll down for a pint, compared to driving ten miles to some dank Scottish watering-hole. On my first visit the pub was deserted and I introduced myself. Obviously Patrick was not in the publican's lexicon of first names and he said doubtfully

"Oh, like Nigel Patrick?" mentioning a comedy actor of the time.

"Just like that," I replied. The next time I visited, the pub was heaving. Even so the publican did his best to introduce me

"This is Nigel." It was too noisy to correct him, so for the rest of our time there I was Nigel in the pub, which greatly confused my friends, and me too sometimes.

Meanwhile, I had to hop on a bus which crawled across the city to arrive at last at Combe Down, and Foxhill, the offices of the Ship Department. The combined intellectual capacity of the site was, no doubt, formidable, featuring a large proportion of the Dagger Engineer Officers and of the Royal Corps of Naval Constructors. The appearance was a lot less promising – the sprawling single storey blocks of 'Admirality Hutments', the acres of blank grass, often cut up by injudicious car-parking, the grey-suited figures ambling around, and seemed a long way from the bar-taut, smart as paint Royal Navy that it served.

Two strange structures overlook the city. On the north side is Beckford's Folly, a lighthouse-like building erected by the notorious Beckford, sugar baron extraordinaire of the 18th century. He had constructed a lavish house for himself in South Wiltshire called Fonthill Abbey, but it was so jerry-built that after six months the spire collapsed. Not before, however, Beckford had been able to entertain Nelson and Lady Hamilton there. On the south side of Bath, the encircling hills were embellished (?) by a one-dimensional Sham Castle, put up by the busy Victorians to add drama to their sky-line. Somehow these two oddities, the Folly and the Sham, seemed to reflect the two Admirals who gazed balefully across at each other, Director General Ships and Director General Weapons. Bedded down under these DGs, we wouldn't have entertained such cynical thoughts.

The Ship Department ran on what was known in those days as a 'matrix' structure. This meant that the Ship Sections, for ship classes present and future, acted as a focus to the Specialist Sections, which served in equipment and advice to the appropriate Ship Section. MOD finances were not at the time very complicated, but the specialist Sections got some of their money as "payment" from the Ship Sections they served, and some by 'Direct Grant'. There was a wonderfully flexible and percipient Chief Finance Officer called Neville Lewisohn, who was a master at switching funding between left and right pockets in a blur of monetary Mandarin so that no one could quite follow what was going on, but, miraculously, the money never quite ran out. Undoubtedly a good egg.

My section, DPT 2, was a Ship Section for new-build submarines (mechanical engineering) and thus part of a group headed up by a Chief Constructor. Once a month seven or eight of us went off to Barrow for two days of meetings. Vickers operated a little Piper Comanche aircraft with 11 passenger seats, and this flew from Colerne or Lyneham airfields to the little airstrip at Barrow. The three pilots on rotation were all ex-Fleet Air Arm, and they took great delight in teasing the RAF ground staff at their airfields, by informality and general insouciance. When we got to Barrow we booked into the somewhat greasy Duke of Edinburgh Hotel, and started meeting our opposite numbers amongst the local Overseers with the submarine officers standing by, and visiting the building boats, the mock-up and the appropriate drawing offices. After a few beers and a meal in a local pub we all turned in at the D of E, whence we sprang the next day, mopping bacon and egg from our chins, in time for the Monthly Ministry of Defence Progress Meeting.

(The other way of getting to Barrow was on the sleeper. This dilapidated old train, made up of the rejects from smarter services, used to leave Euston at 10 pm, arriving at Barrow at 4.30 the next morning. You could stay onboard till 7 am, and then go over to the D of E for breakfast. The batteries in the train were so shot that, without the electricity generated by the locomotive, they lasted for about 10 minutes. The experienced traveller would leap out of bed at 4.30 and shave briskly by the increasingly brown light, then back to bed. Newcomers to the service could be distinguished by their unkempt appearance, having tried to get up in total darkness).

Although Barrow was not particularly dark or satanic, the shipbuilders stuck to their traditions, and in the meeting room strong tea was served straight from a large aluminium kettle by faded waitresses in apron, cap and cuffs. I have never seen such a congregation of smokers, all puffing away on Capstan Full Strength. Picking out the speakers across the room was quite a challenge in itself. There were however only three main players, the Chief Constructor from Bath, the Principal Naval Overseer, (another Chief Constructor), and the Vickers Director responsible for submarines, George Standen. The rest of us were a huge cast of extras, only occasionally called upon for a few words.

The reports made by these luminaries varied little from meeting to meeting. George said that good progress had been made against the build programme, especially in those areas which triggered stage payments; the PNO cautioned against complacency, and emphasized the key role of his staff in ensuring quality; and our man from the Bath Project Team said that there was no more money. All were well aware that the recent completion of the four Polaris boats, two at Barrow and two at Cammell Laird's in Birkenhead, had been achieved under a team led by Admiral Rufus Mackenzie, to time, budget and quality; this remarkable success was now the yardstick, challenging and inconvenient though it was.

In due course the meeting ground to its conclusion and we all adjourned for lunch in the Management Dining Room, to be regaled with a bottle of Worthington and the One O'clock News. Time then to beetle back to the airstrip and our flight home. The next day we set about the actions resulting from the meeting. This usually meant a number of letters written by my draughtsmen which were put to me to sign. Many of them were in no sense in the Queen's English, and I started sending them back. In due course the wise old Chief Draughtsman came to see me and said:

"Commander, although you're supposed to sign these letters, they are in fact communications from one of our draughtsmen to one of theirs. They understand each other well. You could spend a lot of time improving their letters unnecessarily."

Point taken, from then on I signed all manner of rubbish!

In due course I moved across in the box, and took over DPT1 from Bob Hill, old Manadon friend and fellow Am-Dramist. This was an interesting job, comprising two novel elements: notional oversight of DSMP, the so-called Dreadnought Submarine Prototype, a fully working reactor and its associated machinery and systems, used for R&D and training; and Programme Officer for SIP, the Secondary Plant Improvement Programme.

My occasional visits to DSMP were good fun, not from a technical point of view, but because it was situated at Dounreay in the far north of Scotland; the travelling was great. Frequently the only passenger on the Vickers flight as we flew on from Barrow, I was then invited into the front seat alongside the pilot. The flight over the

Grampians was wonderful, gazing out over range upon range of rugged peaks. Who said that the UK was overpopulated? The pilot gave me some earphones, so I could listen to the radio chit-chat. I used to wonder idly what I would do if the pilot suffered a heart attack. I reckoned that I could fly the plane OK, straight and level anyway, but hadn't a clue about the radio systems, so would probably be unable to make contact with anyone, and would fly silently on to oblivion, a rather good analogy for the legendary failure of engineers to communicate. Rather obviously it never came to that! When we arrived at the UK Atomic Energy Authority airstrip the first pass was to chase the sheep off the runway, and to decide whether to land along or across it, such was the cross-wind. Once we had landed I was asked to help push the plane backwards into its refuelling bay. Vintage stuff.

Managing SIP on the other hand involved little travelling but a lot of interesting work. It had been recognised early on that the secondary plant in our nuclear boats was no match for the reactor systems, and a modest amount of money was put aside to help. The sum was £2 million a year, but not much of it was readily available, because substantial proportions were forward committed to a few large, not always promising, projects. One was called the 'pump-in-pipe', a worthy attempt to simplify vulnerable sea-water systems by embedding both a pump and its motor inside the pipe without the usual shaft, gland and external motor. Like the biblical quotation "Jesus Christ, the same yesterday, today and tomorrow" it seemed in a permanent state of 'getting there', whilst the Pump Specialist Section and their chosen pump manufacturer consumed endless thousands without any conclusion. For all I know it's still going.

We ran SIP in conjunction with YARD Ltd, the consulting engineers who had derived from the original Yarrow-Admiralty Research Department, a joint venture designed to put some research into the more pragmatic areas of ship propulsion. YARD had some very competent engineers who, over the years, made many contributions to the Navy's effectiveness, though they were so diffident it would be hard for them ever to claim the credit. But they were thoroughly pleasant to work with, and I learnt a lot. With the small change left over in the budget, I was able to initiate my own modest project, aptly described as Solutions looking for Problems. The idea was to note advances in a wide spectrum of technologies and see how they could be applied in our area. We explored some fascinating by-ways together, though many of them turned out to be cul-de-sacs.

It was about this time that I revisited my interest in Maintenance. Dagger Bob Hill was waxing eloquent and erudite on Reliability, a kindred subject, but much more amenable to a quantitative approach, brimming with differential equations. Maintenance was a qualitative business, to do with artificers dismantling working bits of machinery and then poking about inside with greater or lesser efficiency, adroitness and effect. Whilst at Bath I had discovered that most maintenance, as prescribed in the sea-going engineer's bible (or one of them) the Planned Maintenance Schedule, was proposed by the manufacturer and nodded through by the appropriate Specialist Section. The Manufacturer wanted his equipment to be seen as very reliable, and he also wanted to sell the Admiralty lots of spare parts. He therefore naturally over specified maintenance, which does not always improve reliability anyway.

I came to the view that, apart from short-term servicing, oiling and greasing and the like, the whole of the massive list of time- and hours run-based maintenance could be scrapped, to be replaced by On Condition Maintenance – i.e. only carried out when the symptoms demand it. I wrote an article for the extremely starchy Journal of Naval Engineering to say as much. I had some difficulty with the extremely starchy Editor because I wanted to call my piece "Where exactly does it hurt, Mr Feed-Pump?" partly to attract some attention in this sombre tome, and also to add a little levity to such a pedestrian subject. I eventually prevailed and felt pleased when a few colleagues took to greeting me with "Well, hello, Mr Feed-Pump!" It would have been too much to hope for that a revolution would ensue, but some progress has been made (think stately rather than dramatic). A more dynamic Director of Fleet Maintenance could have started by doubling all time intervals proposed by manufacturers, and then again until something happened, but their jobsworth view was that their Division existed to manage maintenance, not to reduce it.

Years later, back at Bath for another job, I met a handsome young Chilean Lieutenant.

"Ah, Captain Middleton", he said, "You are the author of Where Exactly Does It Hurt, Mr Feed-Pump? For years I have carried it everywhere in my brief-case." So fame at last, of a sort.

There was a good feeling about DPT at the time. Whilst the Director, Harry Tabb, was a Constructor, as were a couple of Assistant Directors, Brian Wall and Keith Foulger, and Bernard Vieyra, who was a 'MOD civilian' electrical engineer, there was a strong naval presence amongst the management, from ADSM, our genial boss Spam Hammersley, through old hands like Hugh Thompson, Bud Fowler, Vic Buxton and Vic Snarey, down to youngsters like Bob Hill, Ben Pickard, John Fuery, Rob Walmsley and me. There was a ghastly canteen called – wait for it – The Shipshape Bar – which we avoided in favour of one of the many pubs which ringed Foxhill within walking distance. Occasionally a visiting contractor could be persuaded to buy the beer. Larger, more formal parties were held either in the Civil Service Club, a plain building (opposite the Bath Clinic) which was surrounded with excellent sports pitches, or at The Rockery, a strange semi-underground Tea Rooms. Simple pleasures, amply sampled.

Meanwhile we had been busy at home. 14 Brunswick Street had been fairly superficially modernised for an executor's sale by the relatives of Fishy Edwards, its last owner. We got an idea of what might have hastened his demise as we demolished an ancient summerhouse in the garden. As we dug down, we came across layer upon layer of empty gin bottles; there were hundreds of them. One of my least favourite tasks was to remove a half wall in artificial stone – 'bumstone', which had been inserted as a feature into the otherwise delightful Georgian sitting-room. Of course it been built to last, probably thousands of years, and Janey remembers finding me on my knees, surrounded by rubble, clutching hammer and chisel in bloody hands muttering:

"If Irish paddies can do this job then so can I!" Not necessarily true, but the wall eventually succumbed to brute force and liberal use of the F-word. We were able to insert a nice period cast-iron fireplace, a skill Wiz has certainly inherited. Another Sisyphean labour was preparing the good oak floorboards for sanding. Fishy's repair scheme for the ubiquitous lino had obviously been to cover the holes with small patches, held down with rings of tin-tacks hammered home. When the covering was removed the heads of the tacks came off too, leaving the pins — perfect for ripping up a sanding belt. Each pin had to be pulled out or hammered down using a nail punch. It was, in the end, well worth it.

There were good cellars there, pretty damp, which in our two year spell we had no time or money to improve. At the front there was a capacious coal cellar, with an iron grillage in the street through which the coal was delivered, an excellent arrangement. One evening there was a knock at the front door. Outside stood two smartly dressed West Indians, complete with trilbies. They were, they explained, elders of their local church, down on the London Road, almost next door to the Porterbutt Inn. That morning the son of one of them had been passing our house on his way to unlock the church. He had been swinging the keys round his finger, until they shot off and disappeared down our coal-hole. Could they come in and retrieve them? Of course they could, we replied. Unfortunately however we had had a delivery of coal that very afternoon. Not to worry they said, heading down below. As these two fairly black men disappeared into our totally black and unlit coal cellar, all Janey could say, between splutters of mirth, was:

"They'll need a spade!" We compromised with a shovel and at last they were successful, their whiter grins preceding them as they emerged. You couldn't make it up.

There was schools activity too. Wiz had happily settled into the local Primary at Larkhall, a ten minute walk from home. Toby's eccentric College of Knowledge in Yorkshire had acquired a delightful new Head, Fred Sessa, an American Quaker, but even he couldn't hold it together and closing down noises were soon in the air. We liked what we had seen of the Quaker ethic, and went over to Sidcot, near Weston-Super-Mare to have a look. This was one of the earliest of the Quaker schools, and had been taking boys and girls as boarders since 1802. We went in some trepidation, expecting an outbreak of Thees and Thous, and our relief must have been obvious when the charming Head, Michael Brayshaw, ushered us into his study with those most welcoming of words:

"Good morning. It feels like time for a gin and tonic."

It turned out to be a brilliant place, and Toby started there soon afterwards, to be joined by Wiz a couple of years later.

We had acquired an ancient frame tent, immensely heavy (the framework was all heavy gauge steel pipe) and rather baggy, though commodious. It became known as Billie Whitelaw – full of character *and* wrinkles. We had some great holidays in Devon and used to pitch camp at Sidcot in Tom's Field, where there were many other parents, and not a few of the extreme Quaker variety, all sandals and contorted, plaited hairstyles.

Many people, naval or not, seemed to spend the rest of their life in Bath, becoming more and more Bathonian every year, but before long the crooked finger of the Appointer beckoned, not to be gainsaid. It was, he told me, time for some 'broadening', and I was to go to Latimer National Defence College. We were beginning to get the hang of this moving business. We sold the house with regret but without difficulty for a modest profit, although this did not allow for the hard work and money that we had put into its improvement. We'd made a big effort to leave the house spotless and were naturally distressed to hear that, hours after our departure, it had been broken into by squatters, who apparently took a lot of getting out. The seamier side of Bath. This apart, however, we departed with a hop and a skip, and a whistle on our lips for leafy Buckinghamshire.

* * * * *

Latimer House is a beautiful Elizabethan mansion set in the delightful Chess valley, near Amersham. Well, not strictly Elizabethan, as it had been burnt down in the 18th Century, and rebuilt. Rather strangely the rebuild incorporated the original chimneys, one of which may well have been part of the problem.

During World War 2 the house and its estate were requisitioned by the army, ostensibly for use as a supply depot, but in fact to be used as an Interrogation Centre for important prisoners of war. The local doctor, who had acted as Medical Officer there at the time, enjoyed the odd drink and could be persuaded to enthral the bar with his understated anecdotes.

After the war the estate was re-opened as the Joint Services Staff College. The newly joined students were employed, during their time off, in restoring the flower beds which were in a dreadful state. The long-standing gardener remarked that it reminded him of the war, when at one stage his vegetable garden was being dug over by no less than fourteen German generals.

By the time that we arrived in 1976 the course had been restyled as the National Defence Course, and confined to UK nationals; a pity, as some of the most interesting and colourful officers had previously come from abroad. The course was also extended from six to ten months, and was sometimes described as a six month course crammed into a year. In the interim the site had been exhaustively developed, with a handsome lecture theatre, the Cormorant Hall, additional bachelor accommodation, the Cardboard Castle, and a number of married quarters. Wartime huts served for seminar rooms and studies.

We were, by design, a mixed bunch. Equal numbers of RN, Army and RAF, all Commander-equivalent ranks, plus some MOD civilians and a couple of coppers from Hong Kong and the Met. All about the same age and male, apart from two women, both destined to lead their respective services later on.

The making of the course was that most of us were married and lived on site with our families. It was an excellent milieu for socialising, with a wide swathe of kids of similar ages in the holidays. We all got on very well together, though of course the cultural differences between the services was a constant source of wonder and entertainment. From a naval perspective the army spent a lot of time fussing about the different regiments they belonged to, and how no two officers should ever be dressed precisely the same. We lived opposite a nice chap from the 14/17 Lancers (The Vulgar Fractions) who, despite having a moderate sized quarter and several children, insisted on reserving one bedroom as his dressing room. The RAF wished to be identical throughout, with some bickering between pilots and navigators.

OFFICE JOBS, AND TUBBY'S FLAGSHIP

Their wives operated in a tightly formed phalanx, even going on formation trips to the Family Planning Clinic. Janey was invited to join them, and when she declined was given the riposte "but there'll be sherry!"

The course had been invented with the strapline, 'Never Another Narvik', after some lamentable lack of interservice co-operation there. In truth there had been some convergence since then in operational matters, first seen to some advantage in the Falklands and later in Iraq and Afghanistan. The same could not be said for the support and logistics elements, which remained obstinately single service. In the Falklands I discovered that a single sparking plug had three different reference numbers, and no service could access another's data base for spares or equipment. In some despair I wrote to Peter Herbert, who had been my boss earlier on and was now, surprisingly, the Vice Chief of the Defence Staff. He wrote back to tell me what a percipient and useful letter I had written, about which he could do absolutely nothing. Percipient? Bollocks, a flash of the blindingly obvious more like. One day, perhaps, the combination of a truly purple Procurement Executive and some decent IT in the support area might solve the problem. Who knows?

Work was far from exacting. On Mondays the working week started at 11.15, and on other days at about 10.00, after a five minute stroll from our quarter. Janey, who was by now cooking at two schools, used to get quite fractious at these late starts, delaying her own programme. I used to slope off to the seminar rooms for a fag, to get out of her hair. Most days featured a lecture by a distinguished visitor. These varied in quality from the excellent to the mediocre. The group who produced the best lectures were, overall, the military – few of them were natural speakers but they did their homework and produced well structured talks. The worst were the 'military academics', somewhat ordinary at that, who had had one idea (probably PhD) years ago and were still peddling it around in a thoroughly slapdash manner. The star of the show was a diminutive, unassuming Reader in Current Affairs from the LSE called Philip Windsor. He gave several talks on matters of moment, and used to stroll out onto the stage, hands in pockets, not a note in sight, and talk fluently and persuasively for forty minutes on his chosen subject. You could have printed it out exactly as presented. Brilliant!

Quite a lot of our activities involved role-playing, and, on the insistence of the army, appropriate fancy dress. A fez was de rigueur for playing the Turkish Ambassador at yet another Middle East Peace Conference. Our syndicate studied, in depth, the Vietnam conflict, an interesting and moving story of high expectations and fairly abysmal achievements. We had to produce a thesis and I, for some reason, chose "The Ministry of Defence as an Organisation". What led me to select such a dry subject I cannot imagine, and I was allocated an appropriately dry supervisor from Brunel University. We met a few times and struggled to outdo each other in turgidity, and to keep each other awake. One of the traditions was that each service should 'host' a formal dinner, emphasising the minutiae of etiquette special to themselves. The army, of course, had grave difficulties in thinking of themselves as a single service rather than as a loose collection of Regiments and Corps. However they achieved a compromise, and the icing on their particular cake was an enormous Piper Sergeant Major in full fig, who droned his way around the room. Later I approached this august individual and asked him if I could buy him a whisky. He looked down at me, and to my great surprise said, in a little, slightly gay voice

"Well, actually, I'd prefer a gin and tonic".

The final summer was a magical time. As our visiting lecturers reached a crescendo of magnificence (Secretary of State, Chief of Defence Staff, etc) our work declined sharply, and we had plenty of time to concentrate on the Course Concert (more fancy dress), together with various championships of cricket and tennis, and endless parties, dinner, street, garden and barbeque. In between these events Janey and I walked the local woods, vainly trying to keep tabs on our collie, Froya. We'd retreat to the best pub for miles, the Bricklayers Arms at Flaunden. Always known as the Bricks, a barrel of Adnam's Best Bitter would arrive from Southwold in the boot of someone's car. Nectar. The Bricks had a tiny bar, about eight feet square, in which it was impossible to have a private conversation. Now that Wiz had joined Toby at Sidcot there seemed to be very little money for holidays, and I said as much to Janey over a pint. The reaction was immediate.

"You can't let him say that to you", the drinkers said to Janey. "You deserve a holiday, make sure that he gives you one!"

Finally, in that golden summer, we walked one last time through the lovely grounds of the estate, and made love romantically in the long grass and the setting sun. We then went off to buy a little house near Portsmouth, for I had a new job to go to. The course had been an intensely enjoyable experience of bonding, full of interest and fun. Whether it did much good in terms of 'Narvik' is less certain. Many of the baleful MOD papers written in the next few years may have had their origins in Latimer, where a form of dead official prose was encouraged.

As is the infuriating custom in such circumstances, when the removals people came their van was too small. In married quarters there is a natural reluctance to do much to a garden you will only have for a short time, so you compensate by collecting huge quantities of potted plants, none of which could be fitted into the van. My job, it transpired, was to insert all these plants into the car and drive the 70 miles down to Little Beck, in Bosham. I set off early in the cool morning, and enjoyed waving at the passers-by from my fronded jungle. As the journey progressed the sun shone, and the wild life started to wake up. By the time we got there I was sweating, slapping and swearing at the crawlers and biters. All part of moving.

* * * * *

Little Beck was a rather tired, semi-detached house, which soon responded to treatment. Its plus points were a shady garden and a winning position on an unadopted lane and the millstream, chuckling merrily along throughout the year, and bright with flowers, ducks (in profusion) and small birds. The house was full of homemade structures, fashioned from matchwood. They were all nailed together invisibly, and a few blows from a 'eavy 'ammer was the only way to dismantle them. Bosham was the remains of a beautiful small sailing village, surrounded by the reeds and marshy inlets of Chichester Harbour. It was beginning to become somewhat infested with second homes or families on extended holidays. A bit like Bath, the tourist aspect soured the sense of community. We signed up at the Bosham Sailing Club, and, on repairing to the bar, were greeted by an ancient member:

"Welcome to the unfriendliest club in the south of England," he said, raising his glass.

I noticed that he did not offer to buy us a drink. Still and all, we loved it there, with the water on the doorstep, the beautiful Sussex Downs inland, and Chichester up the road.

But what were we doing there, you might well ask. Fair question. I had been appointed as Commander (E) of Blake, another Tiger Class cruiser, like Lion. (Never heard of a big cat called Blake? Well . . . , oh never mind!) Blake had been converted from a major gunnery platform into a helicopter carrier: Y-turret had been removed, and an enormous hangar and flight-deck were in its place at the back end. In the hangar lurked, on a good day, four Sea King helicopters, tightly huddled together, rotors furled. Beautiful it was not, but it gave the ship some contemporary relevance, I guess.

I relieved Vic Buxton, another submariner who I'd known in Bath. Bright but a bit too sharp for some. Abrasive. I didn't understand why, on my arrival, I was made much of by the Weapons Engineer Commander, a fellow I'd never met. After he left, I learnt that they had been at daggers drawn throughout the preceding refit, and that there 'had been scenes.' Our interfaces were so minimal I couldn't see what the problem was. My job was so delightful that it was unnecessary to squabble with anyone. The Senior Engineer, David Mutch (Not Fucking Much as he was known on the lower deck), was a tough, rugby playing extrovert, who used his huge energy and enthusiasm to keep our rambling department in apple-pie order. Rambling it was, with over 200 souls. I rashly asked the redoubtable Fleet Chief Stoker, Yorkie Loveday, how many hands would sail with us the next day, and he replied, darkly:

"I'll let you know when we've been at sea for a couple of hours." David, who had been expecting another submarine ignoramus as his boss, was surprised at my Lion experiences, of which I could remember just enough.

There was a massive overhead steam line which passed from the forward boiler room to the after engine room without going through the intervening machinery spaces. For years it had been lying fallow, and almost my only direct order was that it should be brought into use. After some days of pressure testing, checking the pipe hangers, working out where the drains were and if they functioned correctly, and sorting out how the fiendishly complicated Automatic Quick Closing Bulkhead Valves worked, the line was brought into use with creaks groans and trickles of brown water. David thought that this was all a bit of a waste of time, but was later on generous when it saved our bacon a few times.

By this time Blake was one of the oldest ships in the Fleet, and I often described her as 'Industrial Archaeology on the Hoof.' Looking at a 1916 Jane's Fighting Ships, what stood out was the mass of advertisements for marine engineering components; almost all the advertisers had products installed in Blake, probably little changed from the 1910s. Despite the MOD's general desire for anonymity, all manufacturers were allowed a discreet name plate, and the roll-call was impressive:

*	Main turbines	GEC/AEI
*	Boilers	Babcock Wilcox
*	Turbo Generators	WH Allen
*	Every sort of Pump	Weirs of Glasgow
*	Electrical Switchgear	Evershed and Vignoles
*	Steering gear	Brown Brothers
*	Sootblowers	Clyde
*	Steam Vac Air Con Plants	Foster Wheeler
*	Auxiliary Generators	Ruston&Hornsby, Brotherhood
*	Steam valves	Cockburn
*	Electrical Components	McGeoch, Parker Pen Co
*	Steam Traps	Yarway
*	Air Compressors	Williams & James
*	Food Mixers	Hobart
*	Hydro-extractors (spin driers)	Amazon
*	Gauges	Budenberg

Etc, etc.

We were due to go 'on deployment' round the States, and decided that the hangar should be used as a display of various departments' skills and interests. I went to the Science Museum to see if they could help, and they came up with a few dusty exhibits from their store at Wroughton in Wiltshire. However the most popular part of our show was our own 'Black Museum', of bits of torn and twisted metal, each one witness to some grinding mechanical disaster.

When we were at sea I spent quite a lot of time on the bridge. Blake Parker, the Captain, a rather old-fashioned man, felt somewhat at a loss in the rudimentary Operations Room, listening to the chatter of the warfare staff.

"Ah, Chief," he would say to me, tearing off his earphones, "come out onto the bridge with me and tell me something I understand." And we would gaze out over the grey seas whilst I fed him the old comfort food of tales of feed water consumption and dodgy distillers. No accounting for taste!

Although the Admiral, Tubby Squires, did not have a dedicated engineer on his staff he still had to have one, and so I became the Staff Engineer Officer. This was an undemanding role, but one which allowed me to attend his daily briefings. These were conducted in a white hot atmosphere by Max Lawson, the fiercely competitive Staff Officer Operations. Under his direction, various lesser staff officers got up spoke and sat down, accompanied by a plethora of wall-charts, vugraphs, clips of video and all the other appurtenances of the media of the time. Finally, with a flourish which owed a lot to a circus ring-master's art, Max said:

"And *that*, Sir, is today's brief!" Tubby, a notoriously undemonstrative man, would mutter a barely audible "Thank you" and shuffle out. Talk about the smell of burst balloons.

We went down from Portsmouth for an exercise, and came to anchor in Plymouth Sound, at Jennycliffe Bay. As the Captain took a final sweep round with his binoculars before going below for a gin his eyes alighted on something on the beach.

"Good God," he cried. "Looks like a body. Chief Yeoman, the cruiserscope." This was an enormous telescope, no doubt dating back to the days of Jutland. The Chief Yeoman unearthed the massive instrument, and focussed on the beach.

"Yes Sir, definitely a body," he reported, never one to lightly disagree with his Captain. A flurry of activity ensued, and the Coastguard was informed. In the dwindling light we later saw a police car arrive at the top of the cliff, and a couple of coppers cautiously descend the path to the beach. As viewed through the cruiserscope, the officers gingerly approached the body, which promptly sat up, revealing two heads emerging from a sleeping bag. Slight embarrassment all round.

The ship went to Portland for a work-up, which did not trouble us much. The Work-Up Staff, habituated to the Leander frigates which formed the bulk of their work, were somewhat foxed by the primitive Ops Room set-up, by the massive - but usually silent - guns, by the complexity and versatility of the marine engineering world (the Sunken Gardens, in the Oily Rag — ship's newspaper — demotic) and by the huge numbers of ratings available to man the various Damage Control Parties. I suppose everyone learnt a little.

We were then off on our deployment. First stop, rather prosaically, was Brest, where the Commander (S), Tony Thorpe and I arranged for our wives to come out for a long weekend whilst we toured Brittany. The girls' arrival had been facilitated by a French naval officer we had met earlier, who scooped them up from the ferry at Roscoff, gave them breakfast and delivered them to the ship. As a farewell gift he gave us a bottle of his own home-made Calvados. We sampled this in our hotel room in Beg Miel; it was so potent that we tipped it down the loo, which promptly and irremediably turned black — an awful warning.

As we set off across the Atlantic towards Bermuda, I was asked to produce a piece for the Public Relations people in the MOD, for possible onward transmission to the dailies. It never made it, but, amazingly I still have a copy. This is what I wrote:

. . . . . AND WE ARE THE CRUISER THEY SENT

Under the fierce blue of a Caribbean sky, the ships were spaced out in a large circle. From the centre you could just see them all, smudges on the hard horizon. The Seventh Royal Navy Deployment group was under way.

In the past few years, as Britain's global responsibilities and influence have diminished, deployments have become a feature of naval life. They combine the political aims of 'presence' and diplomacy with the military aim of cross-operating with other navies in blue water. They sometimes provide a sales pitch, most of all for the Navy itself. They provide an opportunity for young men to see the world, which the retreat into NATO has done so much to reduce. Without group deployments, with all their carefully prepared publicity, it is doubtful whether the service could recruit and retain the manpower which is its life-blood. Deployments are, to the Board of Admiralty, 'very good news indeed'.

HMS Blake, a helicopter cruiser, is flagship of the group. Here resides the Flag Officer First Flotilla, Rear Admiral 'Tubby' Squires (or, sometimes, since the inaugural visit of the group to Brest, 'Le Tubby'). The Admiral and his staff control, cajole, blame and encourage their ships with a ceaseless stream of signals (how the Navy loves its signals!), clattering out by radio, flag and light. The Main Communications Office, wallpapered with radio transmitters and receivers, is in a continuous state of frenetic activity.

The group consists of, besides Blake, the Fifth Frigate Squadron, Hermione, Leander, Juno and Ambuscade. The Support Group comprises the stores ship Stromness, and the fleet oilers Tidespring and Green Rover. Under all lurks the nuclear submarine Conqueror. Birmingham, a new Type 42 destroyer, and Resurgent, an ammunition ship, join up with the group later on. It is, these days, a not insignificant collection of naval strength.

Blake, the oldest ship of the group, is fondly known by her ship's company of 800 as Old Snakey. She is an extraordinary hotch-potch of a ship, designed pre-war, partially built, then halted, during the war, finally completed and commissioned in the '50s as a conventional cruiser. In the late 60s she was converted to her command and helicopter role, by the expedient of removing her elegant after six-inch gun turret and replacing it by a flight deck and a hideous box-like hangar to house the four Sea King helicopters. Old Snakey has style however, whatever her looks. To many of her men she is a way of life, not just a ship. Some of them come back to her time after time. 'It's good to be back.' Despite her multitude of compartments, her unspeakably hot machinery spaces crammed with aging machinery, and the prodigious demands she makes to be kept running, fighting, clean and sparkling, she has us all in her spell. Like an old lady whose lipstick doesn't quite match her lips, her character and individuality shine through. Only to outsiders is she ugly.

Visitors to Blake marvel as they wind their way through her labyrinthine passages. They expect, of course, to see the massive, oil-soaked gun turrets, the little rooms packed with electronics, the shining, cramped mess-decks. What they do not expect are the little signs of domesticity that make the ship a self-contained organism – the blue lamp outside the Regulating (Police) Office, a solitary chef frying an egg for a latecomer in a galley the size of a garage, the butcher hacking up sides of beef with nonchalant skill. Nor do they expect to find the small contingent of 'unofficial Chinese', as they are quaintly termed, who run the laundry, the tailors' shop, the cobblers' shop, and cut 800 men's hair to something approximating to official length. There is an amazing multiplicity of offices, Air Department Offices, Stores Offices, Catering Offices, Pay Office, Admin Office, Signals Offices, Medical Offices, the Schoolroom, Command Planning Offices and Operational Offices. The Padre, however, lives in the Vicarage, not the Religious Office.

The two engineering offices sit side by side in the main passage, as different from each other as chalk and cheese. The Marine Engineers' Office is a used, full, noisy market-place, scattered with drawings and spare parts, with a press of sweating artificers clutching grimy bits of tortured metal. Here the eternal battleground between man and machinery is enlivened by laughter, determination and occasional despair. The Weapons Engineers' Office next door is more cerebral. Calm, clever men draw neat diagrams and discuss in measured tones this modification, that 'rather neat' way to fix something. Everyone knows them as 'greenies', a nostalgic reference to the long-gone distinctive cloth of electrical officers.

The Bridge and the Operations Room are known collectively as the Ivory Tower by the Oily Rag, the scabrous ship's newspaper which somehow always just manages to emerge from the Marine Engineers' Office each day the ship is at sea. Execrably spelt, abominably printed, the paper is a fascinating pot pourri of report, opinion and prejudice. Perhaps most prevalent are the unending 'stitch-ups', the local phrase for put-downs. It is also very funny.

Atop the Ivory Tower the Captain reigns, spending hours enthroned in his high chair with its white duck cover, as he stares out across the sea. Tanned, pipe perpetually half alight, his subjects approach carefully, to be gently, or not so gently, castigated for some shortcoming in their department. Quirky, idiosyncratic, humorous, aloof, the Captain's sway is total. During exercises he abandons his chair and pipe with a sigh and installs himself in the gloom of the Operations

Room. It is dark in there, lit only by the ultra-violet light used in the numerous displays of radar information. It is tightly packed with men gathered like conspirators round the plotting tables, drawing or moving tell-tale pieces and muttering urgently into throat-mikes. The jargon is incomprehensible to the bystander.

The group is away for six months and is an experience of extremes. The delights of foreign ports are in sharp contrast with the real distress that many sailors feel at leaving their loved ones at home for so long. These days we are a domesticated navy, unversed in the rough ways of the old seafarers. Or are we? To many men the zenith of the deployment is the great opportunity for the mythical once-in-a-lifetime 'run ashore'. The most commonly used words in this context are to 'strangle' (to meet someone who offers you hospitality), and to 'trap' (to secure sexual liaison with a girl). "Did you trap?" "Did I ever, essence she was." And in truth sometimes she is. But to suggest that strangling and trapping are the principal aims and activities of the diverse 2000 men in the group would be unfair. There are of course official functions, frequently of great dreariness. There are uneven but friendly sports contests with local teams. There are the sightseers, laden with cameras, forever bumping away from the jetty in buses bent on the definitive castle, church, square, anything truly 'tipico'. There are the 'rabbiteers', nose down for the unique bargain, lugging back bulging bags of local artefacts (rabbits). There are the sad solitary drinkers and the boisterous collective ones, spacing out their drinks with straggling ambles through the town. There are the well-connected, who dash off to spend the weekend 50 miles away with old friends. And there is a surprising number of men who 'don't go ashore very much', preferring to recover from the masochistically punishing pace that we impose on ourselves at sea by relaxing with a beer in the mess.

In harbour, there is a constant swirl of people in and out of the ship. Duty watches change, men come back for a meal and to compare notes with their friends on what they have done and what they have missed. The ship's routine grinds on, equipment has to be mended, decks cleaned, rubbish removed, the Staff always have another exercise to plan. There is an extensive lore of runs ashore. Traditionally, the four day visit to a port starts off with the obligatory 'first night in self destruct run', to be followed by a day of introspection and retrenchment. The next day you are duty and on the last you meet the girl of your dreams — too late. A naval house magazine (not the Oily Rag) published an elegant article — A Theory of Port Visits — which counselled patience, stealth and pacing oneself, and ended with the phrase 'The first turn of the screw cancels all debts'. Staff officers have been known to spend so long planning the perfect run ashore that by the time they got there the town was dead for the night.

The group has five months of this gruelling activity ahead of it. The itinerary passes through the Panama Canal and then tracks northward up the western seaboard of the United States and Canada, alternating visits and exercises. The flowers that were budding in our gardens when we left will be long dead when we return in December. For some of us it will be our first real trip abroad, for others the last. For all of us, and, we hope, for many of the people that we meet, it will be an unforgettable experience. And that's what it's all about.

As we continued towards the Panama Canal, there was one of those bangs in the night from deep down in the Sunken Gardens. It turned out to be a Main Feed Pump which had effectively disintegrated, quite beyond any repair on board. This was a serious matter; one of four large pumps which shovelled all the water into the boilers to provide steam. More in hope than in expectation we signalled for a replacement. To our delight two days later it was on a plane to Bogota in Colombia, to rendezvous with our visit to Cartagena. A Sub-Lieutenant was despatched to the capital with a man from the Consulate to help its final passage though the labyrinthine bureaucracy. There was a certain amount of difficulty since the Spanish for 'the pump' is 'la bomba', and no-one was *quite* sure what lay inside this large packing case. However, sanity and a few dollars prevailed, and Sub Lieutenant Parkinson eventually reappeared in a lorry with La Bomba on the back.

Cartagena was a typical third world sea-port, full of colour, vivacity and disease. Half the ship's company went down with food poisoning, for the local oysters looked delicious and were available and cheap. The other half contracted VD, for the local girls looked delicious and were also available and cheap. The Surgeon Commander, who had so far lived the life of Riley, seldom straying far from the Wardroom bar, suddenly found himself earning his salary. Whilst we were there, the Defence Attaché, Colonel Chavasse, came down from Bogota for an official function, at which he had to wear his Mess Dress. This includes, for cavalry officers, the absurdly tight trousers which they call overalls. About a million miles away from the loose, white, oil impregnated garments which *we* call overalls. The evening over, he came onboard to change, and leave his uniform in the Admiral's Secretary's cabin. The 'overalls' are so tight that the mess boots are removed with them and remain tucked into the trousers on the hanger. The next morning a steward came in bright and early to rouse Brian Jones, the Secretary, with a cup of tea.

"Morning, Sir," he said cheerily, glancing at the kit, " I didn't know you were entertaining Douglas Bader last night."

The Panama Canal has the sadness of a Thai temple, with the jungle gnawing at its entrails. To be sure the lock system is magnificent, the great towers stand proudly, the machinery hums smoothly and the uniformed staff move with alacrity. Over all though hangs the sense of death, of thousands slaving through the high heat and humidity until brought low by disease, mainly malaria. An economic benefit bought at fearful cost, that we were glad to leave behind us.

After a stop at Acapulco (drinking Margaritas whilst watching lithe Mexican boys dive into rocky ravines far below) we arrived at San Diego. As usual, we signalled ahead for some provisions to be waiting for us when we got there. This signal included a large quantity of ice for our party that evening. We had learnt from the experiences of HMS Eagle that, in the States, it was necessary to specify Party Ice, which would then be delivered in bagged cubes, ready for the glass. She had simply ordered "4 tons of Ice", and on berthing, there it was, a single block sitting on a railway truck.

We planned to do quite a lot of maintenance in San Diego, making use of its extensive US Navy facilities. But first, our crying need was to do something about the Washing Machines. We had been supplied with new ones before we left UK, and now all of them had developed the same fatal defect. Furthermore there were absolutely no spares of any kind, anywhere. As we were in white uniform at the time, with a heavy ceremonial programme, this caused the Chinese Laundry crew to wave their hands about hysterically, the Laundry Officer to throw his toys out of his pram, and the Commander, Hugh Orme, a man of sorrows and acquainted with grief, to frown even more than usual. It was up to my department to Do Something. We stripped a machine down, diagnosed the defect and designed a repair modification. All the machines were shipped ashore to a contractor who manufactured and fitted the modification to them and returned them, working perfectly, in 36 hours. Considerable relief all round. Hugh, otherwise known as 'Commander Speaking' for that is how he used to introduce himself in his frequent messages on the ship's broadcast system, cracked a rare smile and bought me a drink.

San Diego had started out as a frontier town, staring over the barbed wire at Tijuana a few miles away. The arrival of a considerable chunk of the US Pacific Fleet had added riches and respectability, but apart from the world-renowned Zoo it had never gained much kudos, partly because it is so close to Los Angeles, whose influence in the area is overwhelming. I spent a lot of time sailing at the Naval Air Base at Coronado; it was perfect dinghy weather, though the water was surprisingly cold if you fell in. I went up to LA for a weekend to stay with an American judge and his wife that I had met at a party.

When the time came to leave San Diego, David Mutch and I were eager to give a party for the Americans who had helped us, the Base Maintenance Staff and some Contractors. We wanted to ask officers and enlisted men, who had done most of the work. Hugh ruled that officers and enlisted men could not be entertained in the Wardroom at the same time (Why? ask Nelson) so we made our own arrangements, and threw the party in the Forward Engine Room. This provided the opportunity to smarten it up a bit, and by the time of the party it was gleaming, with a bar set up on the Manoeuvring Platform, and bowls of nuts and crisps gracing the HP Turbine bearing pedestals. Tony Thorpe offered potted plants, but that would have been going too far. The party was a huge success, and I shall not forget the Captain, Fleet Maintenance and Repair, an enormous, grizzled man with a very substantial stomach.

"Goddamn," he cried, throwing down beers at an impressive rate. "Drinking beer in a goddamn engine-room! Goddamn!" Goddamn, indeed.

For the first time in my life, I had half a steward to see to my cabin. Steward May was a delightful lad, if a little naive. After I joined Blake, on our first day at sea, he summoned me urgently to the cabin. There was, he said darkly, a Problem. Consumed by anticipation, I beetled along.

"Sir," he said portentously, "I'm afraid that Mrs Middleton has made a mistake when she packed your bag. She's put in some tablecloths." How Janey would have hooted. Part of our contract was that we would never pack anything for each other, including tablecloths.

"Those are not tablecloths, Steward May," I replied, "those are sarongs."

"We did 'sarongs' on course, Sir," he said, "but I've never seen one before." Well, now he had. He enquired earnestly about boiler cleaning. What was a boiler and how was it cleaned? Was it stewards' work? It certainly was, I said, and arranged for him to join the boiler cleaning party for a day. I noticed that after that his natural curiosity was markedly less evident.

San Francisco was a pleasant change after the bleached-out blandness of Southern California. We berthed at Fisherman's Wharf, right in the centre of this amazing city. It is one of the few American conurbations in which one can walk comfortably, and of course there is always the tram system. The endless wire rope that drags the cars along through a slot in the roadway runs continuously, and late at night it was eerie to hear it softly whistling and clunking to itself as it pursued its labyrinthine course. Tony Thorpe and I found ourselves in a quiet bar in mid-afternoon. The only other customer was a truck driver, a portly man with thinning hair and unshaven jowls.

"Hey Bud," said the bartender to him, "you going to the Ball on Thursday?"

"Yup."

"What you gonna wear?"

"I thought my blue dress."

On, on to Vancouver, beautiful city of the North, surrounded by endless conifers, so different from the palms and oleanders we had just left. The locals said that they felt much more natural kinship with the Americans of Seattle, Oregon and

California than with their fellow Canadians over the Rockies, but I'm not sure that these claims were reciprocated. We sailed a match against the Canadian Navy, in very low 18ft. half-deckers. It was blowing quite hard, and every now and then one met a semi-submerged 100ft. tree-trunk, refugee from some logging operation up country. Very challenging.

It was time to start for home, and we travelled uneventfully until we were back in the Caribbean. There one of our helicopters fell into the water after both its engines failed simultaneously. Built a bit like a boat, it floated quite happily surrounded by its flotation collar deployed around it, whilst we rushed over to help. We rapidly lowered all our boats to make room on the boat-deck, whilst the helo's rotor blades were removed. The boats were hoisted aboard our Stores Ship Stromness and the Lift then started. The weight of the bird was greater than the crane's overload capacity, but slowly, with the Chief Electrician holding on the overload breakers, and with wisps of smoke appearing from the motor, the helicopter came on board and subsided with a sigh, as much from the spectators as anything else. Helicopters are like oak trees, not so big when they're up in the air, enormous on the ground in an unfamiliar place. This particular cuckoo bulged out of its nest in all directions, whilst the air engineers washed it down with copious quantities of precious feed water. They also, to universal amazement, produced 40 gallon drums of WD 40, a substance we had only seen before in hand-held aerosol cans. Nothing is too good for our helicopters, but there was relief when we could unload this one ashore, using a slightly bigger crane, and get our boats back.

The final visit of the deployment was to Fort Lauderdale, where the US Corps of Engineers had built the Intercostal Waterway, which promptly became the second home of the multitude of super-rich 'snowbirds', who came down from Chicago to avoid the winter there. We had a shooting match against the Fort Lauderdale Police, and I remarked to one that there must be a substantial underclass catering for the needs of these pampered creatures.

"Want to see it?" he asked , and took me for an eight hour patrol of the poor suburbs that the tourist never sees. The first thing that he did was to give me a huge 0.45 revolver with the instruction "When I say shoot, shoot!" Fortunately he didn't.

Soon we were home and it was wonderful to be back with Janey and the family. She had kept herself busy in her usual cheerful way, starting up a coffee shop in Bosham, and working in the Haut Brion restaurant in Emsworth, a perilous cycle ride away. But we had missed each other as much as ever, and were glad it was all over, for ever, we thought. With this outing it seemed that my seagoing days were over, and I would be destined, henceforth, to life in what is picturesquely called a Stone Frigate ie a desk. And had this excursion, linked in so many ways to an older, less earnest navy, been of value? Well, to the country, and those that we visited, I don't know. And to me? Of course, new interesting experiences. And what had I added to Blake? Very little, I'm afraid, in such a top-heavy and overmanned environment – except perhaps a little of what the French call *ton*!

CHAPTER 8

Stone Frigates, Mostly

I was about to embark, although I didn't yet realise it, on 15 years of assorted office jobs, with one short return to the coalface in between. A manifestation of the Peter Principle, no doubt, and a counter to any feelings of superiority which might result from increased responsibility and rank. All these appointments were intensely interesting in their different ways, but it has to be said that one desk is much the same as the next, unless you are sitting at it, and over the period there was another, darker shadow. As you move up in the bed more and more of your time is taken up with resource management, and it became painfully clear that the Royal Navy had been contracting in size ever since I joined it, and was continuing to do so. Managing down resources over a long period is enervating and demotivating, and I was lucky to have ridden an isolated area of growth, the nuclear submarine programme, for a few years. Anyway, this period of my life did not, for obvious reasons, generate quite the succession of stories and memories that I had enjoyed so far, so I will be brief. (Prolonged applause from yawning audience?)

From Blake I was sent to the Ministry of Defence in London, a prospect that appealed and appalled in equal measure. The modifying feature was that I was not going to the Main Building, where the Naval Staff worked prodigiously hard till nine in the evening, fortified by industrial quantities of NAAFI sherry. No, I was going to work for the Second Sea Lord on personnel matters in the Old Admiralty Building, all that was left of the original Admiralty after the civil service had annexed a large chunk, and Admiralty House, fronting onto Whitehall, had been bagged by the Government as a rest home for ministers. I worked in a garret, appropriate to my position, a cramped office in which four of us sweated in summer, shivered in winter and peered up through the skylight at a view reminiscent of Oscar Wilde's, from Reading Gaol.

Within the MOD at that time there were a couple of genuinely powerful directorates, Naval Plans and Naval Manpower Planning, both of which were close to the vital ingredient, money. Plans was highly prestigious and was regarded as an essential stepping stone to the highest ranks of the Navy. The Directorate of Naval Manpower Planning (DNMP), on the other hand, was not highly regarded, and was seen as a stepping stone to oblivion. Both these 'power shops' were surrounded by a diaspora of ineffectual advisory directorates, most of which have now been rightly shipped out of the MOD.

The Directorate of Naval Manning and Training (Engineering) was advisory. It was supposed to curate the structure, welfare and training of the engineering branches, but in practice the structure was dictated by DNMP, subject of course to affordability, the welfare by the Directorate of Naval Service Conditions, together with the personnel divisions of the Civil Service, and the training by the sprawling empire of the Commander in Chief, Naval Home Command. Thus, although we spoke knowledgably, wisely and forthrightly, it was mostly to each other – one way of ensuring an appreciative, if small audience. Small we certainly were; four commanders of various engineering specialisations, including my old friend Peter Strelley, and our boss the dear man Captain Colin Robinson, shrewd and warm, but not inclined to go to war in the great internal battles that raged round the MOD, battles largely generated, I suspected, to keep the participants amused. Colin was about to leave the Navy and embrace his passion, dealing in maritime pictures, at which he was subsequently most successful.

A few months after I had started I was summoned to call upon my ultimate boss, the Second Sea Lord. Admiral Sir Desmond Cassidi had a reputation as a hard man, a bully who drove his staff to desperation. I was too far down the food chain to be in any way affected by this, but I approached our meeting with circumspection. After his cowed secretary had ushered me into a large office on the sixth floor of the MOD Main Building he shook my hand perfunctorily and started:

"How does your perception of the job you have come to compare with your preconception before you arrived here?"

Blimey, 'Good morning' would have been nice. However I was able to say:

"It doesn't. I was in a cruiser in mid-Atlantic when news of my appointment came through, and of the 800 men on board none of them had ever heard of DNMT(E)" Fifteen all.

"So what have you done about it?" he rasped. An ace?

"I have written an explanatory article for the Journal of Naval Engineering," I replied. He circled in for the coup de grace.

"But that's only read by officers," he crowed.

"I have copied it into the Naval Engineering Review" I replied with just a glint of superiority. Game? Game it was. Sir Desmond snapped open his brief-case and fumbled about inside, eventually producing a plastic lunch box.

"Would you like a ham sandwich?" he offered. Indeed, game, set and match. I never looked back!

We were renting a flat in Pimlico during this job, and weekending at home in Bosham. Janey was working for her old employer from Bath, the property developer M.P. Kent, and used to go over to his flat in Deanery Street, almost next to Park Lane and the Dorchester. Our landlord was a rather thirties character called Oliver, or Olly, Berger, a former Colonel (Guards, I guess) now working as a Retired Officer in the MOD. He wore a long black overcoat, which matched his little moustache. Olly insisted on being paid rent in an arcane way, every four weeks rather than monthly ("then it'll always be on a Tuesday, d'you see, dear boy?") and half in cash, half in cheques made out to a variety of recipients. It hardly seemed worth the fuss. He and his wife lived in Eaton Square in some style, so they probably owned half of Pimlico.

It was a pleasant 20 minute walk to work, past the excellent Tachbrook St market, then through Victoria, cutting across St James' Park and Horseguards Parade. I sometimes used to wear a bowler to protect my thinning cranium, something which would be unthinkable now. When I did I invariably got a salute from the cavalryman on guard under the arch at Headquarters London District. These salutes sounded like a battery of kitchen implements being thrown down some stone stairs, and were properly acknowledged by the merest elevation of one's umbrella tip. No hat = No salute!

At lunchtime Peter Strelley and I would go out for a beer, often to the stygian Duncannon Arms opposite Charing Cross Station. Here we were sometimes joined by friends from the Main Building, who would make our hair (what was left of it) curl with horror stories from the real world, as they saw it. We lapped it up but did not envy them their sojourn on the treadmill.

I can't recall much of what I did for DNMT(E), but I do remember going in at five o'clock one summer morning to write a paper on "Frodsham". This distinguished man had written a study on the future of engineering. Well forgotten now, but at the time it seemed as if he just might change the world. He didn't.

It was a shock to be promoted to Captain from this job, especially as I'd rather suspected that coming to this obscure garret had been a coded signal from my Appointer. It was even more of a shock to be told that I would be going to be the Flag Officer Submarines' Chief Staff Officer (Engineering), very much more than I could have hoped for. "Calloo, callay, oh frabjous day" etc.

This promotion virtually guaranteed me another nine years naval employment, and was the trigger for a rare outbreak of personal strategic thinking. We were bursting out of Little Beck, and needed somewhere bigger; at the same time it seemed likely that the majority of this nine years would be spent in Bath, so that was an obvious focus. FOSM was based at Northwood, in North West London, an expensive suburb which we had no wish to move to.

We put Little Beck on the market, by the simple expedient of mentioning it to the itinerant greengrocer, Charlie; within half an hour we had a phone call. In the four years that we had been there, whilst the house doubled in price, the field over the stream had been turned into a bungaloid development, and the jungly patch next door had had a house built on it right up to its boundaries, so we were beginning to feel hemmed in. Our potential buyers came from Chelsea and were enraptured by the light and space as they saw it. When the day came for them to sign the contract, he was running in the London Marathon, and we scanned our tiny TV throughout the race, anxious lest our buyer would have a heart attack before signing; a heartless (ha, ha!) if practical approach. At the same time we were looking for somewhere to move to. We had fixed on Warminster as a centre of search – commuting distance from Bath, but on the edge of the lovely countryside that surrounds Salisbury Plain. The first place we looked for was, supposedly, in a village off the A36. The Old Post Office. We eventually found it, not tucked away in the village, but right *on* the A36. You could have leant out of a bedroom window and struck a match on a passing lorry. Shudder and move on.

We did move on, to have a look at Greenhill House, in Sutton Veny. We wanted space? Here was space, eight bedrooms and "extensive cellars". The house, built in 1840, was a fine four square building originally the residence of the Master of Foxhounds, with stables attached. It fell, as such places do, on hard times, and was eventually snapped up by a developer. He built four new houses in the grounds, and converted the stables into a terrace of four more. Left with the main house, and a modest garden, planning permission was refused to turn it into flats. It was consequently given a lick of paint, and put on the market for a song. We liked what we saw, although there was a lot more rot than we had realised. Bloody surveyors! Still we bought it and, after a few initial jolts, had a great time there. We loved the village and stayed for twelve years.

We were in a hurry to move in, and, experienced in the delays and procrastinations of solicitors, I was somewhat brisk with the chap we'd found in Warminster to act for us. I used to ring him every morning from the office to ask him what he planned to do for us that day, and rang again in the evening to see if he'd done it. When we eventually met, at completion, he shook my hand and said

"It's been most, er, exhilarating, working with you, Commander."

Anyway we were in six weeks after we first saw the place, so it worked well.

We had a lot of fun at Greenhill House, which responded very well to 'the treatment'. We chopped down an enormous yew, which let some light into the garden for the first time in years. The Council's 'approval to fell' in this Conservation Area arrived six weeks after the tree was down. We paved the kitchen yard with beautiful (and pricey!) Yorkshire flags, turning a dreary utility area into something vaguely Kensingtonian. And we declared war on the dry rot. A competent, but deeply rural, team came up from Dorset, and hacked, sawed, chipped and squirted until all was well. The foreman, Clarry, used to bring a lemonade bottle full of cloudy liquid with him every day, and the lads enjoyed passing it round at mid-morning. One day Janey asked for a sip, which nearly blew her head off.

"What's in *that?*" she gasped between tears.

"That's Dorset Sunrise," said Clarry proudly. "I'll tell you this, a chicken went in there last night; wasn't there this morning." An oblique reference to the old West Country habit of feeding rough cider with meat to 'give it some body'.

All too soon it was time to lay down my paintbrush (and my chequebook) and start work at Northwood, not a part of the world that I really liked, though quite handy for John Betjeman's Metroland. This monument to the Cold War had started out as a country house which found an alternative role in the 1890s as a high class knocking-shop, royally patronised. I met a very old lady, living locally, who told me that, as a little girl going past Northwood House in a carriage, she had been told to turn her head away – presumably to avoid the dreadful sight of the Prince of Wales emerging, doing up his flies! The estate was acquired by the RAF during their expansionist phase in the 1930s and became the Headquarters of Coastal Command. In the '60s, when the Home, Mediterranean and Far East Fleets all combined in one Commander-in-Chief Fleet, he too moved to Northwood, to optimise the prosecution of Russian submarines, and to provide a secure base for the direction of the deterrent. A large underground bunker (The Hole) was built, and NATO responsibilities followed. The CinC was now CINCEASTLANT, and FOSM was COMSUBEASTLANT. The RAF regrouped to High Wycombe as CinC Strike Command, and the Northwood faction became Air Officer Commanding 18 Group – what's in a name? At some early stage during their tenure the RAF had contrived to burn Northwood House to the ground, but the footprint was soon covered with unpleasant looking buildings redolent of the 1960s.

I took over from Geoff Bown, a fiercely intelligent 'greenie', who, like some others of his peer group, gave the disconcerting impression that you could never aspire to replicate his standards of competence. 'Cheerful Good Humour' was never likely to be engraved on his tombstone. When I arrived I went in to see the Admiral, Tubby Squires. We spent a couple of minutes musing on my new job, and a further twenty in pleasant reminiscence about our shared time in Blake. When I emerged from Tubby's office Geoff was hovering, with steam coming out of his ears.

"What *were* you talking about?" he whispered urgently. "In six months I've never had more than five minutes with him." I couldn't resist it. "It's the way you tell 'em, Geoff", I replied. Not the best way to start a turnover.

Very few of us had our families at Northwood, and there wasn't much 'unaccompanied accommodation', so we found digs with the diaspora of withered widows and divorcees in the area. I took over Geoff's digs and asked him what he did about an evening meal.

"I've found," he said sententiously, "that it's easiest to eat the same thing for six months at a time."

"Oh," I said dubiously, "what is it just now?"

"Cheese on toast," Geoff declared, "and because you've arrived early, you can buy some of the makings." He flung open a freezer, to reveal serried ranks of sliced white loaves, and blocks of industrial Cheddar. I paid the modest asking price and jettisoned the lot after he'd gone.

My office was next to the Chief of Staff's (Terry Thomson, then Dick Husk), and we had a little hatch through which we could communicate without walking round. It was rather reminiscent of the porthole between the two engine rooms in Adamant. I always thought of this office as the Engineer's Revenge; many of the staff worked down in the air-conditioned Hole, but from my window I could see grass, trees and the off-watch WRNS playing tennis. 15 – 0 ! We all seemed extremely busy. FOSM at the time was the focus for all submarine thinking, and we were the meat in the sandwich between the vociferous seagoers and their Squadrons and the more stately (ie pessimistic) brothers on the Naval Staff. There was a cadre of extremely bright commanders on the FOSM staff, all demonstrating their brightness by producing endless brilliant papers on their favourite topics. All of which had to be staffed 'upwards', that is through Dick and me. As a Captain (E) I was suddenly expected to be well versed in *all* forms of engineering, and I was hit with the bow-wave of the software revolution that was engulfing us. I used to say that I could tell you anything about a Target Acquisition, Classification and Tracking System (TACTS) except how to recognise it. I was heartened that, in amongst this welter of over-excitement on the weapons engineering front, the old relative certainties of the marine engineering world, of safe to dive certification, of effective full power hours expended and of innumerable interesting defects were in the safe hands of John Macgregor and Rim Wood.

Apart from all this clever-clever staff work, we had, in today's jargon, a substantial duty of care for our far-flung flock. There were 29 submarines in the Flotilla at the time, with a new build emerging every year from Barrow, and tails were definitely up! But like any proud parent we could not forebear from fussing over our charges, and spent a lot of time visiting and chatting to the crews and squadron staffs.

I became aware at this stage that I was no longer 'one of the boys'. The cadre of commanders in the service was a true band of brothers, aged 30 – 50, the building bricks of any staff. Suddenly, on becoming a Captain, you were no longer entirely integrated with your former friends, and were exposed to a degree of isolation that I, for one, had certainly not expected.

Perhaps to compensate for this, FOSM had a gathering every six months for the Captains (SM), their wives and us. These proved to be very pleasant, if not overly productive events. We had a new Admiral, Peter Herbert, an amiable fellow, if not over-bright, for whom doors opened effortlessly and propelled him, slightly bemused, to become, eventually, Vice Chief of the Defence Staff, and a full Admiral. Peter was living in a residence at RAF Uxbridge and entertained 'le tout ensemble' there. He did not have a strong head, so it was perhaps unwise of him to insist on personally orchestrating the change of seating between courses, something his Chief Steward could have achieved in his sleep. Peter stood, swaying slightly, list in hand, as chaos developed around him; tables with a single female, husbands and wives staring at each other in surprise, others with ten men all squeezed together – we probably aided and abetted the anarchy.

WAR!

On 2nd April 1982 Argentina invaded the Falkland Islands. The measured pace at Northwood faltered for a moment, then continued, quickening noticeably. John Fieldhouse, the Commander-in-Chief, went into almost permanent secret session with senior advisers and emissaries from the Government, the MOD and the Foreign Office. It soon became clear that Terry Lewin (Chief of the Defence Staff) and Henry Leach (First Sea Lord) had persuaded Mrs Thatcher to go for it, and the Northwood drum beat speeded up accordingly.

On the submarine side it was relatively easy. Three SSNs were despatched south in great secrecy and at high speed. A couple more were warned off. Otherwise, mostly normal; we still had the deterrent to maintain and many other quotidian tasks.

The business of the Headquarters as a whole was:

* a. to select the most suitable ships to be sent south;

* b. to select the Commander of the Task Force;

* c. to start the ball rolling for enhancement packages for the combatants, using the Treasury reserve to acquire systems meriting 'urgent operational status';   and

* d. to evolve an overall plan, and from it appropriate Rules of Engagement.

The selection of ships was fairly easy. The First Flotilla was mostly at sea already, in and around Gibraltar, and, since they were a thousand miles on the way to the Falklands, it made sense to send them on. Not much was known about what the Argentinians were up to, certainly not their navy, so capability selection was not much of a problem. The second echelon of ships needed to be started from home ("Make ready. . ..''), including the two carriers, the amphibious group and the numerous merchant vessels (Ships Taken Up From Trade, STUFT) required for ferrying and logistic purposes.

Sandy Woodward, my former Captain, was the Flag Officer First Flotilla, and so was the natural choice for the Commander of the Task group, though I gather there was some high level discussion. Major General Jeremy Moore, Royal Marines, was to be the Land Forces Commander, and they could hardly have been more ill-matched, Woodward egotistical, incisive and vociferous, Moore, modest , withdrawn and quiet. There were problems!

The matter of enhancement was a game for any number of players. Each ship deployed (or on call to be deployed) could have its capabilities improved by various bolt-on equipments not currently budgeted for. The warfare staff first identified the shortcomings of each ship that were susceptible to enhancement, and the engineering staff then decided what equipment was available "off the shelf", and how it would be integrated into the ship's systems. A submission was then sent to the MOD who, on a good day, awarded the concept "Urgent Operational Status", and submitted it to the Treasury for approval and funding from the government's contingency account. The Second Permanent Under Secretary in the MOD was spotted pacing the corridors of the main Building, gloomily muttering

"There will be a Reckoning."

You might think that the other major task, of defining the Rules Of Engagement, would be quick and straightforward. But there was a mismatch. The Plan, usually articulated and agreed in conversations between Woodward and Fieldhouse, could change in minutes, depending on events and perceptions. The new ROEs however had to be finessed not just through the MOD, itself a slow and labyrinthine process, but through Ministers and perhaps the Cabinet, which added an order of magnitude of delays, requests for further information and obfuscations. Not surprisingly the extant ROEs were frequently appropriate to the last Plan but three.

During all this buzz of activity at Northwood my job remained virtually unchanged. I was asked, as a matter of great urgency, for a policy for spares in the south Atlantic. I considered the matter for all of 30 seconds before declaiming, dictatorially, "Reactive not contingent". I was mildly gratified to hear this snappy little phrase being repeated round the staff like a mantra. What was that all about? Our submarines were supported by a whole catalogue of spares, some harder to come by than others. A typical example was the ALN wireless mast, an essential but vulnerable part of any boat's ability to communicate. These beauties were about 50 ft. long (90 ft. when fully extended) and were kept in a transit box two feet square and fifty five feet long (obviously!). They could only be flown around in the back of a Hercules. I did not want these and similar precious objects being sent South on the odd chance that they might be needed, to languish God knows where, and be lost to sight and vulnerable to damage, theft or vandalism. When I visited the Falklands some time later I saw that my decision was entirely right. Next to Port Stanley airstrip was an area known by the army as Tin Pan Alley, in which hundreds of containers of spares and stores stood, many locked (keys doubtless lost) and unmarked, slowly sinking, unloved, into the Falklands bog. Hopefully there were no submarine spares among them!

The mood in the Headquarters was determined throughout the conflict, and increasingly sombre as our ships started to be hit; the loss of Sheffield was a huge shock. We hadn't lost a warship in a shooting war since World War Two, and, to be frank, had scarcely credited the Argentinians with either the capability (Super

Entendards, Exocet) or the competence to deliver them. Our intelligence must have been dreadful. On FOSM's staff we were delighted when Conqueror sank the Belgrano, though faintly incredulous. The Mk 8 ** torpedoes she used had become notoriously unreliable with age, and the Flotilla was holding its breath for their imminent replacement, the Spearfish heavyweight torpedo. Throughout the short campaign everyone at Northwood was firmly in favour of the whole enterprise, very different from the almost universal doubts and disapproval of George W Bush's invasion of Iraq twenty years later. The losses of Coventry, Ardent, Antelope, Atlantic Conveyor and Sir Galahad were grave and heartfelt blows to us all, but, despite this tragic and unnecessary loss of ships and lives no-one doubted that we should press on and prevail, which of course, in the end, we did. Soon the shooting was over, and the Task Force was trundling home, leaving the staff to arrange a rotation of warships to keep the hard-won peace in the South Atlantic.

During the war there had been one crucial occasion when Peter Herbert, FOSM, was held up coming from his residence at Uxbridge to the Headquarters. The road crossed the traffic- choked A40, and he missed a vital meeting. It was decided to find him a new residence, closer to the Hole, and a suitable house was found in Rickmansworth. It was called Primrose Cottage, not an obviously military or maritime name. Peter appeared in the office one day to announce that he had decided to call his new dwelling Holland House. Dick Husk and I gulped a bit, and pointed out that, although the Holland 1 early submarine had recently been raised from the deep near Plymouth, Holland House was widely known as an aromatic Dutch tobacco, and as a garden furniture retailer. What I didn't say was that I had already arranged some new name boards to be made for 'Dolphin House'. It was therefore with some relief that, the next day, we heard from Peter that he'd decided to call it Dolphin House after all.

Soon after that I was on the move. I can't say that it felt as if I'd contributed much to the job, though my superiors and subordinates all seemed quite satisfied with my performance. I guess that there are some jobs where you just get through it, and this was one of them.

I had been asked to become the Chairman of the Committee for Naval Nuclear

Operator Qualification and Training and Technical Safety Panel, rather obviously known as the 9-letter Committee. Whilst this was a prestigious job, and a compliment to be offered it, I was not enthusiastic. Like Ettore Bugatti, who said "I build my cars to go, not to bloody stop", I would, I thought, find it difficult to espouse nuclear safety, in all its ghastly totality, at the expense of getting things done with a very modest risk. Nor was I keen on spending another couple of years weekend commuting to London. I went home to get on with the house and see something of the family. All was going smoothly there, Janey was well established as the cook in a nursing home in the village, and Toby and Wiz were both flourishing at Sidcot.

In due course I learnt that I was to go to the Falklands for six months to take charge of Naval Party 2010, the group set up to provide afloat maintenance and support for the maritime element down there. The separation would be the usual disagreeable shock, but otherwise this sounded interesting, an Absolutely Bloody Final stretch at sea, in new completely different surroundings, about which, unlike so much of my career, I would be able to talk freely. Go for it!

And so I did. Janey drove me over to the airport one dark November day. I was somewhat buoyed up by the thought that it would be spring 'down there'. The journey was sufficiently unusual for me to write about it at the time.

It was something of a relief to be on the way. However often we do it, the poignancy of leaving family, home and country remains as sharp as ever, allayed in this case by the fluttering anticipation of new experience. The dark lanes of Oxfordshire and their pretty, modest villages had never seemed so quintessentially English as we drove to Brize Norton.

The air-base presents the feeling of a major hospital – a round-the-clock operation conducted by slightly tired, cheerful young men and women with an air of easy professionalism. Only the shadowy bulk of VC10s and Tristars on the tarmac hint, like a discarded theatre trolley, at tomorrow's operation. After checking in baggage and being assured that, yes, in all probability there would be a plane with a seat on the morrow it was time to repair to the Gateway Hotel.

This RAF transit mess maintains the weary atmosphere of an establishment designed for the consumption of musak, fortunately on this occasion without the musak. But, glories, there was unearthed a small bar, aglow with a variety of officers, clad in the many subtle gradations which signal to the knowledgeable their tribal origins. With all the cautious bonhomie of new boys at school we greeted each other; we acknowledged sheepishly our common destination and cemented this mutual fate by the exchange of whiskies and enjoinders to 'keep a sense of humour'. In a dark corner a girl, struggling to maintain her composure, bravely told her young husband "by the time you get home, I'll have finished painting the house". And so, sombrely, to bed.

Even before we boarded the aircraft the next day we stood huddled, peering drearily at a dull dawn, already depersonalised, numbed and numbered by the System. In a straggling crocodile we crossed the apron to the waiting jet, with the apathy of men whose destiny is no longer their own. In fact, the flight was comfortable enough. We set down at Dakar for fuel and the passengers debouched, standing smoking at a safe distance from the bowsers. We marvelled at the heat and light of Africa, and at the occasional black man who drove his truck past to prove the foreignness of it all. But, so quickly institutionalised, we were glad to scurry back into the womb of the aircraft and climb onwards towards Ascension.

We crossed the equator as the sun set in a brilliant band of prismatic reds, but the natural drama was not matched by any of the pleasant sailors' ceremonies I knew, no dripping Neptune, no shaving with giant wooden razors. By the time that we reached Ascension it was dark. Twinkling all alone in the limitless sea, the old volcano seemed a miraculous and perfect haven.

The warm wind washed over us as we stumbled out. Here the ground crew were British once more, bronzed, in shorts and desert boots. The RAF may be quick, but they are also inclined to be dry, and it was with considerable relief that some of us found ourselves later installed before a glistening glass of lager in the Exiles Club. This echo of old colonial splendour occupies one of the few decent buildings on the island, a fine verandahed house built in 1783 to house the officers of the garrison. Run now by Cable and Wireless, whose satellite trackers stand like great white ghosts in the sere landscape, the club buzzes with a mixed bag of English and Americans, civilians and military — all thirsty!

A few bleached-out blonde women permeate this male enclave, conscious of their rarity value, blasé of the honey pot effect. Equality of work equals inequality of play in such isolated societies. Nobody minds much. Driving back through the hutted town we saw men lazing on their balconies, a six-pack at their feet, a video's coloured glow illuminating their tanned faces.

Sleep in a portakabin was a fitful affair, hyped up by the novelty and surmise, lulled — but not much — by the ancient air conditioner which provided no cooling but stirred up the air and added a few clanking decibels. Four am seemed an unpropitious time to start the day.

The twelve hour journey in a Hercules from Ascension to the Falklands has attracted its share of legends, and the drowsy passengers, waiting to board, took some masochistic pleasure in telling them to each other. If there are difficulties with refuelling, or with landing, or with the aircraft, those twelve long hours can extend, interminably, to twenty. Diversions to Brazil or Uruguay are not unusual. A return to Ascension is commonplace. The trip appeared spiked with menace.

Sit in your car for twelve hours with the engine running, the seat upright and a sheet over the windows. Take a good book, a box of dryish sandwiches and some cartons of soft drink. Leave the radio off. It's a bit like that, and as we droned steadily south, ear defenders reducing the vibration, we sank into a semi-coma, conversation impossible, each man and woman an island; desultory alternation between sleep, reading, introspection and looking at our watches. How the carpet of time crept on.

Half way along, we refuelled. The sedate dance of the tanker, trailing its shuttlecock-ended refuelling hose, and our own thirsty Hercules was conducted with a fine precision. We had to dive slightly to lift our maximum speed to match the tanker's minimum, but it was scarcely dramatic, revealed only by an imperceptible change in the feeling through the seat, and by the lazy uncoiling of the altimeter in the cockpit.

At last we dipped down and caught a first glimpse of Port Stanley. Lines of white houses with pink and green roofs straggle along the blue area of the harbour. All about lie the impedimenta of a defeated and of a victorious army. We bumped, skidded slightly, trundled to a halt, and emerged, owlish and dazed.

The Falkland Islands is an archipelago of hundreds of separate islands, all rich in wildlife, but only a handful inhabited by humans. The only two of significant size are

West and East Falkland, the latter the location of Port Stanley, the only settlement of greater than hamlet size. In 1982 the population of the islands was 1800, of which over 1500 lived in the 'capital'. The outlying countryside, the 'camp' as the locals call it, was bleak, and lightly inhabited if at all.

Bearing a passing resemblance to the Orkneys, the islands are low, devoid of trees (the two exceptions were marked on the chart "tree, conspic."), the higher elevations being rocky outcrops, much of the rest being gorse, tussock grass and unrelenting bog. Sheep have been farmed there for many years, primarily for their wool, as they were, in the main, scrawny beasts whose meat did not appeal.

I arrived in the spring, and already the predominant features of summer weather were established. There was a lot of sunshine, and not much rain. The skies were marvellously clear and blue, and the sun burnt with an intensity that belied our latitude, due to the exceptional clarity of the atmosphere compared to the northern hemisphere. The night skies were fabulous, with little or no light pollution. A westerly wind of thirty to forty knots blew almost continuously. In my six months stay there were two days when the wind dropped totally flat, an occurrence so rare that everyone rushed to take photos of the sea without its habitual white horses. The combination of sun and chilly wind meant that everyone who worked out of doors soon had a deeply sunburnt face, but the tan stopped abruptly at the neck.

Port Stanley consisted mostly of white painted little houses, terraced or semi-detached, in the English suburban style of the 1930s. Every roof without exception was of corrugated iron — what the army calls 'wrinkly tin'. The town's only general store was run by the Falklands Islands Company, an English company with its roots in providing coal to coaling stations all round the world, and with a pretty good stranglehold on the islands' economy. The general store obviously did not run to Farrow and Ball, nor yet to Dulux, and every roof was painted in either Strident Red or Strident Green. There was a large church, the Falkland Islands Cathedral, built in the 1890s to replace its burnt down predecessor. Close by was the Hospital, much of which also burnt down whilst I was there. The town had a number of drinking dens, necessary because it was estimated that 50% of the population were alcoholics. The best of these was the Upland Goose, which would just about have passed muster as a down market English pub. Not surprisingly, at the time everywhere was festooned with Union Jacks and other fervent displays of nationalism. A largish house near the Cathedral sported a huge old-style conservatory, facing north (naturally), and stuffed with geraniums. This was Government House, the residence of the Civil Commissioner, Rex Hunt and his wife Mavis, a gregarious and entertaining couple who, from a position of comfortable and total obscurity, had been thrust onto the world stage, without, apparently, too many regrets.

Rex's droits de seignieur were severely diminished when the UK Government, immediately after the war, imposed upon the islands a Military Commissioner, supposedly of precisely equal status to Rex. If the chemistry had been right, this would have been fine, as they both had quite different jobs to do. When I was there, however, the Military Commissioner was Major General Spacie, an austere and humourless man, the exact opposite of Rex.

I was waiting for a boat on the windswept, decrepit 'Navy Jetty' in Port Stanley when HMS Endurance, the Antarctic Patrol Ship, arrived to join station. As was the custom she was to fire a gun salute, and, faced with two Commissioners, had decided to fire one salute of nineteen guns and one of seventeen, according to some ancient rubric. No one ashore knew who was entitled to what, but in any case the thing about gun salutes is that you don't know how many guns will be fired until they finish. Both Commissioners turned up on the jetty, in full fig, to take the salute(s). Rex's ostrich feathers outshone a mere Major General's cap by a mile, and they both stood, not speaking, ten feet apart, facing out to sea. As Endurance started banging away they both puffed themselves up ("this is for *me*") and took imperceptible little shuffled steps forward, so as to be ahead of the other. Lurking some way behind, I was in tears at the prospect of both of them stepping out into oblivion, but they stopped just in time. When the gunnery had finished they both retired, flushed with success, to their transport, still without a word to each other. Rex's was the red London taxi that he always used; the General left in a Mercedes jeep, left behind by the Argentinians. As a bit of Ruritanian comedy it could not have been bettered.

There were about 5000 military personnel on and around the Islands, compared to the twelve Royal Marines who had comprised the garrison before the war. About 1000 of these were naval, and most of the rest were army, including a wide variety of deployed lads manning little Rapier installations on most hill-tops, and a heavy team of sappers clearing mines and laying a few rudimentary roads. The British Forces in the Falkland Islands Headquarters – BFFI HQ – was installed in a former school in Port Stanley, augmented by a variety of containers and portable and temporary buildings. Many of the troops slept in two large floating hotels, called 'coastels', which lay alongside near the airport. The troops affected to hate them ("steel coffins etc"), but to a sailor they looked more than adequate. The senior officers of the HQ, of which I was a country member, had their own little mess in a portakabin; they referred to themselves ironically as the Junta, the very name the Argentinean Chiefs of Staff had adopted.

A bit of background-setting: what was *I* doing? I was accommodated in some comfort in the MV Bar Protector, a North Sea oil rig supply ship requisitioned to support the maritime element. She was manned by Stena line staff, and my Naval Party consisted of about 80 technical ratings and four officers. Bar Protector was a highly effective modern vessel, incorporating contemporary IT based features that the poor old RN could only dream of, with good workshops, accommodation, a huge working deck and a flight deck. She was diesel electric and her thrusters could hold her in position on a sixpence, all controlled by a joystick or computer. We used to take one of the four frigates or destroyers and two conventional submarines alongside, give the crews a chance to relax, and carry out some remedial work, most often welding of fitments on the upper deck where the Falklands seas had ripped the structure apart.

My own role often consisted of acting as a confessional for the Commanding Officers of these ships. Much the same age and rank as most of them, I was, by virtue of my branch, not seen as part of their command structure nor as any kind of threat, and they felt able to unburden themselves to me, often at some length. I also spent quite a bit of time at the HQ, helping to knock some sense into a chaotic staff system which had started with nothing more than sheafs of signals clipped roughly together. As Bar Protector moved round the many coves and inlets of the littoral, this often involved me in some interesting journeys. With scarcely a road to its name, and a lot of military movement all over the place, a network of helipads had been established, serviced by Bristow's commercial helicopter firm contracted for the task. These were frequently in the middle of nowhere, surrounded by bog, and consisted of a hard-standing, twenty feet square, with a small portakabin (= garden shed) for protection if you got stuck there for a day or two.

I developed, through hard-won experience, two rules for handling the Bristow's system, which was ostensibly to run to a timetable which it never quite achieved:

* a. never ask where a helo is going until you are inside it and strapped in; and

* b. always take the first helo that arrives, regardless of destination. There may never be another one.

Bar Protector spent a lot of time in San Carlos Water, where the main British landings had taken place. Despite its grim reputation as 'Bomb Alley' during the war, it was in peacetime a secure, sheltered anchorage with picturesque scenery. Already a moving memorial to those lost in the war at sea had been erected. Across the bay was the large building used to house a refrigeration plant, just one of many failed ventures to make the Falklands sheep pay their way. During the war this had been used as a field hospital, made famous by Surgeon Commander Rick Jolly's memoirs. On the wall I found inscribed the caption of a cartoon of the time:

The Falklands? Two bald men fighting over a comb.

Back in Stanley there was a signpost with boards showing how far the major capital cities of the world were away, all measured in thousands of miles. At the bottom there was a new addition:

RAF Buchan 8327 miles. Not far enough.

Messages from the heart, one felt.

The days of the laptop were still in the future, but I had brought out with me a Boots portable typewriter and one of those old black and yellow books 'Teach Yourself to Type'. The perfect medium for this exercise was 'Blueys', airmail forms which could be sent anywhere post-free. Friends who had not heard from me for years were surprised to suddenly get a badly typed missive describing some minutiae of Falklands life, but it helped and by the end of the trip I was quite competent. Sadly this skill soon withered when I got home, and this book has been typed using two fingers on a much more forgiving computer keyboard.

Christmas came and went, in the manner of celebrations away from home, somewhat forced and over-reliant on alcohol to synthesise the party-spirit. Like everyone, my thoughts were with the family, and I was happy to know that Janey had the children with her at home for love, support and fun. Toby (I'd forgotten to say) had started at Sheffield University, doing Geography, having been Head Boy and a considerable cheese at Sidcot. Wiz was still there, and before I came home I was to hear that she had got a place at Birmingham University to read Drama and Theatre Arts, a course you she had her heart set on.

Around the Christmas season there was a lot of peer group entertainment, a bizarre occurrence since the food was the same everywhere, whatever the victuallers had sent down from UK, ditto the wine which was NAAFI red or NAAFI white and that's that. However it stopped the social niceties from getting too rusty. Bar Protector was always very popular, particularly with the army, as it was one of the few places that they could get chips. Due to some quiddity of army victualling rules they could never amass enough cooking oil to fry off their chips, a weakness not shared by the navy.

A Concert Party descended on us, straight out of It Ain't 'Arf 'Ot, Mum, complete with Jim Davidson, talking about eating goldfish, but not actually doing it on this occasion, a couple of slightly battered chanteuses in fishnet tights and not a lot else, and a small man with an accordion and some blue songs. As entertainment it was not great, but it *was* greatly enjoyed; a bit of colour and silliness was something that we all needed.

New Year had always been celebrated on the Islands with the Annual Horse Races, which took place on a fairly level bit of rough ground near the town. Each race was a simple dash over about half a mile in a more or less straight line. There were a dozen or so nags, all of which ran in all the races in different colours and possibly with different names. The locals knew precisely what was what, but the military hadn't a clue, betting on names, the colour of the jockey's eyes etc. The three bookies could be seen planning their next European holiday on the proceeds, but it was a good day out notwithstanding.

Wherever we went the wild life was marvellous. Five sorts of penguins. The Megallanic, or Jackass, locally named for its braying call. These lived in burrows and would emerge and attack your boots if you tapped by the entrance. The Rockhoppers were the most populous; huge colonies – hopping rocks with great aplomb before plunging into the water for breathtaking swims through the surf and waves. The Macaroni and Gentoo were more withdrawn, gentle souls of the penguin world. There were a few King penguins, but they, like the Emperors, really belonged further south, and appeared solitary and introspective out of their comfort zone, such as it was. In the water dolphins, seals and sea lions were all present. The dolphins looked for any ship underway to swim alongside, generally in pairs either side of the bow-wave. The seals bobbed about close inshore, for all the world like old men in a jacuzzi. The sea lions basked on the beach, occasionally letting out one of their enormous, mournful roars. In the air black-browed albatross and giant skuas made majestic outriders. The soggy ground underfoot probably bore unique treasures amongst the fescues, bents and anemones, but I was too ignorant to spot them. Just slopping through it was enough.

As if all this was not sufficient, we went off for the highlight of the trip, a visit to South Georgia. We travelled the 800 miles through the most atrocious weather, an unwelcome reminder of how sea-sickness can strike anyone at any time. I lay in my bunk groaning in concert with the ship's structure, and dreaming hopelessly of sitting under a tree, the only cast-iron cure for the ailment. Much of the extreme weather was due to our transit into the Antarctic Convergence Zone, and out of the Roaring Forties. As we approached the island, the weather moderated enough for us to pick up some British Antarctic Survey people from a speck on the chart called Bird Island, where they had been working.

We sailed into Grytviken Harbour on a glorious, windless and cloudless day, with the sun sparkling on the glacier (one of 150 on the island). We rounded King Edward's Point where the Argentine submarine Santa Fe lay wrecked, under the windows of the British Antarctic Survey headquarters building, and anchored opposite the old whaling station. In days gone by South Georgia had been a major centre for whaling, principally by Norwegians, and there were three whaling stations (Grytviken, Stromness and Leith Harbour) together with numerous outlying developments. Whaling only took place in the Antarctic summer, and each winter the crews would depart for home, leaving the bases as if they had stepped out for five minutes. In 1965 they left, never to return.

Twenty years later, weather and passing sailors had taken their toll. Many of the wrinkly tin roofs had collapsed under the weight of snow, or had been ripped off by the wind. A whaleboat had sunk alongside. Many artefacts had been looted. Just about everything was rust-coloured.

Before we went ashore we were briefed that it was absolutely necessary to take full protective clothing with us. Whilst the sun might be shining, the weather could change in a trice, and katabatic winds of up to 100 knots could howl down from the mountain tops. In the event the weather remained perfect all day, and the beach was dotted with our sailors sunbathing, whilst their enormous mounds of clothing sat unused beside them.

It was fascinating to wander through this Marie Celeste scenario, trying to work out the functions of many large sheds plentifully equipped with heavy machinery. Whilst the greater part was involved with the processing of whale meat, including freezing and canning facilities, there was a sizeable maintenance base for the fishing vessels, together with everything needed to support a large workforce. It was overall a fascinating but mournful experience, everything broken, rusted and beyond repair, a time capsule slowly dissolving, without diminishing the scar on the natural landscape.

One bright aspect in the gloom was the Chapel, a pretty, freshly painted, Norwegian wooden building, which had been respected and enhanced by visiting sailors, who had also left an amazing collection of trinkets and tributes on the grave of Ernest Shackleton which lay in open ground nearby, guarded by an extremely large and unfriendly sea-lion.

We moved on to Prince Rupert's Bay, and made our way to what appeared to be a garden shed set in the middle of a colony of 30,000 King penguins (all numbers are approximate). The shed had been occupied by Cindy Buxton and her colleague who were making a nature film for Anglia TV when the war broke out. They were visited by a masked SBS man who told them that they were now safe. They didn't know that they hadn't been. This shack too had the Marie Celeste feel to it, bedclothes, cooking stuff and books all in chaotic evidence, but it must have been a sharp spot when the katabatics descended, no doubt. Remarkable women in a remarkable place, and never could they have been surrounded by so many dinner-jacketed suitors. The penguins were a delight, fearless, inquisitive, one could almost say humorous, and all with the most exquisite grooming imaginable. A bit of teenage fisticuffs breaking out in the background. An amazing day.

Time to go – from South Georgia and for me soon after, from the Falklands. It had been an unusual experience, occasionally quite brilliant, often mind-numbingly tedious. Overall there hung an atmosphere of sadness, for the futile war, the senseless loss of life, the bald men and the comb, the whaling and its demise, the first symptoms of climate change. I was more than ready to abandon the melancholy soaring of a solitary albatross for the inconsequential chattering of a flock of starlings.

My successor was a sour and humourless man. I had a quarter of an hour to exchange pleasantries with him – lots of mine, very few of his. As I was stepping into the boat he asked me how I arranged to address the whole Naval Party. I, not one for ceremony, said that I usually popped my head into the Senior Rates' Mess, and asked them to pass the word. Before we were out of earshot I heard the broadcast:

"All members of Naval Party 2010 fall in on the work deck now."

O tempora, o mores!

The trip home was enlivened (hardly the word) by the presence of several elderly Islanders who had been in the hospital when it caught fire, and were being sent to England for more medical attention. Janey, sweetly meeting me at Brize Norton, was alarmed when the plane was met by a fleet of ambulances. Had there been some dreadful in-flight disaster? She was relieved to see me unscathed, bronzed (from the neck up) and unusually thin after my sojourn down south. It was, hopefully, our last significant separation.

After a spot of leave I was asked to conduct a study into the recruiting, selection and early training of officers. I enjoyed this and came up with a selection of interesting recommendations. I may have made a tactical mistake in indicating a critical view of Dartmouth, a Whited Sepulchre Grade 1, not to be dissed in any way. I thought that, at the time, it was smug and introverted, and did not stand comparison with the Royal Marine arrangements at Lympstone. I suggested that collocating the RN officer training with that of ratings, well carried out at HMS Raleigh in Plymouth, might be wise. The Second Sea Lord, Sir Simon Cassels, was a patrician perhaps more suited to the 19th than the 20th century, and he suppressed my study – he said that I had exceeded my Terms of Reference (bravo, what are they for except to be exceeded?). I was disappointed, but not greatly so – I had done my work, what was done with it was no longer my problem. I was however rather bucked by my old friend Chris Wood, who was embedded deep in the Naval Staff and somehow got a glimpse of the forbidden document. He said that he thought it was the best paper on personnel that he'd seen in years. I owe you a pint, Chris.

The contretemps did not affect my next appointment, which was still 'in personnel', as Captain Naval Drafting. This was the titular head of an organisation of 150 souls which arranged the careers of all naval ratings, 55,000 of them at the time. A distinction is made between Appointing, the officers' system, which takes full account of personal characteristics to try to put round pegs into round holes, and

Drafting, which confines itself to technical attributes, preference and liability for sea or shore service, and cares not for the shape of the peg or of the hole. In the days before there was much in the way of computery it was an intensely bureaucratic process, involving every sort of paperwork known to man, Kalamazoos, rotating card systems, Cardex (is that the same thing?), files galore, and every Drafting Officer's personal, compendious notebook. Strict rules had to be adhered to, in the cause of fairness to all, but, despite every effort, Drafty did not always get it right. Not for nothing was our motto:

"Often courted, seldom loved."

We were accommodated in a Kremlin-like 60s block in Gosport, called HMS Centurion. We shared this with the Naval Pay people, no doubt on the basis that we could share their data. Above us we had set a Commodore, who was supposed to encourage cooperation. Being of a naturally cynical bent (he was, after all, a Pusser) he decided to let the two halves of his empire flourish separately, a wise decision.

During the week I stayed in a flat on the front at Lee-on-Solent. This was in the middle of the Costa Geriatrica, though curiously, between the spokes of the Zimmer frames, you could see the youthful but advanced wind-surfers zipping past, often in full flight. Janey used to come down sometimes mid-week, and the distinctive sound of our plucky little 2CV approaching was always a happy moment. The flat had one bedroom built out at the back, facing north over the airfield; it had three outside walls, and underneath was the car park where the faithful Ford Escort was kept. The bedroom was bitterly cold in winter, and for the first time ever I bought an all-night electric blanket. One morning, after a particularly hard frost and a withering north wind, I went down to the car park to find my car completely encased in a block of ice, like the bear in the Fox's Glacier Mint. There was no question of opening the door to start the engine – I couldn't find the door. A water main in the roof of the car park had burst directly above the car. I summoned my Secretary, Lieutenant David Marsh, and between us we gently eased off an estimated 150 lb of ice. The car then started perfectly. People said afterwards 'Why didn't you take a picture?'

It had not taken me long to suss out what was wrong with the drafting scene. The manpower structure had got grotesquely over-complicated, even more inexcusable in a shrinking navy, and, taking into account the various 'additional qualifications', there were over 500 drafting categories. The whole drafting business was posited on the curious conundrum: youngsters joined the navy to go to sea, but once there decided that they did not want to go to sea anymore. So they had to be sent, and in a way that was scrupulously fair. A nightmare, not least because over the years more and more rules had been invented, all of which added up to removing the ability of managers (ie the Drafting Officers) to manage with care and flexibility.

I proposed that there should be a reduction in ranks, starting with the leading hand, which could be a brevet rank at the behest of the Commanding Officer. People, particularly technical people, particularly weapons systems maintainers, should always return to the same class of ship, perhaps to the same ship. Extra sailors should be sent to ships to allow the CO to play the sea/shore system according to individual preference and expedience. These were not particularly radical proposals, but I had bargained without the then current Director of Naval Manpower Planning, an anchor-faced man dedicated to the maintenance of the status quo, who had been one of my predecessors. He told me sternly to carry on drafting in according to the rules, and to leave the bright ideas to others. With such a block nothing could happen, and, though there was plenty of sympathy for my views, I had made the mistake of not brigading opinion into an effective striking weapon. I was learning painfully that solutions were simple; getting them accepted and actioned was not. Twenty years later I was delighted to hear the Second Sea Lord of the day announce, with a flourish, that he had decided to delegate elements of drafting to individual ships and squadrons, just as I had suggested.

A prophet is without honour in his own country.

Notwithstanding all that I enjoyed my life as Drafty, though I was not too cut up to be drafted myself in 1987 to my final job as a Captain, back in Bath as Director In-Service Submarines (DISM). Two more years and I would be up or out, of which the latter was statistically far more likely. Interesting times. It was good to be finally able to commute to work from Greenhill House, as we had originally intended, and to end my naval career (as seemed likely) doing a job I could understand, surrounded by kindred spirits.

The job itself was wide-ranging, covering all aspects of design and support for all our submarines, including those nuclear boats queuing up to be scrapped. We carried out safety assessments and design reviews, arranged work packages for dockyard refits, obtained – often with great difficulty – spares, and specified changes required for safety or operational reasons.

One of the most demanding activities was the management of the safety of nickel-aluminium-bronze (NAB) castings, which formed the greater part of the seawater cooling systems in the nuclear fleet. These, crucial to the safety of the boats, started to deteriorate *ab initio*, and it required a great deal of work to justify their continued use up to a certain point, and then say "enough". Fortunately John van Gruytheusen, a brilliant young Constructor, dealt with all this with considerable aplomb, as I struggled to keep up with him. There was in fact a lot of struggling to keep up as DISM, not least with the weaponeers, who had conceived a far-ranging update of sonar systems for all the newer boats, and then launched me into the MOD to explain why this was necessary and how it would be managed and funded. I must have succeeded, because I read recently, twenty years on, that the update has now been fitted throughout the much diminished flotilla.

There was a special MOD Committee, chaired by Mike Livesay, the Assistant Chief of the Naval Staff, concerned with the availability of the Polaris boats. I used to turn up once a month with the usual engineer's *via dolorosa* of defects and dangers ahead. There were occasionally, though, more pressing problems. The primary side of the nuclear propulsion plant, fashioned from the best materials to exacting standards, had been fabulously reliable and successful for years, but everything starts to break down in the end. This is known as the far end of the bathtub curve (incidence of defects against time) or, more vaguely, as Entropy. In this case the problem was with the downcomers, screens bolted inside the steam generators to guide the flow of 'secondary' water, pumped in cold from the condensers, passing over the primary/secondary tubes to emerge as soggy steam at the top. The downcomers, totally inaccessible from outside, were starting to break loose. My colleague and good friend Andrew McVean, who was the Director Nuclear Propulsion, and I used to address the Committee. Andrew, using his doom-laden Scottish voice, would explain that if these components broke loose they could affect the flow, cause noisy rattles, and perhaps perforate the tubes themselves (the worst case). I, the eternal optimist, would put these problems into perspective with other threatened material failures, and conclude that disaster was unlikely. The Committee, transfixed like rabbits by our brilliant if divergent headlights, bravely decided to do nothing (well, what *could* they do?). In the end the design contractors, Rolls Royce and Associates, produced a remarkable solution combining complex jigs with an ingenious procedure to fix the problem without cutting a hole in the steam generators. The process was graphically described as 'wall-papering the hall through the letter box'. It worked!

It was about then that my Dad died. He featured largely in the early chapters, but has not had much of a mention since. He was lucid and twinkling right to the end, and lasted surprisingly well, considering his wartime troubles. We used to go down to Wimbledon fairly regularly to see him and Mum, and always got on well, though being given a large glass of banana liqueur and an in depth interrogation on the defence scene from A to Z was not perhaps the best end to the day. We'd always got on really well, and it was sad to lose him.

During my time as DISM I got increasingly irritated by what I saw as a peculiarly English vice of adding complication to engineering systems instead of getting the fundamentals right. It so happened that I had a secretary, Jill, whose typing speed was so phenomenal that the batteries on her machine were always running down because they had no time to recharge. I felt no compunction about asking Jill to type an article which was published in the Naval Engineering Review, (not, I have to say, to rave reviews, but engineers were always a pragmatic lot). Here's some of it:

THE DRIP-TRAY PHENOMENON

Once upon a time an artificer, working on a submarine pump, was distracted by hot liquid dripping on his head. It seemed to come from a tight bundle of small-bore pipework. Without more ado he wired up a tickler tin as a drip-tray.

Eventually the tickler-tin topped up and dripped on the head of a passing engineer officer. As he was wearing his divisions (well, his only) cap, this irritated him and he asked another artificer to fix it. He, being an ingenious fellow, drilled a hole two-thirds of the way up the tickler tin, sweated in a short length of tube, and ran a poly hose from the tube into a nearby scupper.

Sometime later, the chief tiff tripped over the poly hose. "Bloody calliante set-up," he muttered. "We'll get the chippies to make a proper drain tank". It was stainless steel, with a funnel at the top and a cock for a stoker to drain it down. The MEM employed on this agreeable task dropped the bucket onto his trainer, whereupon it broke his toe. The ship's investigation concluded: "The tank should be fitted with an electric pump". Another MEM, detailed off to run the pump every so often, forgot (not surprisingly, because it only needed pumping out once a month) and the flat flooded minutes before Captain's Rounds. "What it needs," said the DMEO, "is float-switches", "and an alarm in Manoeuvring", growled the MEO.

Time moves on and the scupper blocked; once again the flat was flooded. Another chief tiff wrote an S1182 "provide the drains collecting tank with an overboard discharge, hull valve and back-up, tested to deep diving test pressure". Years later the design authority doubled the scantlings all round, added a syphon breaker, a vapour trap, two pressure gauges, an inboard drain, full lagging to naval engineering specification, and persuaded a dockyard to do the work. FOSM's noise team were horrified – "a noise short" they said. Flexible pump discharges were fitted and the tank and its (by now multiple and complex) fittings were noise and shock mounted.

Sometime later, the First Lieutenant observed a thin stream of oily water dribbling from under the casing. "What it should have had", said the MEO (another MEO) "is a separator tank – trust the design authority". And eventually it got that too. There was now little room in the flat, and an artificer (another artificer) working on the pump was not best pleased to feel a drip from the drain pump discharge flexible. He wired up a tickler tin as a drip-tray. . . . .

This little fairy tale, codenamed the Drip Tray Phenomenon (DTP), will be familiar to everyone. It highlights two national characteristics:

An inability (or reluctance) to fix the leak ie to use simple engineering skills to perfect the system,

An enthusiasm for designing out fundamental problems by the use of ingenious, complex and costly palliatives.

Our ships bear witness to our apparent inability to get the basic engineering right. The design assumes that everything that can fail will. Components are developed and tested and proved to amazing standards of reliability, with astronomic figures for mean time between failures. Nevertheless, we duplicate, build in redundancy, and cross-connect everything within sight. And then we provide maintainers, expensively trained, to repair this intrinsically reliable item, and spares to enable them to rebuild it.

Of course we understand that it is more **interesting** *to design back-up and supporting systems than it is to perfect the fine and tedious detail of a single reliable system, and then impose the quality assurance discipline to ensure the requisite standards of fabrication. We must also understand that ship and equipment design and construction is not occupational therapy, but is intended to provide value for money and thus demands the 'Keep It Simple, Stupid' (KISS) approach.*

Because I have used a childish mechanical analogy, that does not mean that electrical engineering is free of the DTP. Perhaps the most striking contemporary example is that of computer-based systems, where our fondness for DTP encourages us to paper over hardware deficiencies with software solutions — solutions whose provenance, relevance and quality assurance are often hard to discern or assess. The current, sustained difficulties in weapons system integration bear witness to the piling of drip-tray upon drip-tray, the wearisome tendency of operational staffs to strain after operational perfection, (egged on by DTP-rich contractors) and the presence of the Pareto principle — the last 10% of capability causes 90% of the cost. Did you know that a significant proportion of modern electronic equipments' cost is directly attributable to the Ministry of Defence's standards for in-transit shock resistance (the kick-it-off-the back-of-a-lorry test)? This obscure requirement, called up in code from the depths of NES 1000, and applied without reservation to all contracts, adds millions to our procurement bill, when all we wanted is a better box. KISS, and KISS again.

Perhaps we could agree that a ruthless determination to avoid the DTP in design, and to draw unfavourable, forceful attention to it when we encounter it in service, could do much to increase our received value for money, reduce training and spares costs, and improve operational availability. And perhaps we could agree that the classic design aim of simplicity is as demanding and as satisfying in its achievement as any amount of self-indulgence in the Drip-Tray Phenomenon.

This was, as it turned out, my final diatribe, my last effort to kick against the pricks. I was about to become a prick myself. One of the few down sides of my DISM job was working for Bill Sanders, a senior Constructor whose reputation as being difficult to work with I found entirely justified. He carried a ferocious chip on his shoulder and regularly took pleasure in telling me that I would never make an admiral.

It was therefore with special delight, tinged with considerable surprise, that I heard from Hugh Thompson, genial and astute Senior Naval Officer, Bath, that I was indeed to be promoted. Later, as Hugh and Rosemary sat in our garden with a bottle of bubbly, we drank an ironic toast to Bill Sanders – an ecstatic moment!

CHAPTER 9

Upward, Outward, Onward

It was a pleasant stroke of symmetry that now, near the end of my naval career, I was once again involved with Gieves, now Gieves and Hawkes. As I've mentioned, they were key players at the outset, but, in the intervening years, they had retreated from the waterfront and their prices did not compare with many more utilitarian naval tailors. Not for nothing were they known as 'Thieves'. However with promotion to Flag Rank there was, for once, a decent allowance, and it was of course important, on this auspicious occasion, to Get It Right.

There was quite a lot to get right. I had been principally in a shiny grey suit for the past two years, and my current uniform was pretty well time expired. Now everything had to be smart as paint, newly laced, fitted with flag officers' buttons (I'd never realized that they were different) and immaculate enough for representational display – always a challenge for a plumber. The new cap alone, with its double row of scrambled egg, cost £150. Even my sword needed some attention to remove some accretions of rust and verdigris. Mr Gieves' man observed obsequiously that there was no change to the inside leg measurement – no surprise there, but that the waist measurement would need easing all round. I'll say.

I had been appointed as Chief Staff Officer (Engineering) to the Commander in Chief Fleet, another job at Northwood, but this time with a Residence (!), a Retinue (!), and a Secretary and PA (!). A month ago I'd lived at home and got by on half a secretary, high speed Jill. What had changed? My fortunes, I suppose. Janey and I smiled, lay back and enjoyed it.

None of these benisons was quite of the highest class, but they were all more than adequate. The Residence, Friar's Mead, was a large 1930s house in Stanmore, built for the RAF in their great expansive movement, and handy for their fighter HQ at Bentley Priory. We still got mail addressed to long gone Air Vice Marshals who had once lived there. There were several other RAF houses in the vicinity, and our garden backed onto RAF Stanmore, some sort of logistic centre. Our Jack Russell, Bertie, was a great escaper and often hopped through the fence to find refuge in the Sergeants' Mess, whence he was retrieved by the staff car, barking furiously.

The Retinue was sheer delight. It consisted of a Petty Officer Steward, a Leading Cook and a Driver. The Petty Officer was firstly Polly Perks, and then Dave Potts. Polly was languid and good looking. He could have had pretty well any woman that he wanted, and in the end he did, which was a great shame because his wife was as charming and lively as he was. She made the tactical error of remaining at home in North Wales, too far from the errant Lothario. He was very efficient and quite unflappable. Dave, on the other hand, was round and pop-eyed, with goggle glasses; he was devoted to his wife Steph, and, later on, to their much longed for daughter Laura. Sadly Steph died soon afterwards, and Dave faced the difficult task of bringing up his daughter on his own. He was also efficient, but quite flappable, with a dry sense of humour when not panicking. Like all our staff, he became great friends with us, for years after our naval times were over.

The Leading Chef for most of our time was Karen Smith, a glamorous and delightful six-footer, who cooked extremely well, while personally existing on bought-in junk food. She had the Royal Marines security boys in the palm of her hand, and they used to spend an inordinate time checking out Friar's Mead, for the chance of chatting up Karen in the kitchen. She said that she only put up with it because they always brought their absurdly friendly Rottweiler security dog with them.

The drivers were usually youngsters with six months between jobs, but were all nice boys who could drive well, and cheerfully turn a hand to a spot of stewarding or whatever, under the despairing tuition of the PO Steward. The Staff Car was supposedly one of the perks of the job, but I didn't enjoy it much. The Vauxhall Carlton of the day was not a great car, and the back seat was fiendishly uncomfortable. My Secretary tried to encourage me to work there on trips, and even went to the lengths of equipping me with a heavy precursor to the laptop, complete with pre-Windows operating system. If I worked I felt sick, and whether I did or not I got back-ache. Otherwise great.

I visited a lot of shore establishments, often for a formal parade. It was protocol to drive through the gates at the precise preordained moment, lights blazing, to be greeted by flags, bugle calls and salutes. Fortunately all these places had a lay-by nearby where we could lurk until the time was right, to the second.

In the office my every need (including some I didn't know I had) was catered for by Commander Richard Coupe, my secretary, and by Third Officer Millie Heazell, my PA. In theory he managed the infeasible amount of paper that poured continuously across my desk, and she arranged my diary, visits, transport, entertainment and all the other activities of a "busy executive". In practice they presented a seamless front of support which I could not fault.

The CinC was Ben Bathurst, who I had last seen when, as a Cadet Captain, he had beaten me so erratically at Dartmouth. I hoped that this had now stopped, and so it seemed it had, for he was affability itself, once one had got used to his disconcerting habit of looking over your shoulder, as if forever scanning the horizon for better company. We didn't collide very often as he was frequently away on MOD or NATO business. His Chief of Staff, on the other hand, I saw almost every day. After a dull start with Peter Dingemans, on the way to retirement, and a man who found it difficult to be genial, there was a burst of life when Roy Newman, his successor, arrived. Roy was "known to be difficult", and was sometimes called the Navy's Rottweiler for his aggressive approach and tendency to shake his victims in his teeth. He had spent some time in submarines, entering in the Polaris 'bulge' as a fully fledged Torpedo and Antisubmarine officer, and therefore regarded as something of a parvenu or Johnny-come-lately by the old guard. In fact I got on with him very well, as I would not be bullied, and our minds, interested in novel alternatives, ran along the same lines. We concocted together a radical plan for base-porting the fleet in the future. Once again our prophecies were ignored, and it is only now, twenty years on, that they are being implemented almost exactly as we envisaged. The premature disposal of Portland, with its capacious natural harbour, and the sidelining of Rosyth, a dockyard sized almost precisely to accommodate today's refit requirements, have denied the new plan the essential flexibility that we had built in.

My immediate subordinates were, however, much less satisfactory. Both engineering Captains from the surface world, they seriously disappointed me; one was a rigid traditionalist, the other slightly mad. Neither had what the French Marshal Beaufre referred to as the "essential gaieté of the service officer". How right he was, and how lacking they were. I was surprised, and saddened, that such out and out jobsworths should have risen so far. Fortunately there were many other excellent officers at Northwood, and I found a lively bunch to work on what was called the Fleetman project, which looked into the separation of the top-level (4*) responsibilities of the CINC from the lower level tasks (2*) of running the surface fleet. The solution was obvious, but there was a lot of detail to be sorted out before we moved. There was some resistance from the usual suspects, particularly from Nick Hill-Norton, then Flag Officer Flotillas Three, who shared his father's charm and energy, but not his rapier mind. It seemed natural justice that he ended up as the first Flag Officer Surface Flotilla, where he continued to make difficulties! Trying for everyone.

Stripped of the large Fleet Engineering Staff, and my two dodgy deputies, I was able to expand my role to include elements of personnel, shore communications and discipline, together with logistics, the coming subject, and my title changed to Chief Staff Officer (Support). This allowed a proper convergence of support disciplines which I welcomed, whilst giving the Chief of Staff more time to concentrate on warfare and operations. This came into its own when The Iraqis invaded Kuwait, and we were soon cobbling together a large Task Group to sail for the Gulf, enhanced, of course, by all manner of operationally essential goodies, procured outside the normal labyrinthine processes.

World changing events were in progress, but at a lower level the worker bees still pressed on with their mundane activities. For Janey and me there was a constant load of hospitality; Admiral Clanky was finally Entertaining! In what, I fancy, is now a fairly obsolete overkill of ritual partying, we provided lunch, dinner and accommodation to our peers, staff and every description of visiting fireman, plus, if we were lucky, a few of our own dear friends. Janey was the gracious hostess non pareil, and the PO Steward did a very passable interpretation of Jeeves at his most – cool. Every so often there would be a gathering of the Fleet Flag Officers and their wives, and as the resident engineer I was entrusted with the less, er, mainstream guests – those who did not belong to the inner circle of the Command Mafia. We put up the Commandant General Royal Marines, Robin Ross, the Hydrographer John Myres, and the Commodore Minor War Vessels (now no doubt reclassified as Major War Vessels), Graham Johnston amongst many others. We had a very good time.

France was not at the time within the Integrated Military Structure of NATO, but a French Captain was resident in the Headquarters as an 'observer', and perhaps to help prevent collisions between our submarines and theirs. He was an extremely swarthy native of Finisterre, whose wife used to shave his head every third day. When they came to dinner we provided some Pernod in their honour.

"A drink for peasants," he grunted, reaching firmly for the champagne. He did a good job of 'épater les bourgeois' in the suburban road where he lived, by barbequing a large pig on a home-made spit-roast, well marinated with pungent herbs. He proceeded to sabre his champagne bottles with his sword, firmly in the cavalry tradition. Stylish, n'est pas?

On another occasion we had some very old, and slightly infirm friends to stay. On the morning after a dinner party Michael staggered down stairs, and said to Dave Potts:

"It was a real complement for you to leave out the condoms for me, but I regret that they remain unused". We all looked rather blank, whilst Dave slid away to investigate. Minutes later he returned. "Those were not condoms, sir, those were Alka-Seltzers."

After a couple of years I got the expected call to go and call on the First Sea Lord.. Of course I had met Julian Oswald, one of the most genuinely delightful naval officers you could ever hope to encounter, many times, but this was different – this was my future. After a few minutes of pleasantries in his capacious office, where the Secretary, the Principal Staff Officer, the PA and sundry other staff lay like guard-dogs outside his door, he articulated the no doubt time-worn phrase:

"I'm very much afraid I have no further jobs for you". He said it with such genuine sincerity that we both smiled wanly at each other, and moved on to talk of other things. Yet it was no surprise to me. The Flag List promotion pyramid is pretty pointy anyway, and much of its machinations are aimed at getting the favoured few promising candidates into the right positions for experience and visibility. My job as CSO(S) suppressed any unique contribution I might feel moved to make, and my inclination – towards strategic planning – was marginalised by the need to get on with the grinding staff work. Jock Slater, who had relieved Ben Bathurst as CINC, kindly nudged me towards getting better known by the top honchos, but after 38 years in the navy I did not feel disposed to flaunt myself in such a way. The one job I would have liked was Director General Naval Manpower and Training, but the Second Sea Lord's team were not voting for me (too uncomfortable, soundness uncertain), and in the end the job went to a smarmy, conformist pusser.

After a few hours of due consideration I decided that I was delighted to be on the way to new adventures. The navy had done better by me than I probably deserved, and there was a new life out there. I was awarded the CB (Companion of the Most Excellent Order of the Bath), well known as an indicator of impending departure, but nevertheless a welcome honour. I had survived my time without a single medal and if I was going to end up with just one, the CB was ideal. Wiz drew a wonderful cartoon of me and the Queen in the bath together, true companions! I went to the Palace to receive my gong, and we had a boozy lunch to celebrate.

Shortly before I was due to leave Northwood, the MOD embarked upon one of its periodic Flag List culls, this time informed by the dubious tenet of Front Line First. (Dubious because such a one dimensional view of military forces takes no account of the depth of support needed to ensure sustainability). My post was declared vulnerable because I now had few battalions under my command, and because in many of my duties I advised, liaised and facilitated, not military activities which got a tick in the extremely small civil servants' box. My relief had already been appointed and indeed served for a few months before getting his marching orders. He was lucky to have been promoted at all, but, right in character, decided to sue the Admiralty Board for wrongful dismissal. I believe the case is still going on, like Jarndyce v Jarndyce. I was delighted to hear, a few years later, that, after trying to do without the post, it had been reinstated. He, of course, had not been!

We embarked upon a final flurry of farewells, including several dinners. Because of the vicinity of Friar's Mead we were asked to a senior RAF dinner party, where Janey was seated next to Sir Peter Harding, the Chief of the Defence Staff (until his removal for sexual indiscretion!) Afterwards, when I asked her how it had gone, she said that for a few moments she had been a world expert on the Eurofighter aircraft, about which he had talked continuously throughout the meal, but that she had already forgotten most of it. That's my girl! I went to a wonderful submarine engineers' dinner at Dolphin, where I addressed many old friends on our shared life and hard times in the 'Trade'. I was dined out by the small cadre of engineer admirals in Nelson's daycabin in HMS Victory, into which we just fitted neatly. Janey and I had lunch with the Oswalds in their flat in Admiralty Arch, since sequestered by John Prescott. On my final day I said goodbye to the CINC, Chief of Staff and my own staff, spent fifteen minutes telling my successor how to do the job, exchanged my uniform cap for a bowler with a naval cap tally round it, and climbed aboard a strange contraption to be towed ashore and applauded one last time. Back to Friar's Mead where we loaded the two dogs, two cats, and the last of the potted plants into the car, said a tearful goodbye to our faithful retinue, and set off for Wiltshire. For me, the naval experience was over.

It was not quite a case of "with one bound he was free" for there were some tidying up activities to complete. Easily the most tedious was a course on Business Appreciation, run by the Polytechnic of Central London, which had just been rechristened as Westminster University, though our course remained firmly buried in the past. We sat in a seedy office block in Holborn, whilst a series of dead-beat lecturers did their inadequate best to prepare us for the outside world. All I can remember is a short fat man who had come to tell us of his experiences in industry, which in his case was the rag trade.

"When I was in Rayne's Stockings . . ." was how he always started his lectures, and we all instantaneously had a powerful image of him in bra and panties, squeezed into shiny black stockings – it quite made our day. Overall though, it would have been better to read Eric Newby.

I suppose that I should end my tale right there, but the corollary of 38 years in one job is to see how institutionalised one has become. I decided that I wanted a clean break from the Navy, no running alongside the bus, jumping up to see what was happening inside. I also felt it important to keep well away from the public sector, although there were many Health Trust jobs going begging at the time. A head-hunter told me 'All you need to do is get yourself a portfolio of Non-Executive Directorships, say five', but it was a time of recession, and no-one seemed interested in my particular talents. I hunkered down for the long haul.

The conventional wisdom was that for every 10 job applications you made, you might get one interview. For every 10 interviews you might get one job offer. Faced with such daunting statistics one's immediate thought is "they don't apply to me", but in fact they seemed remarkably accurate. I made 140 applications, had 12 interviews, and, eventually, one job offer. I don't know if I was institutionalised, but many of the interviewers certainly were. They seemed to think that I would have grand expectations, of cars, drivers, secretaries, flunkies. Some wished I was grander – "I don't suppose you've got a K? Oh, well, pity." Many of the smaller organisations, trade associations, smaller charities and the like, had not recruited anyone for years, and seemed to have no idea how to do it. In several interviews I had to help them out – "I think that this is where you ask me about my financial experience." I was shortlisted for the Sail Training Association and, after a brilliant final interview (though I say it myself), learnt that they would never employ a naval officer after some bruising encounter in the past. I was similarly shortlisted by the Friends of The Elderly and, after a tense hour in a room full of fierce women in hats, heard that they had had their hearts set on a female candidate from the outset. What wastes of time. Later both outgoing Chief Executives confided in me "You're lucky you didn't get the job."

Half way through this protracted process I rather took my eye off the ball, and we moved houses. Greenhill House was too big for the two of us, and Toby and Wiz were only occasional visitors. We also wanted some more land. We found a beautiful, run-down house with two acres of wilderness 15 miles away, in Chilmark, and two months later we had moved. There was a lot of work to be done.

I decided, as I resumed my job search, that this was a dismal activity. After 38 years, the Navy had given me no help whatsoever. Most head-hunters and executive search companies were desperately inefficient and frequently offensive; interviewing boards were generally inept. I didn't want to change all this; I just wanted to be far away from it.

At last my chance came. I was summoned to an interview as the Chief Executive of a charity. The interview took place in Imperial College, and I was confronted by four distinguished men: Sir Denis Rooke, formerly of British Gas; an FRS chemist and former Vice Chancellor of Oxford; a former Permanent Under Secretary; and the former chairman of M&G Securities. A formidable team who asked me searching, relevant and structured questions for exactly half an hour before I was ushered out. The next morning, I had a letter in the post. I was to be

The Secretary to the Royal Commission for the Exhibition of 1851

A moniker worth waiting for, though it took me a month or two to remember who I now was.

After the Great Exhibition, when the mighty building had been taken down piece by piece and transported to South London on horse-drawn carts, the Commission, led by Prince Albert, invested the profits in buying 80 acres of South Kensington, still amazingly farmland in 1852. Albert's aim was to form a centre of intellectual excellence to match those in Paris and Berlin. It certainly worked. The Commissioners applied pressure on the Government, which eventually led to the Victoria and Albert Museum, the Natural History Museum, the Science Museum and the Albert Hall being built on their land, together with the Royal College of Art, the Royal College of Music and the precursors to Imperial College. Round these clustered a rash of smaller organisations , such as the Royal College of Organists, and the National Schools of Needlework and Cookery, all keen to muscle in on this synergistic gathering. It was an area which exemplified the implacable confidence that the Victorians had generated amongst themselves.

By the 1890s, after all this building activity, the Commission was coining it in, and started its famous Science Scholarships, supporting post-doctoral scientists in a way that had previously only been done by private patrons.

So I found myself plunged into a fascinating mixture of Victorian culture and contemporary science and engineering. The 1851 remained the theoretical hub of the South Kensington development, known as Albertopolis. On one occasion, at a rather delicate private view taking place in the British Art Library of the V&A, no doubt in recognition of some 1851 funding, the curator placed into my gloved hands an original Leonardo da Vinci notebook. 'Please do look through it,' he purred, whilst the assistant curators, ranged round the wall, went several shades of white. They had been taught that absolutely no-one, but no-one, ever handled the priceless treasures. What really struck me was how similar this little book was to my own engineer's notebook in the past, and I felt a surge of communion with the great man, spanning the centuries.

I went to visit my scattered flock of brilliant post-docs. I found myself, one stifling July day, sitting in the Condensed Matter bungalow at Oxford University. Itself a fairly incomprehensible subject, the specialised bit that my charge was studying was even more arcane.

"How many people *really* understand what you're doing?" I asked.

"Do you mean in the world?" he replied "About six." Clearly I was not going to be one of them.

My life was therefore a wonderful bridge between the two cultures, a concept I recognised as much as I abhorred it. Why has this schism occurred? I blame the philosophers, who were charged with the custody of all knowledge, not just

Wittgenstein's utterances. The V&A had been intended to be a Design Museum, featuring all artefacts, but was deflected into Fine Arts and Craft, possibly by William Morris. So the Science Museum had to be built to cover the shortfall.

When I first took post, Sir Denis Rooke told me that for the past 25 years the 1851 had been making a surplus, and that the Charity Commissioners were becoming fractious. "Do what you can," he said gently. Two years later, at the annual gathering of the 1851 Commissioners, I was able to announce that we had made an operating deficit of £200,000. This news was greeted with a round of applause. Was I in Wonderland, I thought, and was I Alice?

There were four of us in our little office in Imperial (of which the 1851 remained the landlord). Myself, Pat my secretary, a part-time accountant and Valerie, the archivist. With an indulgent and preoccupied Board of Commissioners and Committee Members I had almost total freedom to get on with the job as I saw fit, a remarkably refreshing situation after the slow, fine grinding of the MOD. We modernised everything in sight, spent an inordinate amount of time trying to get engineers interested in our grants in the same way that scientists were, encouraged industrial design and started a new award in architecture. I loved it all, but after eight years daily commuting from Wiltshire got through to me, and I took my leave of a unique, totally philanthropic and thoroughly admirable organisation.

The Times kindly printed a letter from me:

Sir,

After 48 years of fairly continuous employment , I have just retired.

*My working colleagues ask incredulously "What are you going to **do**?" My retired friends seek to reassure me "I've never been so busy".*

This preoccupation with activity seems a singularly British trait. In Italy, I feel sure, a similar announcement would be greeted with cries of "Bravo! Is your hammock comfortable? Is your cellar sufficient?"

Personally, I do not plan to overdo it in retirement. However, I might try a few more letters to the Times.

To my surprise I received several letters in reply, one or two from women offering a variety of solace. I easily turned them aside. I was going home – for good!

CHAPTER 10

Mrs Middleton's Husband and
The Master Armourer

I set out to write a reasonably consistent commentary of my naval career. Looking back it seem more like a series of vignettes, with some shocking lacunae. I'll just try to set the record straight at least with respect to some of my family whom I left hanging in mid-air as I swerved off down yet another rabbit-hole, in pursuit of yet another anecdote. I could also mention a few other things which have been a continuous, intermittent or occasional influence upon me over the years. If that isn't a euphemism for sweeping up unconsidered odds and ends I don't know what is.

My parents featured largely at the start of this book and, as in life, my life and theirs drifted apart as I got older. Dad finished with ICI about the same time that we were getting married, and they moved to Wimbledon when he got a job with the MOD as a fuel technologist. This involved inspecting army barracks heating systems and he spent a lot of time in Germany, where he was accommodated in the officers' messes there. He came back goggle-eyed at the excesses in some of the cavalry messes – a million miles from his own rather austere naval experience.

Mum was pleased to leave the burning-glass of village life, and luxuriated in the suburban milieu, nipping up to town to visit the Spanish Club, and see art movies in the Curzon Cinema in Mayfair. She clearly retained some 'grande dame' style. At her local butcher, in Raynes Park, an underling offered her a cheap cut. The butcher sternly remonstrated with the lad. "Mrs Middleton wouldn't want anything that isn't full price". Dad, on the other hand, was appalled at being thrust into conflict with the Residents' Association, the usual uneasy combination of eccentrics and apathetics.

We used to see them quite often, noting with love, and a little sadness, the inevitable signs of ageing. When we stayed with them Dad always used to keep me up late, asking interminable questions about the Navy and the Defence scene generally, whilst plying me with libations of a peculiarly disgusting banana liqueur which he seemed to have laid down in bulk. It was only when this rendered me speechless that the interrogation stopped.

Eventually, Dad had a heart attack, and returned from hospital briskly demanding some Capstan Full Strength and a scotch and soda. He had done well, considering his wartime illnesses, but two years later he had a stroke and died quite quickly. It was 1989. Mum, showing her customary chutzpah, promptly sold the house and moved into a residential home near Croydon. It was not great, but she was proud of her initiative, and eked out a simple life together with some good friends that she made there. She was very pleased when I was made Rear Admiral, and used to come and stay at Friar's Mead, where she charmed everyone with her style and humour. She followed Dad to the grave in 1996, and of course, whoever you are, a mum's death is a defining moment in all our lives.

Netta, my sister, was five years younger than me when she was born, and five years younger she has stayed – funny that. When we were young that was a big gap. I started boarding from the time she was three, so we never had a chance to be close. Of course now five years difference is nothing and we get along very well, though that early lack of closeness can never quite be overcome. She went off to Trinity College Dublin, to our Dad's delight, where she met Dick Barham, whom she married soon after they graduated. She once famously said to Mum, in all seriousness, "I wonder what would have happened to Patrick if we hadn't got him into the Navy?" Good question. Netta and Dick moved to Kent, where, in due course, he became a stinks master at King's School, Canterbury, whilst Netta moved into librarianship. They had two sons, Nick and Peter. Peter has learning difficulties, and this may have been one of the factors which led me to a trusteeship of CARE.

I was picked off the streets of Sutton Veny by Major General Stuart Green, who introduced me to this fascinating charity. It was started as a single residential home for 'the handicapped' in the 1960s. At the time the fashion for such places was to be deeply rural. This was to protect the residents from prying eyes, and give them the questionable benefit of looking at a cow at close quarters. As a result, and no doubt with much whisky fuelled laughter by the founding fathers, CARE was formally entitled Cottage And Rural Enterprises, a name which confused us all for many years. Later we realised that these country capers were the last thing that was needed, and started to establish our burgeoning communities in suburban areas, where our residents could start to integrate with the wider community, and walk to the pub and shops. This also meant that the numerous young staff (care workers) could get to and from work without ruinous taxi fares. The parents were faintly appalled, but it was the right thing to do. We ended up with eight communities up and down the country.

I remained a Trustee of CARE for 14 years, and Chairman for 8. The other Trustees and staff were thoroughly pleasant, and most of the expansion had been orchestrated by Stuart before I arrived. We had an agreeable and undemanding time fine-tuning the organisation, until my final year when all hell broke out. The Chief Executive was accused of bullying and harassment, and the Trustees swung into action. We had been used to delegating most activities to the Chief Executive, and as a Board we had to suddenly grow up and do our duty. I became closely and continuously involved with employment lawyers and other expensive creatures. The Board, who I might have classified as lightweight before the crisis, rose magnificently to the challenge, and acted decisively in a truly unified fashion. It was a beastly time, and its echoes rumbled on for some months, but the boil was lanced and we eventually got back to normal. This commotion provoked some structural introspection and a raft of new policies, procedures and processes. I decided that was enough for me, and hope that I jumped before I was pushed. It had been a great experience, and we had been able to provide splendid services for our increasingly diverse and demanding client group, despite the difficulties of screwing adequate fees out of the local and central authorities. I miss them still.

Our precious children, too, have been left somewhat hanging in space. Toby left

Sidcot with a sigh of relief and went off to Sheffield University to read Geography. I hadn't realised until then that Geography is one of the few subjects in which you can get either a BA or a BSc. He opted for the latter which involved a lot of statistics – thank heavens for the newly arrived pocket calculators, which could calculate standard deviations if you knew how. Notwithstanding, he enjoyed Sheffield, and, apart from some geography, acquired valuable life skills in victualling and communal living. A variety of girls started coming home, from the gorblimey to the sublime.

After Uni, Toby thought that he had a job tied up with a geological prospecting firm in the oil business, and went off for an exotic holiday on the strength of it. By the time he got back the oil price had slumped, and his job prospects with it. He found a temporary niche in the agrochemicals world, selling Hungarian lupin seeds, but as a career path it seemed unlikely to blossom. After some heart-searching he went for a commission in the Royal Marines, and never looked back.

He scrambled through the fearsome training at Lympstone, where he became known as Bomber, a tribute to him for going at everything full tilt, and we attended his passing out parade one rain-soaked day. Who should be there too but our old friends David and Mary Rose Pulvertaft. David's father and mine had been fellow engineers before the war, and it was a coincidence that David and I arrived at Manadon together. It was even more of a coincidence when Toby and Rupert Pulvertaft also turned up together at Lympstone, and remained firm friends ever since. In such an ephemeral world as the Services it's amazing to have this thread of continuity through three generations. At the parade, David and I both wore bowlers, he, with his lean ascetic appearance looking like a High Court Judge, me considerably more bucolic – a farmer up for the market comes to mind.

Toby and I only met once "on duty". I went to inspect Polar Circle, the ice patrol ship that was to replace the old Endurance that I had last seen in the Falklands. As I stepped on board I was welcomed by my son, who had an amazing year in that very unconventional (by RN standards) vessel, and earned a bridge watchkeeping ticket there. He ushered me to the lift: inside stood a very black Marine in No 1 blues, smart as paint, who gave me a crashing salute. A display of style worthy of the lad.

He worked his way up through the ranks, passing a number of difficult appointments en route, and pausing in 1993 to marry Anna Strowger, a beautiful girl he had met in Plymouth. It was a perfect summer's day when their wedding took place at Anna's parents' house in Modbury, the sun shone, the champagne flowed, the guests were beautifully turned out, and behaved quite reasonably well enough. Rupert Pulvertaft was Toby's best man, and the two were on the top of their form – terrific! A succession of interesting jobs followed, but Toby and Anna thrilled us all by giving birth to twins a few years later. Phoebe and Eleanor were not identical, which avoids subsequent confusion ("Unforgiveable, Grandpa!"). In fact, even at birth they were clearly very different, and so they have remained, delightful but different.

Darling Wiz had finished her time at Birmingham University with a good 2:1, and thereafter decided she would have a temporary hiatus from the world of acting. She got a job with an illustrators' agent and spent a lot of time with buyers and sellers in this specialised market. After this she shrugged, and abandoned herself to the rigours of her chosen profession. The low wages, infrequent opportunities and woeful administration make this a fearsome environment, and I often felt that, despite Toby's obviously demanding life, Wiz was the true tough one, blitzing through penury and disappointment with grace and humour. She never asked for a penny, and bounced along the bottom quite cheerfully, despite an appalling couple of agents. She appeared in Miss Jean Brodie in the eponymous role, a bravura performance, onstage for the whole play. Whilst we knew that this was only a play, it was still a moving spectacle to see your daughter disintegrating on stage, and we still had tears in our eyes as we met her for a beer afterwards. After the usual adventures in the relationship game, Wiz has now settled down with Jane Haslegrove, a feisty Lancashire actor who is a wonderful companion and the greatest fun. Jane is currently on long term contract to Casualty, so has a flat in Bristol, and the pair of them lead a peripatetic life between there and their house in Sydenham.

As for my precious J, I hope that she's made enough appearances in this book to indicate her absolutely central role in every aspect of my life. Companion, soulmate, lover, knockabout chum and wife, she has been steadfast in supporting me in all my professional activities. Now, as I've cast off my former burdens, I take great pleasure in supporting her as Churchwarden, Lay Pastoral Assistant and general good egg around the community. It is a fitting and enjoyable reversal to become 'Mrs Middleton's husband'.

I should just mention our animals, which have been a persistent presence in our lives. We started with Punch, a long-haired miniature Dachshund, a brave and self-opinionated dog who was greatly loved but could infuriate with a single action. When he was very old, and we were living in Bath, he had some dreadful malady and I had to take him to the animal hospital at Churchill, near Bristol. When we arrived the staff took a cursory look at the small quivering object, and said "He's going to have to wait – we've got an elephant coming in." It was true, a mighty pachyderm from Bristol Zoo arrived soon afterwards, and we all watched spellbound as the huge creature lurched towards the giant operating theatre.

When we went to Singapore we had two dogs, Scrumpy and Moppet, a number of cats, and a pair of ducks. These were quite aggressive, and Wiz used to appear from the garden, totally nude, clutching her derriere "Ducks bite me!" They reserved their most ferocious attacks, however, for themselves, charging at their own images in the car's polished hubcaps. Patter, patter, patter, ping! Next up was Za-Za, a beautiful grey and white cat from Cartmel, in Cumbria. As a kitten she ran up the curtains and chimneys, and wrapped herself in loo-paper, but she lived to be a grand (and imperious) old lady of twenty two, and when she died we all wept – she seemed to have been with us forever.

In Scotland we acquired Froya, a Border Collie from a dogs' home. She proved to be a friendly character with an extraordinary attraction to twinkling lights, and a capacity for charging along the beach eating every wave until she was sick from swallowing sea-water. We all have our little foibles, I suppose. It was at this time that we collected the statutory gerbil and hamster, rodents without much appeal to the adult members of the family. At one stage it was necessary to dispatch one or the other. The euthanasia kit consisted of a dropper bottle of ether and a bit of cotton-wool. As I warmed to my grisly task, I noted that the instruction leaflet carried the following warning:

Be careful not to spill the liquid on the animal's skin, as it could cause irritation. Indeed.

We went through the rite of passage of Toby bringing home the school grass snake, which promptly escaped – an uneasy weekend ensuing. We had an athletic rabbit – Twitchit, natch – who promoted an excellent game of family rugby, as we tried to catch him whilst he raced round the garden.

Jemima was a little black cat we got in Bath, an urban creature with the manners of a street urchin, often bringing back chip papers and worse from the London Road. Za-Za treated her with lofty disdain. By the time we got to Sutton Veny we got another rescue dog, this time a very sweet Lurcher called Maurice ("What's a lurcher?" Answer: "A dog you see on a piece of string behind a gypsy caravan".) We decided that we could not have a dog called Maurice, so he became Boris, which suited him much better. He had been badly treated, and needed a lot of TLC to recover from it. At this stage a stray black cat appeared from nowhere, on the day that The Duke of York was married. Hence, Yorkie. Yorkie was a real comedian, forever doing tricks which never quite worked. He was a natural troubadour, and it was no surprise when he disappeared as suddenly as he had arrived. We were sad to see him go, dear boy.

Now in Chilmark, we have an English Springer Spaniel called Bramble, a Parson Jack Russell - Biggles, two cats, a variety of hens, and two geese. The gander, Hector is on his third goose, his first two having died. It's quite difficult to get hold of single geese, as they are generally sold in trios, so I put an advertisement in the local rag:

LONELY HEART

Hector, a handsome 10-year-old farmyard goose, seeks willing, fit female for country walks, mutual grazing and maybe more. Faithfulness guaranteed. Dowry available. No candlelit dinners.

This sparked a variety of offers from the good ladies of the area, and Hector is now suited.

The reader may feel that things have got pretty desperate if I am reduced to describing our animals, but I suppose that I have done it because, as I have got older, I find that I increasingly admire the simple, steadfast qualities of these creatures, so often superior to those of our own, flawed species.

It really is time to finish, but there is one final episode to round off the book. I was apprenticed at the age of fourteen to my godfather, Owen Parry, in the Worshipful Company of Armourers and Brasiers in the City of London . Dad took me down to Armourers' Hall, in Moorgate, and with what I viewed as somewhat excessive enthusiasm relinquished me into the care of my apprentice Master. The Court, who presided at this ceremony, seemed incredibly ancient, probably much the same age as I am now. I later became a Freeman of the Company, and then of the City of London. This has little to do with driving sheep over London Bridge, but is the licence to practice one's trade within the City walls. Later I was elected a Liveryman, which entailed the payment of some 'Fines and Fees'. I baulked slightly at this, and sought Owen's advice. "It's only once," he said "and if you're half the man I think you are, you'll drink it in a couple of years." He was dead right.

The Company has been a constant presence, holding interesting and enjoyable events and introducing me to a wide swathe of pleasant people, and it was a treat to be elected to the Court and, eventually, to be made Master. I had a great year, and for the first time felt that I really understood something about the Company and the City institutions with which it interfaced. As I stepped down, exhausted, at the end of my year a colleague passed me a note:

"There is nothing, absolutely nothing, as passé as a Past Master"

And that, I think, says it all. I pass.

The Plain Unvarnished

1938	PM born in Valletta, Malta
1946 - 1951	St Christopher's School
1951 – 1954	Cheltenham College
1954 – 1957	Britannia Royal Naval College, Dartmouth
1957 – 1959	HMS Camperdown
1959 – 1962	RN Engineering College, Manadon
1962 – 1964	HMS Lion
1964 – 1965	HMS Dolphin
1965	HMS Adamant
1965 – 1967	HMS Ambush
1967 – 1968	RN College, Greenwich
1968	Promoted Lt. Cdr
1968 – 1969	HMS Churchill

1969 – 1972	HMS Warspite
1972 – 1973	Tenth Submarine Squadron
1973	Promoted Commander
1974 – 1976	Directorate Project Team, Submarines
1976 – 1977	National Defence College, Latimer
1977 – 1979	HMS Blake
1979 – 1981	Directorate of Naval Manning and Training (Engineering)
1981	Promoted Captain
1981 – 1983	Chief Staff Officer (Engineering) to FOSM
1983 – 1984	Commanding Officer, Naval Party 2010 in the Falkland Islands
1984 – 1986	Captain Naval Drafting
1986 – 1989	Director, In Service Submarines
1989	Promoted Rear Admiral
1989 – 1992	Chief Staff Officer (Engineering, later Support) to CINC, Fleet
1992	Awarded Companion of the Bath; Retired
1994 – 2002	Secretary, Royal Commission for the Exhibition of 1851
2000 – 2001	Master, Armourers and Brasiers Company